D0953197

Uncovering Happiness

ALSO BY ELISHA GOLDSTEIN

The Now Effect: How a Mindful Moment
Can Change the Rest of Your Life

Mindfulness Meditations for the Anxious Traveler:
Quick Exercises to Calm Your Mind

A Mindfulness-Based Stress Reduction Workbook
(coauthored with Bob Stahl, PhD)

Uncovering Happiness

OVERCOMING DEPRESSION WITH
MINDFULNESS AND SELF-COMPASSION

ELISHA GOLDSTEIN, PhD

ATRIA BOOKS

NEW YORK   LONDON   TORONTO   SYDNEY   NEW DELHI

ATRIA BOOKS
A Division of Simon & Schuster, Inc.
1230 Avenue of the Americas
New York, NY 10020

First Atria Books hardcover edition February 2015

ATRIA BOOKS and colophon are trademarks of Simon & Schuster, Inc.

For information about special discounts for bulk purchases, please contact Simon & Schuster Special Sales at 1-866-506-1949 or business@simonandschuster.com.

The Simon & Schuster Speakers Bureau can bring authors to your live event. For more information or to book an event, contact the Simon & Schuster Speakers Bureau at 1-866-248-3049 or visit our website at www.simonspeakers.com.

Interior design by Kyoko Watanabe
Jacket design by Janet Perr
Jacket art illustration by Leah Pearlman

Manufactured in the United States of America

10   9   8   7   6   5   4   3

Library of Congress Cataloging-in-Publication Data

Goldstein, Elisha.
Uncovering happiness : overcoming depression with mindfulness and self-compassion / Elisha Goldstein, PhD.
     pages cm
"Atria nonfiction original hardcover."
1. Depression, Mental—Alternative treatment—Popular works. 2. Mindfulness-based cognitive therapy—Popular works. 3. Self-acceptance. 4. Compassion. I. Title.
RC537.G658 2015
616.85'27—dc23

                       2014015765

ISBN 978-1-4516-9054-5
ISBN 978-1-4516-9056-9 (ebook)

For Lev and Bodhi,
for teaching me the art of uncovering happiness

You may not control all the events that happen to you, but you can decide not to be reduced by them.

MAYA ANGELOU, *LETTER TO MY DAUGHTER*

Contents

CONTENTS

Introduction

Mahatma Gandhi, the famed leader of India's nonviolent independence movement, once described depression as a dryness of the heart that sometimes made him want to run away from the world. The Dalai Lama referred to it as the thoughts and emotions that undermine the experience of inner peace. Writer John Keats told of the hopelessness that depression created in his soul: "If I were under water, I would scarcely kick to come to the top."

Every part of the mind and body can feel the weight of depression. It hijacks thoughts and feelings, influences behavior and choices, eats away at physical and mental health. It can be a serious medical illness that steals happiness and overshadows sufferers with darkness. It touches all of us, either directly or indirectly. Each year, twenty-five million Americans have an episode of major depression; many have experienced it before and will again in the future.

Depression has many faces. Some depressed people function relatively normally throughout their lives despite ever-present, low-grade feelings of chronic unhappiness. Others become incapacitated with rolling bouts of self-loathing thoughts and murky mazes of negative feelings that clog the mind. Many discover that activities that once felt playful, pleasurable, or satisfying now bring no happiness and are difficult to do. The ability to control thoughts and actions seems lost.

You may have experienced depression in the past. Or you may be depressed right now. Perhaps you have felt its spirit-sapping symptoms—difficulty concentrating, lack of motivation, boredom, fatigue, anxiety, insomnia, irritability, guilt, feelings of worthlessness, emptiness, and sadness, and the incessant nagging of automatic negative thoughts—and have even considered suicide.

"What's the point of living?" you may ask. "No one can help me. Nothing's ever going to change." You may feel so full of despair that, like Keats, you would scarcely kick to come up from under water.

Your feelings are very real. When you are depressed, you *feel* hopeless.

But that doesn't mean your situation *is* hopeless.

Here's the thing about depression: It tells you lies. It makes you believe that thoughts are facts. It can even take away every last ounce of hope in your soul.

In the following pages, I'll show you why there is so much reason to feel optimistic. I'll explain how huge advances in mindfulness, neuroscience, and extensive studies of the depressed brain have brought about major breakthroughs in what we know about depression's triggers and treatments. I'll show you how you can use a variety of straightforward tools and techniques to break depression's hold on you and begin to uncover the happiness that is the essential core of who you truly are.

There is hope. You *can* feel better. By following the steps in this book, you can take back control of your mind, your mood, and your life.

Your Brain's Own Natural Antidepressant Power

When you hear the word *antidepressant*, you probably think of a pill: a medication used to treat your illness. Medications are one kind of antidepressant. But they're not the only kind.

Science is now showing that we also have natural antidepressants within our brains. Natural antidepressants are mindful mindsets (thoughts and behaviors) that build us up instead of tear us down and allow us to help ourselves improve our own moods.

These natural antidepressants can be gathered into five main categories:

1. Mindfulness: a flexible and unbiased state of mind where you are open and curious about what is present, have perspective, and are aware of choices.
2. Self-compassion: a state of mind where you understand your own suffering and use mindfulness, kindness, and loving openness to hold it nonjudgmentally and consider it part of the human condition.
3. Purpose: a state of mind where you are actively engaged in living alongside your values, are inclined toward compassion for others, and possess an understanding of how your existence contributes value to the world.
4. Play: a flexible state of mind in which you are presently engaged in some freely chosen and potentially purposeless activity that you find interesting, enjoyable, and satisfying.
5. Mastery: a state of mind where you feel a sense of personal control and confidence and are engaged in learning to get better and better at something that matters.

By developing these five natural antidepressant fundamentals, which I will show you how to do step by step, you can strengthen your brain's ability to act as its own antidepressant that can be as powerful as—or even more powerful than—the antidepressant medications.

Because you are alive, anything is possible.

—THICH NHAT HANH, VIETNAMESE ZEN
BUDDHIST MONK AND TEACHER

A Note About Antidepressant Medications

I recognize the value of antidepressant medications, and I believe they can play an important role in the treatment of clinical depression. I've seen pharmaceuticals be lifesavers for some depressed patients, giving them the help they need to engage in necessary psychological treatment.

However, I also believe these drugs are heavily overprescribed and overused. For many patients, antidepressants cause more harm than good. They can create a cascade of mental health problems that go far beyond the depression they were prescribed to treat. Too many people get caught in the trap of jumping from one drug to the next or taking multiple prescriptions in order to offset serious side effects caused by individual drugs.

As I see it, the problem with current pharmaceutical treatments is that they haven't caught up with recent discoveries in neuroscience.

A growing number of health care professionals are starting to integrate current science in the decision-making process when treating depression. They are beginning to look at the illness in a science-based, whole-person approach. But still, too many patients, health care providers, researchers, medical organizations, and government-funded agencies rely on outdated information to make decisions and recommendations about the use of antidepressant medications. They operate from the decades-old assumption that mental health can be restored to people with depression only by using drugs to "balance" the chemicals in their brains. That assumption is no longer accurate.

In recent years, research that you'll soon learn about has revealed so much about natural antidepressants, mindfulness, cognitive-behavioral therapy, and other nondrug approaches to treating depression and promoting long-term healing. Antidepressant medications are still a useful tool for treating depression, but they're not the only tool, and in many cases, they're not the most effective tool. It's important to be informed about medication and make the decision to integrate them or taper off of them as part of your treatment in conjunction with your doctor.

Whether you are on antidepressants and they're working for you, you're on them and want to get off of them, or you are not on antidepressants at all, the work that you do through this book is going to support your ability to get better at overcoming the depressive cycles.

THE STATS ON ANTIDEPRESSANT MEDICATIONS

- About 11 percent of Americans over the age of twelve take antidepressant medication.
- More than 60 percent of Americans taking antidepressant medication have taken it for two years or longer; 14 percent have taken it for ten years or more.

- Antidepressants are the third most common prescription drug used by Americans of all ages.
- In the past twenty-five years, the rate of antidepressant use in the United States has increased nearly 400 percent.

Source: US Centers for Disease Control and Prevention (CDC)

A Mindfulness Approach

Mindfulness is the foundation on which everything in *Uncovering Happiness* is built. Put quite simply, mindfulness is awareness. It is the action of intentionally using your five senses to bring complete attention to your experience of the present moment, while letting go of judgments and biases. Although it is rooted in Buddhism, the practice of mindfulness has undergone extensive scientific study in the West and has been shown to be a powerful, effective way of eliciting psychological wellness. It has been used with great success to help people with depression, anxiety, stress-related disorders, chronic pain, addictive behavior, and even chronic stress. Mindfulness is one of the ways that we can take advantage of the brain's *plasticity* (explained on page xviii) in order to strengthen our emotional resilience.

In recent years, psychology researchers have found the practice of mindfulness to be particularly helpful in reducing the risk of relapse in people who have experienced depression. Many studies have found it to be a significant alternative to or support for medication.

Mindfulness works by interrupting the conditioned cycle of thoughts, emotions, sensations, and behavior that mire people in a downward spiral of depression. Using mindfulness allows us to transform our harsh inner critics to voices of support by increasing the capacity for self-compassion that nurtures self-worth and resiliency.

A Self-Compassion Approach

While mindfulness is the foundation for *Uncovering Happiness,* mindfulness on its own is often not enough. The other foundation on which this program rests is self-compassion: the recognition of our own suffering with an inclination to help ourselves. Once we become aware that we're struggling, self-compassion allows us to activate the brain's self-soothing system. This inspires a sense of safety and courage to engage in the behavioral changes necessary to move toward healing.

As humans, we're wired with an automatic negativity bias, paying more attention to what's negative than positive. This wiring is for survival: if danger is lurking, we want to have a quick-response system to keep us safe. The problem is that this same negativity bias turns inward, and we can be too hard on ourselves. With depression, these voices really dig in, striking where we're most vulnerable and evoking feelings of shame, inadequacy, and unworthiness. The cultural stigma of depression as a weakness only feeds these feelings. Part of self-compassion is to recognize that we're not alone with this, it's not something to be ashamed of, and that emotional struggles are a part of the human condition.

Science is now revealing that self-compassion is a key transformative and protective mindset for decreasing anxious and depressive symptoms. The alchemy of mindfulness and self-compassion transforms vulnerability so that instead of it being something we fear will spiral us down, it becomes an upward spiral of self-worth and resiliency.

It may seem difficult to do, but it's a skill that anyone can learn.

Think of this book as your compassionate guide. Even after you've read it from cover to cover, it will remain with you, ready to help guide you through the ups and downs that are part of this unfolding life.

Based in Science

The techniques, tools, and strategies in this book are grounded in a wealth of exciting new scientific knowledge. For decades, psychological treatment was based on observations about people's behaviors, choices, thoughts, and explanations. But the development of technological resources such as functional magnetic resonance imaging (fMRI) has opened windows into the human mind, allowing neurological researchers to understand brain function in amazing new ways that have never been possible before.

Using advanced scientific technology, researchers have discovered, for example, that by using certain cognitive and mind-body techniques, we actually have the ability to change our brains. This is called *neuroplasticity*. Until about the 1970s, scientists believed that once the brain finished undergoing the growth and development of childhood, its structure, pathways, and connections were pretty much set in stone. But researchers began to challenge that assumption, and they designed studies to test it. (I'll tell you about some of the fascinating ones later in the book.) Soon the idea of the "static brain" was replaced by the belief in the plasticity of the brain—science was showing that the brain can actually be rewired through the actions of neural processes, behaviors, and the environment. This was amazing news for people with depression, anxiety, and other emotional health problems, because it demonstrated the potential for the parts of the brain associated with emotions to be made more resilient. We now know, for example, that we can actually grow new nerve connections and activate areas of the brain associated with awareness, learning, memory, and empathy. We can strengthen the parts of the brain associated with resiliency just as we can strengthen the muscles in our bodies. What's more, we can actually deactivate areas of the brain that rev up when we experience the automatic negative thoughts that fuel depression.

What it all comes down to is this: we can build up the sections of the brain that protect us from depression, and slow down the sections that foster depression. Doing this allows the brain's own natural antidepressants to emerge, grow stronger, and contributes powerfully to the resiliency that we need to enjoy good times, survive difficult times, and open us up to lives that truly feel worth living.

Unlearning Helplessness

This book also addresses another crucial area to overcoming depression: unlearning the *learned helplessness* that influences the behavior of so many people with depression.

Learned helplessness is a mental state in which we are unable or unwilling to solve a problem even when there is a viable solution within reach. It occurs when our brains come to the conclusion that we don't have control over problematic situations. Being depressed induces a sense of learned helplessness that can surface again in the future, when depression reoccurs. Learned helplessness teaches us to stop trying to help ourselves *even when we are actually capable of it*, and it prevents us from learning new strategies to prevent relapse *even when those strategies exist*. It is another lie that depression forces us to believe.

Yet just as helplessness can be learned, it can be unlearned. We can begin replacing learned *helplessness* with learned *helpfulness*. Science shows that we can actually grow new neural connections in areas of the brain that process emotional pain, empowering us to recognize our own helplessness and replace it with more constructive thinking and self-helpful behavior.

Once we identify and understand the helplessness habits we fall into during periods of depression, we can challenge and change them, replacing them with new behaviors of helpfulness that allow us to solve problems and pull ourselves away from depression. By *un*learning learned helplessness, we can unearth the inner strength we need to make choices that lead us out of the self-perpetuating loop of helplessness and depression.

The Format of Uncovering Happiness

The following pages integrate the findings of hundreds of academic studies and dozens of interviews with mindfulness teachers, psychologists, neuroscientists, and researchers. (See the notes section of the book for citations.) It also includes stories from some of the people I've worked with who have suffered the burden of depression and who have used the techniques in this book to find their own personal pathways to healing. All of these stories are shared with permission, and pseudonyms have been used to protect each person's privacy.

Uncovering Happiness has three parts.

In part 1, I'll lay out the groundwork for cultivating what I call an antidepressant brain. We'll cover the following topics and more:

- what depression is, and why it happens;
- what the depression loop is, how it works, and how we can interrupt it;

- why having depression once or twice or even repeatedly for years does not mean you are destined to face a future of chronic depression;
- how subconscious conditioning feeds depression;
- why depression is not your fault;
- how to break the habits that contribute to and sustain depression;
- how a transformative method is changing the way we think about human potential; and
- how to stop one very specific force from allowing us to fall into depression again and again.

In part 2, we'll look at the five essential natural antidepressants: mindfulness, self-compassion, purpose, play, and mastery. I'll explain what these are, how they can protect you from depression, how they inspire real happiness, and how to develop them in your life.

Part 3, "The Natural Antidepressant Tool Kit," is a fantastic resource that will give you an array of tools, techniques, and practices to support you throughout your journey. Here you'll find guidance on creating your own antidepressant "cheat sheets," forming your own "get-well team," building healthy habits that you can stick to for the rest of your life, and becoming part of a supportive mindfulness community.

Where I'm Coming From

Mindfulness changed my life; in fact, it may have even saved it. Looking back, I can trace my ups and downs with depression to as early as childhood. In youth, depression can often show up as anger, and my family would describe me during those years as defiant, willful, and angry. Imagine a chubby, freckle-faced kid with a frown and his arms crossed over his chest—that was me. My parents divorced when I was six years old, and I grew up searching for ways to ease the feelings of loneliness and emotional pain. During high school, I started experimenting with alcohol and marijuana as an escape, and in college I discovered psychedelics and amphetamines. The drugs helped me get away from the internal experience of loneliness and grief that had resided within me since childhood.

While living in San Francisco during my twenties, I built a successful career in sales. Yet at night, I lived fast and partied recklessly, abusing drugs and alcohol with a like-minded group of drifting souls. Eventually my despair and shame grew so deep that I isolated myself from my family and friends and lost myself in my addictive behaviors.

Occasionally, in some of the seedier bars I frequented, I would come across a mess of a man who was so strung out that he repulsed me. I remember saying to my friends, "God help me if I ever turn out like him." I thought, since I was managing to succeed at work, I was in control of my self-abusive behavior. But one night, after many hours of partying, I saw the truth of who I had become. When I found myself slumped beside that man and his equally dazed companion in the back of a broken-down limousine, I saw my own reflection in his wasted face and realized I was throwing away my life. I jumped out of the limousine, determined to transform myself.

It wasn't easy, and I admit that I hit a few bumps as I set out to start my life over. My family urged me to spend a month away at a retreat center. During that time, I questioned everything I did and all that I believed. Answers began to come to me as I started to practice mindfulness: I wanted to stop abusing my body. I wanted to find the purpose and meaning of my life. I wanted to be happy.

I wanted to heal myself, and eventually, I realized, I wanted to help heal others who faced some of the same challenges that had nearly broken me.

I went back to school and entered into a playful adventure with mindfulness. I focused on living a more purposeful life, surrounding myself with supportive people and replacing destructive behaviors with healthy choices that fulfilled me. I started to create a life of meaning and purpose that allowed me to feel whole. I was starting to uncover happiness.

After finishing my training as a clinical psychologist, I began running mindfulness-based stress reduction (MBSR) and mindfulness-based cognitive therapy (MBCT) programs focusing on helping people relate to stress better and not relapse into depression. During the years that followed, I saw how effectively mindfulness-based therapies helped people reduce stress and heal emotionally. I began training therapists, physicians, educators, and business people in the combination of mindfulness and mental health. I went on to coauthor *A Mindfulness-Based Stress Reduction Workbook* and authored *The Now Effect* and *Mindfulness Meditations for the Anxious Traveler*. I designed programs to reach a variety of different people, including Mindfulness at Work® for corporations, Mindful Compassion Cognitive Therapy (MCCT) for depressive relapse, and codesigned the CALM (Connecting Adolescents to Learning Mindfulness) program with my wife, Dr. Stefanie Goldstein. As I continued with my own practice and learned from the practice of my clients and students, I discovered powerful essential antidepressant elements that had never before been explicitly integrated into the current mindfulness-based therapies for people with depression.

Throughout this journey, I've gone through profound shifts in how I relate to myself and the world. I've learned that I don't have to be enslaved by the story of the past, and I certainly don't need to believe everything I think. I have a deep sense that I am worthy of love, and that often comes through my own courage in being vulnerable with myself and others. I don't get caught as often in the trap of "What will people think?" but side more with the belief that "I am doing the best I can at the moment, and I am enough." I have also noticed that life has its ups and downs, and I can't control the conditions that happen to me in any given moment, but I can choose, with awareness, how to respond to them.

I now know that uncovering happiness is not about simply being drunk on life but is found in a profound and enduring experience of learning how to lean into loving ourselves and others in good times and in bad. It's a happiness based on a sense of common humanity, connectedness, and purpose. I notice feeling more loving and peaceful with myself and others—not all the time, but much more than before. While I still get hooked at times by self-judgments and negative thoughts, I have learned to be grateful for the good moments and a bit more graceful during the difficult ones, knowing that all things in life come and go.

The guidance in this book is not a miraculous panacea—it can't cure depression overnight, and each step does take effort to implement into your life. I can't promise you that reading *Uncovering Happiness* will make all of your depressive symptoms disappear instantly. But I can promise that the guidelines within these pages will give you the tools you need to begin to break the cycle of depression and release yourself from its grip.

Whatever your experience with depression has been—whether you just have the blues, you have chronic low-grade unhappiness, or you've experienced one or more major depressive episodes— you have the power to change the way you feel. By understanding how depression works and making the choice to nurture your natural antidepressants, you can become stronger and more resilient. Trust yourself; you can cultivate an antidepressant brain and uncover happiness.

If you're not completely convinced that you can take steps to help yourself feel better, try putting aside that judgment. That's your depression talking. Try your best to ignore those doubts for now and take a leap of faith. Soon the experience of truth will begin to crowd out the lies of depression.

Ready? Let's get started.

– john   o'donohue –

PART 1

A Naturally Antidepressant Brain

STEP 1

Understand the
Depression Loop

Clint, a middle-aged executive, had experienced bouts of anxiety and depression off and on since childhood. Raised by an overly critical father, Clint grew up believing that having negative emotions was a sign of weakness, so he buried them deep inside. When Clint was a child, his father would call him a sissy and embarrass him in public when he cried. Later in life, when Clint felt sadness or other difficult emotions, he would close himself down and become numb, avoiding his partner, and burying himself in work to try to hide from his feelings. Clint didn't realize it at the time, but he was caught in a depression loop: complicated feelings (such as sadness) would trigger reactionary thoughts (negative self-talk) and sensations (emotional numbness) that would in turn cue certain behaviors (withdrawal from loved ones and escape to his computer and his work). Anxiety and hopelessness left Clint feeling pessimistic that he'd ever emerge from his depression, creating a negative feedback loop that made him feel trapped.

Working together, Clint and I focused on understanding the cyclical nature of his responses to his feelings. Clint began to see and recognize his own personal depression cues. He began to learn to step outside of his habitual mindsets when uncomfortable feelings emerged in order to take a closer look at those feelings and the reactions they elicited. He identified triggers, thought patterns, and behaviors that were associated with his depressive experiences.

Clint had a breakthrough experience one morning. After hearing some bad family news, he paid attention to his reactions and noticed himself becoming numb and withdrawn. He felt an urge to head to his computer to work, as he had so often before. He saw himself trying to flee from his sadness instead of allowing himself to feel it. This time, though, things were different. Because he had learned how to recognize the activation of his familiar depressive loop, he was more aware and able to interrupt it. He was able to make the choice to step out of the cycle and let himself feel sad rather than hiding from the feeling. As he gave himself permission to experience an uncomfortable emotion, the tension in his body dissipated, and within a half hour, the sadness passed. Clint felt elevated by a sense of freedom he hadn't experienced in quite some time. By recognizing his own personal depressive stimulus, Clint was able to change his response and avoid a negative spiral that would lead him down the path of negative feelings, thoughts, sensations, and behaviors.

Learning to identify the cyclical nature of the depression loop and to recognize your own depression cues, as Clint did, is crucial for uncovering happiness. We're going to focus on that in this chapter, because knowing what triggers your own depression loop is a powerful first step toward being able to overcome depression. Having awareness gives you space to make choices: instead of responding automatically and without thought, you can make informed, mindful decisions that can protect you from depression and open you up to possibilities you didn't see before.

The Truth About Depression

Having a clear understanding of depression, what depression is or isn't, helps sharpen your ability to recognize it in your own life, acknowledge how it affects you, develop proactive responses to your own personal depressive cues, and lay the groundwork for cultivating a brain with natural antidepressants.

Let's begin with what depression *is*.

First and foremost, it is an illness—and like many illnesses, the experience of depression can vary from person to person. Some people have major depression, striking the brain just as an acute case of pneumonia strikes the lungs. People with this kind

FINDING THE FREEDOM IN THE "SPACE"

As you work through the steps in this book, I hope you'll keep in mind a wonderful quote from Viktor E. Frankl, an Austrian neurologist, psychotherapist, Holocaust survivor, and author of the book *Man's Search for Meaning*: "Between stimulus and response there is a space, in that space lies our power to choose our response, in our response lies our growth and our freedom."

The space between *stimulus and response* is the space in which automatic, unconscious thinking often takes over. When a stimulus appears, we may initially think we have no choice in how we respond to it. Someone cuts us off in traffic, and we respond with anger. A critical remark from an employer fills us with shame. But even though it may feel as if those responses are inevitable, they are not. There is a space between stimulus and response, and within that space we have the freedom to choose. That philosophy is at the very core of *Uncovering Happiness*. Start to recognize the space between stimulus and response in your everyday life. Once you become aware of that space, we can use it to make reasoned, conscious choices.

of depression experience extreme symptoms that can severely curtail their normal everyday functioning for varying amounts of time. Others have less serious symptoms that are more akin to the allergies that may last for weeks, months, or years, interfering with their happiness but not necessarily preventing them from living a functional life.

Because depression is not talked about openly, many people are ignorant about it. People sometimes think that depression is made up, a kind of chosen laziness, lack of self-discipline, or character flaw. But they're wrong. Thanks to advances in brain imaging, we know that the brains of people who have depression actually look different on scans than the brains of those who don't, just as the lungs of people with pneumonia look different on scans than those of people with healthy lungs.

Depression causes a range of symptoms that interfere with daily life, happiness, and the ability to sleep, work, eat, make decisions, socialize, and enjoy pleasurable activities. It is so prevalent that nearly 7 percent of adults in the United States will face an episode of major depression this year. Millions more will experience a sense of chronic unhappiness.

There is no one cause for depression. It can be the result of someone's genetics, difficult experiences early in life, or both. Episodes of depression can be triggered by outside events and situations such as a physical or emotional trauma, the loss of a loved one, an accident, a natural disaster, a change of seasons, hormonal changes, pregnancy or childbirth, stress, relationship problems, unemployment, and a host of other causes. Or they can have no visible trigger at all.

Like most other illnesses, depression can be treated successfully in a variety of ways, including medication and several kinds of therapy. Even the most severe cases of depression can improve with and at times be prevented by treatment.

Now let's consider what depression *is not*.

The biggest, most important thing that depression is not is *your fault*. Depression occurs as a result of a combination of genetic, biological, environmental, and psychological factors. People don't choose to have depression, and it's not something they can just snap out of when someone tells them to cheer up.

Depression is not who you are—it involves a conditioned habit that your brain has learned, and that your brain can unlearn. A habit is a routine of some process that we learn and that after being repeated tends to occur subconsciously. Even in someone who is genetically predisposed to depression, the habit is how the brain reacts to the relapse signs when they arise that fuels the downward spiral. After even a single depressive event, all your brain needs is a cue and a conditioned combination of thoughts, emotions, and sensations arise and go to work beneath your conscious awareness. The brain perceives this as a threat and then begins to engage in common behaviors that can be used to avoid this discomfort. Maybe you tend to overeat, isolate from friends, become a couch potato, or procrastinate. Like any habit, the result of these behaviors is predictable, bringing up self-loathing, hopelessness, anger, or sadness, and keeps you stuck deeper in the conditioned reaction that I call the "depressive loop." But one of the biggest errors we make is identifying with this depressive loop as if this is who we are.

You are *not* your depression.

As this depressive habit loop unfolds in your life, the brain eventually creates a story with you as the main character as a depressive person. If you've struggled with this throughout life, family and friends have likely reinforced this identity, calling you a "depressed person." When something is part of who you are, it becomes fixed, unchanging, and a draw for feeling deficient or defective. But when we truly investigate depression, even chronic unhappiness, it's just a passing, fluctuating pattern of thoughts, emotions, and sensations that comes and goes like all other things. It's not fixed at all, and clinging to this identity can be a source of deep shame and sorrow that repeatedly cues chronic unhappiness or more acute episodes. But it doesn't have to stay this way. For the past fifteen years, scientists have discovered the dynamic nature of our brains and how we can create new neural connections throughout the life span.

At the moment it may be difficult, but for now, see if you can begin holding any story that states "I am a depressed person" lightly. As you do, you may come to understand that the all-too-familiar feeling that "something is wrong with me" is not something to be ashamed of, any more than having pneumonia or allergies is something to be ashamed of. You don't choose depression—it chooses you.

Depression occurs in all types of people. Although women are 70 percent more likely than men to become depressed at some point in their lives, millions of men develop it as well. But many try to keep it a secret because men are taught from a young age that you need to be "strong" and that depression is a source of shame, implying "weakness." From an evolutionary perspective, if you're weak, the clan doesn't value you, you're not a desirable mate, and you don't belong. If you're cast out of the clan, your life is at risk. The brain of the modern-day man doesn't see it much differently. Hiding depression only keeps us identified with it and doesn't let it do what it's meant to do: come and go. An increasing number of men understand this better and are speaking up about it and seeking support. On the other hand, many kids can't hide it, as depression comes out as anger, irritability, and willfulness.

Depression is not always obvious. The shame associated with depression leads people to often hide their illness from friends, family, and even their doctors. So if you're walking around think-

ing that you're the only one you know who's struggling with this illness, chances are pretty good that you're wrong. You may very well have friends, neighbors, coworkers, and family members who are depressed. They hide it from you just as you may hide yours from them.

SIGNS AND SYMPTOMS OF DEPRESSION

- Persistent sad, anxious, or "empty" feelings
- Feelings of hopelessness or pessimism
- Feelings of guilt, worthlessness, or helplessness
- Irritability, restlessness
- Loss of interest in activities or hobbies once pleasurable, including sex
- Fatigue and decreased energy
- Difficulty concentrating, remembering details, and making decisions
- Insomnia, early-morning wakefulness, or excessive sleeping
- Overeating or appetite loss

- Thoughts of suicide, suicide attempts
- Aches or pains, headaches, cramps, or digestive problems that do not ease with treatment

Source: US National Institute of Mental Health

Depression as a Side Effect

Depression can sometimes be caused by medical conditions such as thyroid disease, cardiovascular disease, diabetes, and brain disorders. It can also be brought on by medications: dozens of drug classes list depression as a possible side effect, including (but not limited to) calcium channel blockers, beta-blockers, benzo-diazepines, statins, painkillers, cancer treatments, therapeutic hormones, and birth control.

People don't choose to have depression, and it's not something they can just snap out of when someone tells them to cheer up.

The Depression Loop

I've found during my work with depression that it's helpful to envision it as a kind of circular process: an automatic loop rather than a linear set of events. Clients find it useful to think of it as a cycle, a spiral, or even a traffic circle. However you picture it, understanding the circular nature of events that lead to or keep depression alive is an important step toward recognizing how it can pull you into its sphere of influence.

For now, let's use the image of a traffic circle to explain how the depression loop works. If you live someplace where there are lots of traffic circles or if you have ever driven on one, you know how confusing and maddening they can be.

You're driving on a straight road, minding your own business, maybe humming along with a song on the radio, and suddenly a traffic circle looms ahead. It just kind of appears on the street ahead of you. Your mind instantly starts anticipating entering the circle, how the cars may stream in, and how you're going to exit. A feeling of fear or anxiety arises; your hands start to sweat and grip the steering wheel. As you enter, you search for a sign for a way out, and halfway through the circle you realize that you have to switch lanes to jockey for position so you're ready for your exit. Meanwhile, you drive by other entrance points that each admit streams of new cars into the circle. You see your exit, but you realize that you either have to speed up or slow down. If you miss your exit—which is so easy to do—you have no choice but to loop around again hoping that next time you'll make your way out.

Falling into the depression loop is a lot like entering a traffic circle. You're living your life, feeling fine, minding your own business, and all of a sudden you find depression looming. Maybe it's just a feeling you wake up with, a moment when you suddenly fall prey to a shaming inner critic that says something like "there's something wrong with me/you," or a response to hearing some negative news. Once you're in it, you try valiantly to get out. But it's so easy to get stuck.

Just as various roads lead you into a traffic circle, the depression loop has four entrance points: thoughts, feelings, sensations, and behaviors. Any one of these can lead you into the depression loop. Once you're caught inside the loop, your mind goes around and around struggling to get out. Streams of thoughts enter the loop as your brain struggles to figure out "What's wrong with me?" As one of my students says, "The bloodhound is sniffing around for the villain (and much analysis is required)." The brain anxiously defaults to reaching back into the past, referencing and rehashing negative events to try to figure it out. Simultaneously, the brain jumps into the future, planning, rehearsing, and anticipating some upcoming hopeless catastrophe. As all this happens, the brain pours stress into an already stressful situation.

You may see an exit, but as you try to leave the loop, you find yourself blocked by more depressive thoughts, feelings, sensations, and behaviors. Before you know it, the traffic gets even heavier with the addition of streams of fear and anxiety when you begin to perceive that you're becoming trapped in the self-perpetuating depression loop. You're desperate for escape, but, sideswiped by fear and negativity, you become so overwhelmed that you just keep going around and around and around. Soon a sense of learned helplessness sets in: you can no longer even see the exit, so you stop trying to break free and begin to believe you may never escape.

This was a common occurrence for one of my patients, thirty-year-old Sandy, who had experienced bouts of depression her whole life. Typically she would feel fine for a while, but then at times, seemingly out of nowhere, she would become depressed. Sandy would lose interest in activities she usually enjoyed and have trouble finding the motivation she needed for everyday tasks. Feelings such as unworthiness and guilt would begin to flood her mind, and in response, she tended to isolate herself from her family and friends and make choices that fueled her depression rather than pull her out of it.

Sandy experienced depression as a persistently reinforcing loop that dragged her down. Negative thoughts would trigger troubling feelings (or vice versa) that in a short time would turn into an ever-present depressed mood state. This would make it tough for Sandy to get out of bed in the morning. Doing the activities she usually enjoyed felt nearly impossible, and instead of partaking in life, Sandy would often end up sitting in her apartment feeling terrible about herself, eating too much, drinking too much, and sinking deeper and deeper into a morass of gloom.

The Depression Loop

Your Changing Brain

Sandy didn't know this, but each time she experienced a bout of depression and got lost in the depression loop, her brain actually changed. When we practice anything in life over and over again, it starts to become automatic; in psychology, we call that a *conditioned habitual reaction*, and in neuroscience, it's called *experience-dependent neuroplasticity*. Right now eighty billion to one hundred billion nerve cells, or *neurons*, are interacting with what some have said are one trillion connections, called *synapses*, in an unimaginably fast and dynamic network. When we do something over and over—whether it's something we're trying to learn, such as improving our tennis swing; or something we'd rather not learn, like an anxiety response to dogs after being bitten by one—neurons in our brains fire together. As we repeat these actions, they eventually wire together, making the process an unconscious habit. This is called top-down processing. It is the brain's process of drawing from our implicit memories to make sense of the present moment, and it's how the neuroscience of decision making works.

Do you have to think about how to pick up the spoon to eat your morning breakfast cereal, or how to step on the accelerator or brake when driving your car? No, and you can thank top-down processing for that: your brain directs you to do these things automatically. Top-down processing comes in handy when the habit is something positive or neutral. But the brain also has the ability to make decisions beneath our conscious awareness that keep us stuck in the depression loop.

A good way to understand how top-down processing plays a part in depression is to think about its connection to trauma. A trauma reaction is so shocking to the nervous system that it instantly wires the brain to be highly sensitive to any signs of it coming again. The trauma of being bitten by a dog, for example, is enough to create a neural bridge between all of the thoughts, emotions, sensations, and behavior associated with the dog bite. After experiencing the trauma of being attacked by a loose German shepherd, simply walking by a leashed Chihuahua can cue the snap judgment of insecurity and the emotion of fear even though the Chihuahua presents no actual danger. This causes the stress hormone *cortisol* to flood the brain, cutting off access to the part of the brain that recognizes the context of the situation: that the Chihuahua is harmless and really not a threat. Instead, the cortisol launches you into a fight, flee, or freeze response governed by fear and irrationality rather than by reason and judgment. You fear the Chihuahua because of your own automatic emotional and physical responses, not because any real danger exists.

This played out in a less dramatic but equally troublesome way for my client Sandy. One day when she came in to see me looking particularly distressed, she told me that she received an email that a client of hers was angry with her work. In exploring it together, we realized that this kind of cue triggered worries about losing that client, increasing her anxiety, and making her heart race and her breathing to become shallow. Her mind spiraled with negative hopeless thoughts about the future of her business, and she began to avoid doing her work. Sandy knew she was getting depressed, and this spiraled more fear. Her response prevented her from dealing with the client's email in a logical, objective way.

Sandy was ready to start breaking this cycle when she finally recognized her depressive loop for what it really was: a deeply conditioned habit (or trauma reaction). In fact, just understanding the concept of the depression loop was enough for Sandy to start effecting a change in her relationship to depression. She was able to see it in action in her daily life and name it. The moment she saw it occurring, she was able to stand apart from it in a *space of awareness* that was separate from the loop itself and to gain perspective—as did Clint, the client I described in the beginning of this chapter. She no longer felt that she *was* the loop—rather, she was the aware person *viewing* the loop. In this space, she found a sense of freedom and a "choice point," a moment in time when she was aware enough to choose a healthier response.

The first step in uncovering happiness and experiencing freedom from the depression loop is learning how to objectively see this loop in action instead of getting lost in it. The moment we notice the depression loop in action is a moment we've stepped outside of it, into a space of perspective and choice. The beauty is that science is now showing us that through intentional repetition and action, we can change our brains for the better. This is what psychiatrist and researcher Jeffrey Schwartz, of the University of California, Los Angeles, School of Medicine, has coined *self-directed* neuroplasticity. It may seem impossible, but it's not. You'll soon see that you can turn the volume down on the fear that keeps it going and catch the signs that cue the habit in the first place.

The moment you notice the depression loop in action is the moment you're able to step outside of it, into a space of perspective and choice.

Learning to Be Helpless

As I mentioned in the introduction, something called learned helplessness plays a significant role in the depression loop. Before we go any further, I want to tell you more about what learned helplessness is and the hold it very likely has on you.

Once again, learned helplessness is a mental state when our minds decide that we don't have control over problematic situations—even if we actually do have some control. Being depressed induces a sense of learned helplessness that blinds us to our choices and discourages us from trying to help ourselves even when we have the capacity to make things better.

We first became aware of learned helplessness in the late 1960s, when University of Pennsylvania psychologist Martin Seligman and his colleague Steve Maier designed a study to determine what would happen when someone experienced pain repeatedly without any way out. Would he learn to feel helpless and hopeless?

Seligman used thirty dogs in his now-famous study. He randomly divided them into three groups: The dogs in group one were put into harnesses for a short period of time and then released. The dogs in group two were put into harnesses and then received mild electrical shocks that they could stop by pressing on a panel with their snouts. The dogs in group three were put in harnesses and shocked, but they had no control over the shocks and could not stop them. (This kind of research sounds cruel to us today, but fifty years ago, there were different opinions about the treatment of laboratory animals.)

The dogs in group three learned that no matter what actions they took, there was nothing they could do to stop from being shocked.

Seligman wondered what effect a traumatic experience like this would have on the dogs' ability to learn to avoid future suffering. To figure this out, he placed the dogs inside a kind of "shuttle box" like the one you see on the next page, with electrical grids for a floor and a short partition separating it into two spaces. A light would come on shortly before the shock to alert the dogs of the impending electrical current. After a little while, the group two dogs learned that they could escape the shock by jumping over the partition when the light came on. But the group three dogs, who had learned to be helpless, just laid there stoic, immobilized, not expending any energy to leave. Their past experience of not being able to relieve their suffering interfered with their ability to learn to relieve future suffering. This was the first time researchers had shown that having experienced helplessness in the past can interfere with the ability to learn to escape future relapses.

Years later, researchers conducted similar studies with people in which they used brain imaging technology to show what hap-

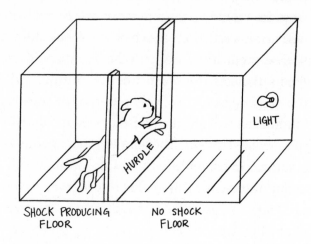

SHOCK PRODUCING
FLOOR

NO SHOCK
FLOOR

pens in the brain in situations like this. They found that the areas of the brain involved in helping a person make clear decisions and feel motivated to follow through are distressed. Even though people who are depressed would love nothing more than to help themselves feel better, their brains become habituated to thinking there is no way out.

When people see someone who is depressed, they don't think of learned helplessness; they often think it's just an issue of laziness, or a lack of motivation or willpower. Unenlightened people believe that if someone with depression simply exerted more effort, he or she would get better. But that's not how it is. This depression myth couldn't be more wrong.

Like the dogs in the shuttle box, how can we learn to see "the light," or signs of relapse that come in order to learn to escape the shock of depression? How can we resolve the longstanding insecurities, unresolved traumas, or limiting core beliefs that continue to keep us stuck?

Another interesting example of this is a study performed in 2011 by researchers at a small lab at the University of Colorado Boulder.

They split rats into three groups; mild shocks were administered to the tails of the rats in group two and group three, while group one received no shocks. Group two had control over escaping the shocks, whereas group three did not. When the researchers studied the rats' brains, they discovered that the rats in group two showed neuron growth in a part of the brain known as the prefrontal cortex. (See next page.) Not only did those rats escape the shocks, but their brains actually changed in reaction to the experience.

This research contributed to a growing awareness of the fact that the brain has the ability to break out of the trap of learned helplessness. Like the animals in these studies, we can discover how to escape the "shocks" of depression. As we do so, we cultivate an antidepressant brain by bolstering activity in the prefrontal cortex and slowing down the action in the amygdala.

Thanks to research on learned helplessness, we have better insights and tools for breaking free from depression.

Brain Names

The brain is an amazingly complicated organ. You don't have to know all its ins and outs in order to uncover happiness, but it helps to know the names of a few of the most important brain structures related to depression:

- The *amygdala* (a-mig-da-la) is an almond-shaped structure in the center of the brain that regulates memory and emotional reactions. The amygdala processes and interprets information gathered by the five senses and then tells the body how to react. It has been coined the "fear circuit" for its pivotal role in our fear reactions. It is often enlarged in a depressed brain, suggesting that we may be more sensitive to fearful cues.

- The *prefrontal cortex* (PFC) is located in the front of the brain, just behind the forehead. It's the *executive function* center of the brain, which is responsible for complex cognitive behavior such as abstract thinking, analyzing thoughts, decision making, rational perspective, and predicting outcomes of choices. It's the most evolved area of the brain. Your PFC lights up when you're engaging in rational and deliberate decision making. It manages your goals and the appropriate responses to achieve them. A depressed brain will often show a general reduction in PFC activity, but with heightened activity in the right prefrontal cortex (known for more negative emotions) and less activity in the left prefrontal cortex, which lights up with positive emotions.

- The *hippocampus*, located right next to the amygdala, is involved in learning, memory, and context. It draws on memories to help us gain perspective and make conscious choices. When the amygdala perceives danger, it cuts off access to the hippocampus. After all, there is no need to learn in that moment, because it's time to fight, flee, or freeze, not to stand still and draw inferences. This is what makes it difficult to learn new ways of

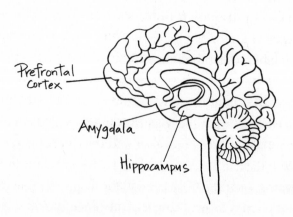

coping in the midst of depression. The hippocampus is also negatively impacted by repeated surges of cortisol, flooding the brain in response to states of fear, which ambush us often during the depression loop. This may be why in a depressed brain, the hippocampus is often smaller in size.

Escaping the Loop

Thoughts, emotions, sensations, and behavior. When it comes to depression, these four elements feed off one another to create a depressive feedback loop. While nobody knows what causes depression, we do know that as this feedback loop repeats over time, it becomes a conditioned habit, so that a single stimulus—perhaps a negative thought, or feeling sad or physically tired—can trigger the looping.

But here's the upside to all this: just as the brain can be conditioned into making the depression loop an ingrained habit, it can also be conditioned away from it. You truly can rewire your brain so that you don't automatically fall into depression whenever certain thoughts, emotions, sensations, or behaviors occur. Having had depression in the past doesn't mean that it's your fate to be in its grip the rest of your life. Understanding how the depressive loop works is the first step to stepping outside of it, gaining perspective, and dropping into a space of choice, possibility, and freedom. When you're driving down a road and see a traffic circle looming, you don't have to enter it. You can veer onto a different road.

This isn't easy, but it's possible—and the more you practice it, the better you'll get at not only pulling yourself out of the loop but also preventing yourself from entering it in the first place.

Depression cues have a range of possible triggers. Some are obvious: major negative life events such as the death of a loved

DEPRESSION CUES

Depression often starts with a cue, or trigger: an initial sense of unease that can be brought on by a subconscious thought, memory, physical feeling, emotion, or some external life event. It can be something as mild as a friend's disapproving expression or as severe as the loss of a job or loved one. The cue is usually followed by:

- **Thoughts**: After the cue, the mind starts to think, and the stories begin. The brain anxiously defaults to reaching back into the past, referencing and rehashing negative events to try to give the cue meaning and context. Simultaneously, the brain jumps into future planning, rehearsing and anticipating all kinds of possible catastrophes that could result from the cue. As it does this, more stress pours into an already stressful situation.
- **Emotions**: The blues or anxiety set in (or set in deeper). As they do, new thoughts continue to flow as you say to yourself, "Why am I getting depressed?" or "What did I do wrong?" or "This always happens to me," or "I'm hopeless." This habitual looping can happen instantaneously and last for days. The more you identify with the narrative, the deeper the spiral of anxiety and depression goes.
- **Sensations**: As thoughts and emotions darken, physical sensations and symptoms such as heaviness, fatigue, insomnia, and appetite change set in.
- **Behavior**: Negative thoughts, difficult emotions, and uncomfortable sensations skew your perception and influence your ability to make healthy choices about behavior. This in turn can lead to even more negative thoughts, difficult emotions, and uncomfortable sensations.

one, health problems, caring for an aging parent, losing a job, the end of a relationship, or financial difficulties. Some are more subtle, such as rejection by a friend, a missed career opportunity, or discovering a family member's disloyalty. Depression cues can be linked to the calendar, and can be set off by changes of season, birthdays, holidays, and anniversaries of losses or traumatic events. Paradoxically, even seemingly positive, happy events—

buying a new house, landing a new job, getting married, celebrating a wedding anniversary, going on vacation, becoming a parent, or achieving a long-anticipated dream—can trigger depression cues. Our own individual personalities, histories, life events, and brain chemistry influence what our depression cues are and how they are activated.

What Are Your Depression Cues?

The first step to stopping the cycle of depression is recognizing your own depression cues and triggers. It's good to think about this when you're feeling better—when you're not trapped in the depression loop—because it's easier to be objective and have perspective. If you keep a journal, you may be able to discern your depression cues by rereading sections you wrote before or during periods of depression.

When you identify your depression cues, put them down on paper and reflect on them. By doing so, you stamp them into your short-term memory and increase your chances of recognizing them in action when you're at the cusp of becoming depressed. Being aware of your own cues and triggers makes it more likely that you'll notice when you're about to be pulled into a depression loop.

When you have a better idea of what your personal cues are, you can become aware of them while they're happening and use them as a depression barometer.

Look back into your past and ask yourself what some of the stimulus points for depression may be for you. Was there a certain event that set it off? If not, can you think of specific thoughts, feelings, sensations, and behaviors that have led you into a depression loop?

When I work with groups of clients or students, we do a brainstorming exercise that helps everyone identify his or her depression cues. Standing in front of a group of people who experience all levels of depression—from chronic low levels of unhappiness. to occasional bouts of moodiness to repeated episodes of major depression—I ask, "What are your depression cues? How do you know that depression is coming on?" For a moment, it's quiet, and then some murmurs begin as one person says something like, "I sleep too much." Another says, "I notice my thoughts become a lot more negative." Another says, "I start isolating from friends and family." As they continue speaking, I write everything down on the whiteboard. This brings an awareness of the many kinds of cues that might ignite depression. Equally importantly, it calls attention to the fact that no one is alone in this, and that although our cues may be very different, we all share this deeply human experience.

At first it may feel uncomfortable for you to identify and write down your depression cues, because it forces you to confront them face-to-face. But try to think of it this way: *knowing them will help you protect yourself from being sucked into the depression loop in the future.*

Here is a list of common depression cues. Use it to help you identify what can trigger your depression.

THOUGHTS	EMOTIONS	SENSATIONS	BEHAVIORS
• "I am fat."	• Anxiety	• Fatigue	• Overeating
• "I am stupid."	• Sadness	• Loss of energy	• Eating a certain food, such as ice cream
• "I've messed up again."	• Irritability	• Feeling heavy	• Talking too much
• "Nobody likes me."	• Impatience	• Clenching	• Sleeping too much or too little

THOUGHTS	EMOTIONS	SENSATIONS	BEHAVIORS
• "I am unlovable."	• Moodiness	• Feeling wound up or wired	• Drinking too much
• "People are avoiding me."	• Fear	• Restlessness	• Going on shopping sprees
• "I am a fraud."	• Emptiness	• Blurry thinking	• Overspending
• "I am never going to feel better again."	• Hopelessness	• Appetite changes	• Risky sexual behavior
• "I am worthless."	• Pessimism	• Loss of memory	• Avoiding friends and family
• "I make so many mistakes."	• Guilt	• Body aches	• Not bothering with activities you usually enjoy
• "I am a bad spouse, parent, child, friend, sibling, student, employee," and so on.	• Shame	• Headache	• Not exercising
• "Things are never going to get better."	• Grief	• Gastro-intestinal symptoms such as nausea or diarrhea	• Watching too much television
• "I don't deserve to live."	• Anger	• Dry mouth	• Spending too much time at the computer or playing video games
• "Everything is hopeless."	• Despair	• Shakiness	• Nail biting
		• Increased or decreased interest in sex	• Hair pulling
		• Trouble seeing or hearing	• Obsessive-compulsive behavior
			• Excessive crying

Worksheet: My Personal Depression Cues

Using the chart below, write down the thoughts, emotions, sensations, and behavior cues that sometimes act as depression triggers for you.

THOUGHTS	EMOTIONS	SENSATIONS	BEHAVIORS

Once you've drawn up your list of depression cues, make sure you keep a copy where you can refer to it often: in your wallet, on your refrigerator, in your online scheduler, and so on. Start paying attention to yourself and your moods. You may want to check in with yourself a few times a day—stop everything you're doing, be quiet for a moment, close your eyes, and ask yourself, "Where am I starting this moment from?" Be mindful of what you're feeling, thinking, sensing, and doing. Go over your list of depression cues. Do you notice any of them occurring now? (As you do this, you may think of other potential depression cues. Keep writing them down; the more you add to your list, the more likely you are to start recognizing them.) If this seems like too much work, then you are welcome to just do a check-in at the end of the day or even the end of the week and see if you noticed any cues. See what feels right for you.

When you give yourself a moment to pause and be aware, you are training your brain to be present and opening up the opportunity to see if any depression cues have been activated. If everything is fine, it can turn into a moment of gratitude, and you can go back to what you were doing. But if you recognize that one of your depression cues has been triggered, you can take action. You can start by acknowledging it and labeling it, and this in and of itself can take the wind out of its sails.

For example, perhaps one of your depression cues is that you start to engage in more frequent and intense thoughtless overeating. Or it may even be more specific: thoughtless overeating of chocolate-chip ice cream. When you take a mindful pause and check in with yourself, you may identify the fact that there has been an increased craving lately for chocolate-chip ice cream. When you recognize this increase, you can acknowledge that a potential depression cue has been activated. When this happens, I want you to label it: tell yourself, "My chocolate-chip-ice-cream depression cue has been triggered. I could be on the verge of entering a depression loop."

Now, the fact that you recognize an increased craving for chocolate-chip ice cream may not mean that you're about to experience a major bout of depression. The cue could, in fact, be completely benign and mean nothing more than that you just feel like having your favorite ice cream. But if you decide to indulge in a scoop or two, it becomes a mindful choice instead of a mindless habit.

You'll learn over time that sometimes your cue is a false alarm—as the joke about Sigmund Freud goes, sometimes a cigar is just a cigar. But sometimes your chocolate-chip-ice-cream cue really will be the sign that you're starting to enter a depressive loop. And if it is, you can take action to protect yourself.

In the next chapter, I'll describe some of the specific actions you can take in response to the triggering of a depression cue. For now, let's focus a little more on why understanding the depression

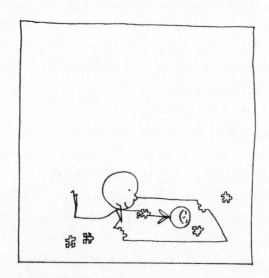

You're worth figuring out.

loop and recognizing and labeling your depression cues is such an important first step.

Once you're aware that one of your depression cues has been signaled, you can learn to objectively see this loop in action instead of getting lost in it. It may seem impossible, but it's not. You'll soon see that you can turn down the volume on the fear that keeps the loop going and catch the signs that cue the habit in the first place.

Name Them to Tame Them

Labeling a depression cue—literally saying its name out loud or writing it down in a journal—is incredibly valuable. Giving it a name can actually take away some of its power and can reduce your chances of falling into a depression loop.

We know this because of some fascinating research by psychologist Matthew Lieberman and his colleagues at the UCLA Social Cognitive Neuroscience Laboratory. They found that the simple process of putting feelings into words—referred to by psychologists as *affect labeling*—can help people do a better job of managing those feelings.

Lieberman and his collaborators showed this in a kind of creepy study—creepy if you don't like spiders, that is. They found that spiderphobic people who label and express their fears about a nearby spider actually reduce their fears and are able to get closer to a spider than are spiderphobes who see a spider but don't label and express their fears. Simply by acknowledging and labeling their fears and putting them into words reduced the distress felt by the spiderphobic volunteers.

Why does acknowledging and labeling feelings help diffuse their power? Lieberman and his colleagues answered this question by conducting studies on subjects while their brains were being scanned by functional magnetic resonance imaging (fMRI). The fMRI machine shows us where the blood is flowing in the brain, which is a direct connection to the brain's activity. They found that labeling feelings actually activates a specific region in the prefrontal cortex, which is less active in depressed people, and reduces the activity in the amygdala, which is more active in depressed people. "If the amygdala is like an alarm clock alerting us to potential threats, putting feelings into words is like hitting the snooze button," Lieberman wrote in an article about his work in the *New York Times*. "The end result is being less distressed in the face of something we fear . . . and less stressed over the long term, which can contribute to better physical health."

When a depression cue is triggered, we begin to feel fear and anxiety as the amygdala heats up. But we want to cool it down by releasing our fears. Recognizing, acknowledging, and labeling a depression cue—and actively understanding that a depression cue can push us into a depression loop—can interrupt fear, cool down the amygdala, and bring the brain back in balance.

As you practice and repeat this, you literally begin to change your neurological wiring and cultivate an antidepressant brain by creating more activity in the prefrontal cortex and less activity in the amygdala.

Here's an interesting psychological fact: when people see a picture of an angry face, their amygdala becomes more active. That's because the amygdala's job is to interpret the data we gather through our senses. Seeing an angry face sets off an alarm of sorts in the amygdala, which activates a series of physiological responses in the body (known as the *fight, flee, or freeze response*) that is designed to help us protect ourselves from danger. However, Lieberman and his colleagues discovered that when subjects see a picture of an angry face and give it a name—anger—brain activity shifts from the amygdala to the prefrontal cortex, which is responsible for analyzing data and making decisions based on that analysis. This is a very simple explanation of Lieberman's work, but it helps explain why it is so useful for people who are prone to depression to use words to label their feelings. Doing so shifts the brain's focus from an emotional reaction driven by fear to a balanced reaction with greater perspective.

As my good friend Dr. Dan Siegel, a psychiatrist at the UCLA School of Medicine says, when it comes to feelings, if you can name them, you can tame them.

We'll talk more about this later. For now, the most important takeaway is that you can begin to make real progress in breaking the depression loop by taking the following steps:

- make a list of your common depression cues;
- take breaks to pause throughout the day, or at the end of the day, to check in with your thoughts, feelings, sensations, and behaviors;
- recognize and acknowledge whether any of your depression cues have been triggered;
- label the cue and put into words the possibility that you may be entering a depression loop; and
- recognize that as soon as you notice the loop occurring, you are in a space of awareness—a choice point—where you can begin to take action.

You can't prevent yourself from ever falling into a depression loop, especially if you've experienced depression in the past. But you can devise a custom-tailored plan and get better and better at putting it into action as soon as you notice your depression cues.

STEP 2

Reverse Bad Habits

Here's a little secret that I've never told anyone: when I was in the corporate world, managing sales teams in San Francisco, I would sometimes play hooky, leaving the office and walking out to the waterfront area known as the Embarcadero, which overlooked the bay. Often it was clouded in a mist of fog. My eyes would drift off in a vacant, empty stare as I wondered what I was doing with my life and why I couldn't seem to get it together. I felt so confused and stuck, continuing to play out my bad habits that left me feeling awful physically and mentally. The more I'd analyze it and try to figure it out, the worse I felt. It wasn't until much later on that I realized a big reason why I kept repeating the bad habits: I was looking in the wrong direction. The real bad habit that was fueling this depressive loop was not something I normally associated with habits. But it absolutely was a bad habit, and it was right in front of me.

My worst bad habit was my thinking.

As I started to learn more about the nature of thought, I discovered that it can become a bad habit when the mind isn't content. This occurs fairly often. The brain registers this discontent and does what it is programmed to do: to try to analyze it and figure out how to fix the pain so that it goes away. However, in my experience and in the experiences of the thousands of people I've worked with, I have found when the brain tries to escape pain, it reinforces the feeling that "something is wrong with me," which inevitably adds stress to the pain and kicks up even more emotional suffering.

This sparks the brain to come up with other ways to soothe distress, which can lead to the unhealthy behaviors that we usually associate with bad habits. *The fact is, we are not our thoughts; not even the ones that tell us we are.*

In step 1, you learned how the depression loop works, and you defined the personal cues that draw you into it. In step 2, you'll delve further into this exploration by seeking to understand which habitual thoughts keep the loop going, how they can drive your brain NUTs (see sidebar), and how to find ways to begin freeing yourself from your own mind. You'll also get a clearer view of the behavioral bad habits that keep the loop going, how to recognize them, and how to use a simple step-by-step process to reverse them. As you do this, you take fuel away from the depressive loop and begin cultivating feelings of trust and self-reliance, which fuels an upward spiral of resiliency.

> ### WHAT ARE NUTS?
>
> The acronym NUTs is way of bringing humor to those Negative Unconscious Thoughts that arise constantly in the brain, beneath our awareness, and that feed the depression loop. Examples of NUTs include deep-seated beliefs that "I am unworthy," "Something is wrong with me," and "Nothing is ever going to change." When a challenging event occurs in our lives, these NUTs become a filter that clouds the way we look at the world—and as a result, they can actually make us feel a little nuts! As we begin bringing more attention to what our NUTs are, we become more conscious of what they are. And, if you'll excuse the pun, understanding our NUTs also strengthens our ability to "crack them," releasing their hold on us.

Habits of Thinking

Have you ever noticed that your head is full of voices? (I am referring to the automatic thoughts that come to you uninvited.) Have you ever wondered about the nature of those voices? How they constantly rehash past events, judge and compare you with others, and anticipate all the potentially worst-case scenarios? Do you hear the voices right now? The ones that might be saying, "Oh yes, I've heard this before" or "What does he mean by 'voices'?"

Yes, that's the one.

These voices are constantly running in your mind, sometimes during moments when you're doing mindless tasks, like when you're in the shower:

"What do I need to do today? There's the doctor at eleven o'clock. I need to buy a birthday present for my niece; what am I going to get her? I never know what to get people. I hope she likes what I get her. I'm never good at getting people gifts. I don't even know why I bother. Ooh, I almost forgot I need to deposit that check today."

Other times when we're not feeling well, our minds can feel like they're going nuts:

[*While looking in the mirror*]: "Wow, I look great today, don't I [*sarcastic tone*]? No wonder I can't get a boyfriend. I hate how I look. I hate where I'm at, nothing's ever going to change. Arghh, why am I so negative? Maybe this is why I have so much trouble in relationships."

Sometimes there are multiple voices at once that argue with one another:

"Another parking ticket? What's wrong with me?" "Nothing is wrong with you; just think of it as a donation to the city." [*Sinking feeling*] "I'm such a screwup." "Stop being so negative! Just think good thoughts [*irritated tone*]!" "Yeah, right, like that's going to make a difference! I tried that a thousand times. Even my own advice sucks. Not only do I keep sinking myself financially, but I can't even see how screwed up I am."

Where I get lost.

Five Major Mind Traps

Whether they are Negative Conscious Thoughts or NUTs, these five seem to earn the highest marks for keeping us stuck in a perpetual cycle of suffering:

1. Doubt

When it comes to the depressive loop, one of the infamous voices that keep us stuck is doubt. Even as you're reading this book, you might notice it:

"This might work for some people, but it's probably not going to work for me." The motive of this voice is to keep us safe from some sense of failure or disappointment, but ultimately it keeps us away from new experiences that can be supportive.

2. Emptiness

Filled with longing to be someplace else or someone else, our minds settle on the belief that the current moment is *never enough,* we're *not enough,* or we *can't do enough.*

In the movie *Big,* Tom Hanks plays a young boy who dreams that when he gets bigger, he will finally be happy. But what he finds is that once he gets his wish, the voice inside still isn't satisfied, and he wants to be a kid again. Many of us hear a similar voice: "I'll be happy when I graduate from school and don't have homework anymore." Or: "If only I could find a new job, everything would get better." Or: "Once I find someone to marry, my life will be perfect." The problem with this kind of thinking is that when the awaited event does occur, happiness may not come with it. We trap ourselves into believing that what we have now is not enough; we'll be happy only when some future goal is met, and we get married, get divorced, get a new haircut, get rich, lose weight, buy new clothes, retire—the list is endless.

Meanwhile, this motive of trying to fix the current moment leaves you in a perpetual cycle of dissatisfaction. If you look at it closely, you'll see that often there is pain underneath that dissatisfaction. By focusing on the idea that you're not where you "should be," your brain is constantly reinforcing the message that something is wrong with you, which then highlights a gap of deficiency that only grows wider as it tries harder. Even after you get what your mind wanted (the new job, the new house, the new partner, and so on), there is only brief relief because although that wanting is appeased for a moment, the voices soon want something else. The root problem is not what you don't have, but the fact that you really don't feel whole or complete.

3. Irritation

At other times, the voices feed irritation. Someone might be walking down the hallway at work humming his favorite tune, and the thoughts come up:

"Does he think everyone wants to hear him? Uh, what is he so happy about anyway? He's probably next on the chopping block."

Meanwhile, who is suffering? We are the ones in pain, but our brains think that if we project our irritation onto another person with judgment, we will stop the pain and somehow find relief. Or when the anger turns inward, it will motivate us to change even though turning anger inward often sews the seeds of depression. Or if these voices of annoyance continue to come up in our relationships and are not discussed, in time the feelings turn into resentment that inevitably eats away at the relationship like a cancer. But our experience tells a different story. Voices of irritation can alert us that something isn't right within ourselves or in a relationship. With awareness, we can use this information to be constructive. When this voice is left unchecked, we can get trapped in it.

4. Sluggishness

These voices also seem to get in the way when we're trying to do good in our lives. Have you ever had the idea of doing something that is healthy for you—maybe hanging out with friends, exercising, meditating, or even just fixing yourself a healthy meal—but then you hear this voice:

"I want to do it, but I'm too tired. I'll do it tomorrow."

When we are legitimately tired—maybe we haven't had enough sleep or have had an exceptionally taxing day—we need to listen to our bodies and rest. But at other times, these sluggish voices are just another sign that we're avoiding being with ourselves because there is a fear that it will be uncomfortable, so it's better to just check out. The motive to shut down is akin to the motivation of our destructive behaviors, such as using drugs and alcohol, which hide our strong and uncomfortable emotions, but eventually the voices of self-blame, self-judgment, and shame creep in anyway, ultimately feeding the depression loop. However, when we can recognize it, we can face it and when we can face it, we can work with it and break free.

5. Restlessness

Still, we have more voices that scream of restlessness. These days our brains are being trained to be noisier, busier, and more distracted. You might be sitting at a table alone waiting for a drink, and as your eye catches the smartphone on the table, the voices start:

"I wonder if I received any new messages. Nope, not one since a minute ago. What about Facebook, anything there? Some new updates, not that interesting. Twitter? Ah, that's an interesting tweet. I wonder when the drink is going to come?" All the while, your eyes dart around to survey your environment, and your leg shakes up and down.

Anytime there is a moment of waiting, most people will reach for their phone to check notifications, emails, surf the web, or play with an app. When there is a space empty of *doing*, the restless voices rise up. We feel compelled to fill the spaces, but what we don't realize is that it's in these empty spaces, as Viktor Frankl says, where we have a choice between doing and being; it's where possibility and opportunity emerge, and where there is a chance to make changes for the better.

All of these burdening voices feed the depression loop. But the fundamental question is, Who is behind all these voices? The true answer is that none of these voices are really ours. The number one pothole we continually fall into is believing that we are these thoughts and that these thoughts are facts. One of the main keys to cultivating an antidepressant brain and uncovering happiness is the realization that you are not your thoughts or the stories they tell. Not the ones that tell you how wonderful you are, not the ones that tell you how horrible you are, and not even the ones that are neutral. Who are you, then?

When you pay attention, you'll find that *you* are the one who is listening.

WHAT LIES BENEATH YOUR THOUGHTS

What would be there if one day all your thoughts were gone? In 1996 Jill Bolte Taylor, a thirty-seven-year-old brain scientist, suffered a neurological trauma: a stroke that took away access to the left side of her brain, which is the part that is more associated with thinking, analyzing, language comprehension, rehashing past events, and anticipating future ones. When her mother visited, Jill didn't know who she was but was able to sense her warm energy through tone and body language. Although her thoughts were gone, she still had her awareness. Consider for a moment that beneath all your thoughts, emotions, and sensations that comprise moment-to-moment experience, there is a calm, grounded, enduring awareness that is always there.

Consider what life would be like if you truly knew at the core of your being that these thoughts were not facts and that you didn't have to buy into them. Take a moment to imagine it. What might come to mind is a scene of you lying on a beach with ocean waves lapping, and if you're lucky, you can take a few deep breaths and actually taste that peace right now just for a moment.

Some people—but not many—have instant realizations or "aha!" moments that allow them to break away from these kinds of thoughts and change the course of their lives significantly. The rest of us need to work at disconnecting from these thoughts because the habit of believing them is deeply ingrained in our brains thanks to many years of practice. One way to start reversing this habit is by practicing playing with the mind. Take a moment to just listen objectively, as best you can, to the voices that are there, even the ones that are just repeating the words you are reading, and even the ones that question the purpose of this simple exercise.

Play with noticing your thoughts a bit, take control, and shout out a quote from Dr. Seuss: "I like nonsense, it wakes up the brain cells." Try not to think of a white polar bear—any luck? Probably not. Try to hold onto the image of the white polar bear—any luck? If you feel a recurring self-judgment, such as "I am stupid," try saying the word *stupid* thirty times really fast, and see what happens to your perception of the word. How does it change? Ask yourself, "I wonder what thought is going to come up next?" and wait; it always will.

The surest way to become Tense, Awkward and Confused is to develop a mind that tries too hard—one that thinks too much.

—BENJAMIN HOFF, *THE TAO OF POOH*

Getting Hooked

Most of the time, the negative thoughts that feed the depressive loop aren't conscious; they come from our deep-seated beliefs and happen instantly as the brain's snap judgments. We need to remember that most of the way we react in this world is driven by our subconscious in the form of perceptions, judgments, and opinions, which occur so quickly that they hook us before we even have a chance. Our minds may judge exercise as "bad" before the conscious excuse of being too tired or having no time emerges as a thought. Your partner was "wrong" the moment he opened his mouth. Without awareness of these snap judgments, the depression loop speeds up, and we find ourselves stuck in a familiar pattern again and again.

This is exactly what happened with my client Julia, who was a successful college sophomore when she learned that a former mentor whom she had long admired had committed suicide after a lifelong struggle with hidden depression. This news caused Julia to spiral into a state of shock and confusion. She thought about all the similarities she had always observed between the two of them, and she worried that if this could happen to her mentor, then maybe it could happen to her. Terrified, Julia fell into a deep depression and eventually admitted herself into a hospital for help.

After leaving the hospital, Julia sought my help. One area we focused on was recognizing the intrusive thoughts that scared her. She told me that many times she just found herself in a funk and riddled with anxiety. I told her that these NUTs can sneak up beneath our awareness and affect our mood. When I told her about NUTs, Julia said, "That's a good name for them because they drive me nuts!" We both had a good laugh, and that seemed to lighten her mood. In the days that followed, she ended up using this acronym to cut some humor into the moments and unhook herself when she found the depressive loop in action. This helped her at times to nip it in the bud. Humor can be a wonderful antidepressant.

Name Your NUTs

In uncovering your NUTs and naming them, you can become more aware of them. You can practice training your brain to make space between your awareness and the thoughts themselves. Getting into that space instantly diffuses their power over you and allows you to breathe easier. As you practice and repeat naming your NUTs, you'll get better and better at recognizing them and setting them aside.

To explore this more deeply, think about your top five NUTs. Spend a few minutes writing them down in the space below or in your journal. When they're captured on paper, you can't help but see the space between your awareness of the thoughts and the thoughts themselves, which allows you to start the process of gaining freedom from them.

In 1980 Steve Hollon, professor of psychology at Vanderbilt University and Philip Kendall, professor of psychology and director of the Child and Adolescent Anxiety Disorders Clinic at Temple University, conducted a study to formulate a list of the top automatic negative thoughts that people experience when depressed. Notice the themes of deficiency and hopelessness that are infused through the list. You can use the findings of this study below to help you create your list. You may see your own NUTs in this list, or you may have others:

1. I feel as though I'm up against the world.
2. I'm no good.
3. Why can't I ever succeed?
4. No one understands me.
5. I've let people down.
6. I don't think I can go on.
7. I wish I were a better person.
8. I'm so weak.
9. My life's not going the way I want it to.
10. I'm so disappointed in myself.
11. Nothing feels good anymore.
12. I can't stand this anymore.
13. I can't get started.
14. What's wrong with me?
15. I wish I were somewhere else.
16. I can't get things together.
17. I hate myself.
18. I'm worthless.
19. I wish I could just disappear.
20. What's the matter with me?

21. I'm a loser.

22. My life is a mess.

23. I'm a failure.

24. I'll never make it.

25. I feel so helpless.

26. Something has to change.

27. There must be something wrong with me.

28. My future is bleak.

29. It's just not worth it.

30. I can't finish anything.

Automatic Thoughts Questionnaire copyright 1980 by Philip C. Kendall
and Philip D. Hollon. Reprinted with permission.

Right now write down your top five NUTs.

1. _____

2. _____

3. _____

4. _____

5. _____

6. _____ *

After you write your own list of NUTs, take a few minutes to think about them. What patterns do you notice about them? Do they occur more frequently or less frequently when you're feeling well? Are they more convincing or less convincing when you're not feeling well? If you tune in to these questions, more often than not, you'll notice that these thoughts occur less often and are much less convincing and believable when you're feeling well and things seem to be going your way. That is proof that thoughts

---

* Extra credit

are not facts. If they were, just like the fact that a chair is a chair regardless of your mood, they would always remain the same.

As you begin to see these thoughts from a distance, you're literally priming your mind to objectively notice them appearing and disappearing more in daily life. You are now relating *to* them instead of *from* them, starting the process of dis-identifying from them, reversing the mind habits that keep you stuck.

Thoughts are not facts. If they were, just like the fact that a chair is a chair regardless of your mood, they would always remain the same.

Crack Your NUTs

Let's take this one step deeper now. Whenever I'm working with people in breaking free from mind traps, I share with them a series of questions adapted from American speaker and author Byron Katie that can help crack the NUTs and expose the lies that they're telling. As you practice continually cracking them, you get better and better at creating distance from your thoughts, dispelling their accuracy and seeing with greater clarity.

To start off, take one of the NUTs you listed above that represents a belief. This might be something like "I'm so weak" or "My future is bleak" or "I'm unworthy of love."

1. Once you've come up with the belief, ask yourself, "Is it true?" Just notice what comes up. You might notice what many people do, that oftentimes the answer is "Well, yes, it's true." This is

the brain initially reacting; it's the autopilot you live with and believe is you.

2. Next, ask yourself, "Is it *absolutely* true?" Can you say that this thought is 100 percent accurate without any doubt? This question gets us to look at the thought again, pause, and gain a bit more distance from it. We have more perspective on the actual thought itself. At this point, many people might say, "Well, I can't say it's a hundred percent accurate; I guess there's a possibility that I can see it in a different way." Notice if this is your experience as you do it with your NUT.

3. The third question asks, "How does this thought make you feel?" Here we're beginning to see the thought as part of a cycle—we might say a part of the depressive loop—that is causing a reaction. Common responses are "It causes feelings of sadness, anger, shame, hurt, or fear." We can go further and ask, "What impact does the thought have on you when it's visiting you frequently?" The answer, inevitably, is, "It cycles me into feeling moody, depressed, or anxious." This tends to lead us to habits of behavioral avoidance such as procrastination, eating, drugs, alcohol, sex—you name it. But in this process, we're stepping outside of it and taking the energy out of the looping.

4. Ask yourself, "What would the days, weeks, and months ahead look like if I no longer had this thought or belief?" Check in here and, as best you can, really imagine this. What comes up for you? Would you feel lighter, happier, or more capable? Would you have more energy, be more motivated, or be less inclined to engage in unhealthy habits? Would it change your relationships with yourself and others for the better? Would you feel more hopeful, open, more alive?

5. Finally, "Who would you be without these thoughts?" This dips us underneath the thinking itself and back to that seat of awareness that is really who we are. If you check in deeply, you might even have a sense that you are aware of being aware right now. This is where you are no longer ensnared by the trivial nature of these mental happenings in your head, but can finally taste the mystery of life unfolding.

You can begin reversing the habits of thinking by (1) actively *playing* with the voices in your head, (2) *naming* the NUTs, and (3) *cracking them* to dispel their lies. This starts to loosen your relationship with thoughts and their hold on you.

Habits of Behavior

Scientists say that habits are formed in a lump of neurological tissue the size of a walnut at the center of the brain called the *basal ganglia*. This area of the brain stores what is practiced and repeated in order to make things automatic. When things become automatic in life, they take less effort, and this frees us up to focus on other things that may be more important.

Think about something as seemingly simple as riding a bike. When you first learned how to ride, you had to really pay attention. You very consciously had to place your hands on the handlebars and then lift your leg over the seat to sit down. Maybe you had training wheels first, and so your mind got used to balancing

ENCOURAGE YOUR POSITIVE THOUGHTS

An important element of uncovering happiness is to notice the positive thoughts that are there and encourage them. Not only does encouraging positive thoughts help us balance our brains' inherent negativity bias, but science also shows that it opens our minds up to greater possibilities. From time to time, you might notice a nourishing thought arise, such as "I'm good enough," "Life is fine as it is," "I'm worthy of love," or "What a beautiful moment." We can be on the lookout for these thoughts and fan the flame with a play on these same questions:

1. "Is it true?" Because of the strength of our inner critics, our minds are often quick to dismiss positive thoughts, so you may notice a quick "No, it's not true. I'm not really beautiful, worthy of love, good enough [and so on] . . ."

2. "Is it possible that it's true?" Here is where we open the door a bit and ask if there is any possibility that it's true, no matter how small our minds may say it is. The answer inevitably here is "Yes, I guess there is a possibility."

3. "If you step into that possibility for a moment, how does that make you feel?" Two things can happen here. You may find that fear arises: the fear of the unknown. What would life be like if I stepped into this light? It reminds me of a poem by spiritual author and lecturer Marianne Williamson that starts, "Our greatest fear is not that we are inadequate, our deepest fear is that we are powerful beyond measure." Remind yourself that it doesn't serve you or the world to be in your small self. However, you might also experience a positive emotion such as joy, contentment, or confidence.

4. "Can I allow myself to linger in this feeling for a few moments?" When we allow ourselves to savor what's good, our "good-feeling" neurons fire together. And as psychologist Donald Hebb put it memorably, "Neurons that fire together wire together," promoting resiliency in the future.

In the following steps, we'll be uncovering our natural antidepressants. But before we do that, we have to uncover the bad habits that arise from these thoughts; the ones that perpetuate the depressive loop.

a little bit. At the same time, you had to multitask, paying attention to the ground and things around you to make sure you weren't going to run into anything. At this point, you couldn't go very fast, and there was a lot of mental (and emotional) effort involved. But as you continued to practice and repeat all the various movements riding became easier. You just got on the bike, and off you went. How did this happen?

Every time you performed a procedure, it was recorded and then chunked together as a memory. This is called *procedural memory*, because it combines lots of processes into one procedure that we can perform without thinking about each of the individual processes as we do them. The procedure becomes automatic, which leaves the brain space to think of other things. Sometimes those things are positive or benign: for example, as you're riding your bike, your mind might wander onto how beautiful the weather is or that the bumpy bike trail needs paving. But sometimes your mind fills with thoughts that have nothing to do with your bicycling: why that last interaction with a coworker didn't go well, for example, or which challenges await you at the end of your ride. The brain doesn't need to be present in order to tell you to pedal or steer, so it goes in other directions instead.

The problem comes when the brain chunks together a number of procedures that are involved with an unhealthy habit. Here's how it unfolded for my client Sherry, after she gave an important presentation at work. After the presentation, her mind filled with thoughts such as: "I can't believe Harry had the nerve to try and tell me how my presentation could've been better. I do all this work, and I never get it right. Oh, I can't believe I have to do this again next week."

This thought was followed by an urge to go to Dunkin' Donuts, along with a squirt of a pleasure chemical in the brain called dopamine. Dopamine, also a key contributor to our habits, sends signals to receptors in the brain saying "This feels good, go get more!" It is secreted when we do pleasurable things, such as eating delicious foods or having sex. It also sets the stage for an unconscious, automatic routine to unfold, as it did for Sherry, who may have gone on to think, "I need a donut and some coffee. But what about watching my weight? Oh, it's just this one time I really need it."

Soon she was at the counter, placing an order for an apple fritter and coffee.

All the different procedures involved in Sherry's navigating to Dunkin' Donuts—steering the car, obeying the traffic signs, applying the brakes, parking between the lines, turning off the engine, walking, ordering, pulling out her wallet, walking to the table, and eating and drinking—are all done automatically in Sherry's brain. Without awareness of the way this habit works, "Just say no" isn't an option; but with awareness, it's possible to change.

In no time, that highly refined sugary donut settled in Sherry's belly, and as soon as it had, the pleasure began to fade, and shame crept in. Instantly, she moved toward the depression loop.

"Why did I do that? I can't tell my husband; he knows I've been trying to lose weight. I'm so weak! What's wrong with me?"

Think about your life. You can give this example with any kind of behavioral bad habits: shopping, abusing drugs and alcohol, gambling, sleeping, isolating, phone checking—you name it. The brain has it all mapped out into one neatly chunked procedure so that you don't even have to reflect on it. It just does it for you and keeps the depression loop fueled.

Where Bad Habits Are Born

One of my favorite cartoons is by Cathy Thorne. It reads, "Today I will live in the moment . . . unless the moment is unpleasant, in which case I'll eat a cookie." It does a great job of illustrating the fact that the brain's drive to avoid what's uncomfortable is such a natural, human reaction. It's not malicious, although sometimes it may feel that way because the brain seems to get us in trouble with that kind of thinking. But it's just the brain being a brain. It's wired to protect us and keep us safe. It follows deeply embedded programming that has kept the human race expanding since inception. As we have found with the *thinking*, the brain's direct path to fix an emotional insecurity is to *avoid it* and move toward something more pleasurable. Feeling stress? Eat another chip. Hanging out with friends seems overwhelming? Stay home again. Feeling hopeless? Pour another drink.

We all have unhealthy behaviors, and they often stem from some habit we developed in trying to protect ourselves during an earlier life experience. When I was six years old, my parents brought me and my two sisters into the living room, and before I had any clue what was going on, both girls burst into tears. My parents proceeded to tell us that they were getting a divorce and that from then on we would be living in two separate places. I stood there blankly. Concerned by my stoic reaction, my mom asked, "What's wrong, Elisha, do you understand what's going on?" To which I replied angrily, "Yeah, I know, what do you want me to do, bang my head against the wall so I'll cry?" I didn't have a clue what to do with this devastating news, I was deeply vulnerable and so being willful was my way of protecting myself.

At that time, we didn't have much money, but we would occasionally go out to dinner. Even as a six-year-old, I thought we should be watching our finances, so often the way I dealt with my emotions was by hiding under the table and refusing to eat. My anger was not about the money but about my perception that it was wrong and unfair that our family had been torn apart. Little did I know at the time, but this way of coping with my feelings would evolve into habitual destructive behaviors.

Years later, I had started a successful career in sales and management selling telecommunications to businesses in San Francisco. But even with awards and money coming in, I didn't feel fulfilled. As I mentioned earlier, I struggled with substance abuse, and the more my inner voices arose telling me I had to stop—and the more calls I received from my family voicing their concerns—the more my old routine of willfulness kicked in. I continued acting out the same pattern of avoidance, hiding under the table of life.

Our earlier experiences led to coping behaviors that were adaptive at the time, but as an adult, they can be unhealthy. As life moves on, the brain does what it does best: it makes habits out of them, freeing the brain to handle more complex tasks.

It's good to know where our avoidance patterns come from because it creates a way of understanding ourselves. Acceptance comes when there is a sense of feeling understood and cared about. If you were standing in a circle of people who you felt understood and cared about you, how would you feel? Sometimes we can get clear on where our avoidance patterns come from through therapy, talking with friends, or journaling.

Jan was a student of mine in her midfifties who grew up in a home with a mother who was a Holocaust survivor. Anytime that

Jan brought up a personal problem, her mother would minimize it, saying, "How could that be a problem compared with being persecuted by Hitler?" On top of that, her parents had marital problems; after their fights, her mom would lock herself in her room. Jan learned to do the same by grabbing a snack, going into her room, putting on her headphones, and drowning out the emotional noise with music and junk food. Even though Jan knew this wasn't a good way to cope, she continued to do it. Years later, she's become better at curbing the habit but still finds herself using food at times as a way to cope with the emotional chaos in life. That's human nature: even when we know better, we still keep falling into the same old potholes that reinforce depressed and anxious moods.

You may remember the old adage mentioned in step 1 from psychologist Donald Hebb, "Neurons that fire together wire together." That describes how anything in life becomes automatic. From the day you were born, you heard people repeat words enough until eventually you started to speak them yourself. After enough repetition, they started to get clearer. The neurons that fired together finally wired together, and you no longer had to think consciously about how to talk, walk, brush your teeth, or eat.

Unfortunately, the same goes for your bad habits.

Why You Can't "Just Say No!"

Many of us try and try to break our behavioral bad habits, and when we fall back into them, we succumb to our mind traps and fall into holes of inadequacy and shame. But while falling back into bad habits is our responsibility, it oftentimes isn't our fault. Understanding the role of the prefrontal cortex and the powerful brain chemical dopamine can explain this important truth.

Remember, when we find ourselves feeling blue, we lose resources to vital areas of the brain that could help us make the healthy decisions to start breaking the bad habits that fuel the depression loop. If you were depressed, and I hooked you up to a brain imaging machine, we'd likely see abnormally low activity in the prefrontal cortex (PFC). With an inactive PFC, it's harder to choose healthy behaviors, regulate emotions, defer immediate gratification, and suppress impulses for longer-term benefits. When the PFC is normally active, we might be able to say, "I notice I'm feeling down right now, and I feel an impulse to eat that pint of Ben & Jerry's, but I know that it's going to make me feel worse. So I'm going to take a few deep breaths and call a friend. This too shall pass." But when we (and our PFC) are depressed, we don't use reasoning—we just reach for the ice cream.

At the University of Southern California Brain and Creativity Institute, neurologist Antonio Damasio has worked for years to understand how we make decisions. In one study, he and his colleagues enlisted patients with damage to the prefrontal cortex to see what effect this had on their decision making. They put four decks of cards in front of the patients. Two decks held cards that were high risk, paying $100 for winning cards and $350 for losing cards. The other two decks were more conservative, paying $50 for winning cards and $250 for losing cards. Patients were not told which decks had more risk, nor were they told that they had only a hundred cards from which to choose.

By the fortieth or fiftieth card, most people develop a *sense* of which is the "bad" deck and which is the "good" deck, but the subjects with prefrontal damage continued to choose cards from the bad deck. They might have known cognitively that it wasn't the best deck, but it didn't *feel* wrong to them. That is similar to how they would act in everyday life, continuing to take high risks and missing the messages that this is the wrong path to follow.

Just like the gamblers who had damage to their prefrontal cortex, when we're depressed, we may know intellectually that avoiding friends and family is an unhealthy decision, but avoidance doesn't *feel* wrong. And so we fall into the same patterns again and again, strengthening the depression loop.

On top of that, when dopamine surges, it sends a signal to the receptors that says, "This feels good, go get it!" and we do. When you have an impaired PFC and a chemical driving your motivation to go get the chips, the drugs, the alcohol, the sex, the clothes, it's almost impossible in that moment to just say no!

But hope is not lost here; there is a definitive way to train the brain to reverse bad habits.

Granted, this is not easy. If it were easy to just change habits, most of us would have changed them a long time ago. Depression affects areas of the brain responsible for learning, memory, and impulse control. Dopamine drives subconscious motivation, sending the signal that "this feels good," and in the absence of learning, memory. and impulse control, that behavior is engaged automatically, which propels the depression loop. Just saying no to unhealthy habits is magical thinking, but with this awareness, you can reverse bad habits.

If it were easy to just change habits, most of us would have changed them a long time ago.

A Formula That Works

We can move away from the depression loop by reversing bad habits. This sounds difficult, but it is actually simpler than you think. It comes down to using an effective strategy: knowing your cues, identifying the routine, knowing what reward the habit is trying to achieve, stepping into the space between stimulus and response, and changing the routine with something healthier that achieves the same reward. Like all habits, as you practice and repeat them, they will start to become automatic.

A great way to see that strategy in action is to consider the story of Charles Duhigg, a writer at the *New York Times* who had a serious chocolate-chip-cookie habit. He ate chocolate-chip cookies every afternoon, and he wanted to stop. He tried, but his resolutions to cut out the cookies never worked. So he decided to analyze his habit to see if he could figure out how to stop it.

His research into the topic showed him that every habit has a cue: some kind of trigger that kicks the habit into gear. For Duhigg and his chocolate-chip-cookie habit, that cue was "time of day"—between three and three thirty in the afternoon. At that point, he'd fall into a routine of standing up from his desk, walking to the elevator, going to the fourteenth floor, buying a cookie, and eating it while talking with his colleagues.

When he really focused on the ritual, Duhigg came to understand that midway through the afternoon, his brain wanted a reward. He had to find out what that was in order to reverse this bad habit, so he carried out an experiment. At three o'clock every day, when the craving came on, he experimented with different behaviors. He tried walking around the block, going to the cafeteria to buy a candy bar and eat it at his desk, and another time just chatting with colleagues.

Duhigg discovered that socializing with friends was his true reward. He learned that he could skip the cookie and achieve the same feeling of having gotten something special simply by spending time with friends. Once he figured that out, he lost twelve pounds. He eventually went on to write the bestselling book *The Power of Habit: Why We Do What We Do in Life and Business.*

Consider for a moment what habit you want to change.

Duhigg's story gives us an interesting experiment to play with, but it may not always be this easy. Some behavioral habits are ingrained more deeply. Sometimes it's wise not to just dive into the deep end but first to practice visualizing the process to get the mind used to it. Believe it or not, this can be a very effective tool for changing bad habits, as a Harvard study showed.

A number of years ago at Harvard Medical School, a group of volunteers piled into a lab to practice a simple exercise on a piano keyboard. Neuroscientist Alvaro Pascual-Leone told the participants to play as best they could for an hour a day, five days a week. At the end of each session, they were hooked up to a brain scanning machine to measure any change in the motor area of their brain, which controls finger movement. As you may have suspected, they found expansion in that area of the brain. But there was another discovery that Pascual-Leone was after.

A second group was taught the same piano exercise but instructed to only *imagine* practicing it for an hour a day for five days a week. At the end of the experiment, the researchers found that this group showed the same level of expansion in the motor areas of the brain as the group that actually practiced playing the piano. "Mental practice resulted in a similar reorganization" of the brain, Pascual-Leone wrote later. Just as visualizing playing piano can create brain change, visualizing making behavioral changes can affect the habit centers of our brains and is a great place to start toward breaking bad habits.

Visualize It

Start by picking one of the undesirable habits that you've identified as fueling your depression loop. Take a moment to picture in your mind the routine as vividly as possible. What time does it occur? Where are you? Who are you with? The more real you can make it and the more detail you can imagine it with, the better.

Next, pause before engaging with whatever the routine is. In this space of awareness, play with the possibility of doing something different. If it's around food, imagine giving someone a call, taking a walk, or sitting in a short meditation practice. This may help uncover what the need really is in that moment. As you move through it, monitor your stress around it. On a scale of 1 to 10, how high is your urge to engage in this bad habit? The idea here is to play with this and see what your experience is. When the stress gets below a 7, and you begin to feel more comfortable in your imagination, you can bring it into real life.

One of my students had a problem with obesity and felt completely helpless when she would drive by a particular bakery in Los Angeles. When we went through the process, she realized that eating cake in the bakery gave her a feeling of comfort, of being loved. This was her reward. We came up with another ritual of placing her hand on her heart or calling a friend as a means of receiving love and comfort. I asked her to quantify, on a scale of 1 to 10, how much she believes she'll be able to do this. She said about a 2. She had every reason to believe she couldn't do it, in the past, every time she drove by the bakery, her prefrontal cortex went off-line. Having her visualize driving near the bakery was a lot safer and could give her the experience of success. I asked her what she noticed after visualizing it, and she said, "As I knew I was getting near it, I felt my heart pumping. I gave myself what I needed: I placed my hand on my heart for comfort and just drove by the bakery. Now I feel more confident that I can do this; it's almost like I've already done it." Belief is the most powerful pill we can take.

As you play with this, you can expect that from time to time you will have bad days where stress can get the best of you, and you find yourself falling into the same old bad habits. Here is a phrase that I use as one of my therapy strategies: Forgive and Invite. As best you can, forgive yourself for the past. There's no value in spending time with those voices of self-judgment; it only steals your energy from moving forward. Now that you're present, invite yourself to reconnect to your intention with the changes you've wanted to make. This helps elicit self-compassion, which we'll explore in the upcoming steps.

Here are the five steps to getting started in reversing bad habits:

1. Identify the cues or triggers for that habit. Writer Charles Duhigg identified that his bad habit was cued by a time of day. Yours may be a certain place, a person, an emotion, a memory, or certain objects.

2. Know the routine and switch it for a healthier one. Note how your routine unfolds. For Duhigg, it was walking to the cafeteria, buying a cookie, and schmoozing with his coworkers. Find different things that are healthier, and experiment to see if they feel satisfying.

3. Figure out what reward you're seeking. Duhigg realized he really wanted social connection, and that was more compelling than the cookie. Experiment to determine what your mind and body really want.

4. Visualize yourself doing it or write down the story for as long as it feels right. If it feels too overwhelming to swap one routine for another at the moment, just lie back and imagine it. Get a sense of how activated your body feels when you don't engage the bad habit and how you feel when you swap it out for something healthier.

5. Experiment with it in your daily life and continue to Forgive and Invite when you wander off the path.

As you start breaking bad habits, be on the lookout to see if you have more energy, smile more, and feel less anxious and more alive.

Anyone can break bad habits. It's just about understanding what the habit is, how it works, and believing that you can do it. The power of belief is amazing. Here's an example. When it comes to studying the impact of medications, researchers measure them against a *placebo*—some inert substance that has no pharmacological effect, to help understand the impact of the active pharmacological substances they are using. For example, some people in a study might be given a new drug for depression. Others are then given a pill with no active medication in it—the placebo. Nobody in the study knows if they got the actual antidepressant or the placebo. The gold-standard studies are *randomized controlled trials*, where participants are randomly assigned to the different groups to significantly reduce any extraneous variables (such as gender, age, personality) from having an impact on the results. When the outcome shows that the placebo has a positive impact, this is called the *placebo effect*. As it turns out placebo rates in randomized controlled trials for antidepressants are quite high—around 30 percent to 50 percent, underscoring the power of belief.

One of the best ways I've seen to bolster belief is through an experience with other people (even if that group consists of just two people). Before we move on, play with this process a bit with your bad habits. See if you can enlist a friend who has a similar bad habit, to support each other.

Pretend your life is a classroom and treat this as an experiment, as if you were engaging your life with fresh eyes. See what you notice. Expect it to be difficult at first, but that's just you pushing through the wiring of resistance that's been built up for a while. Every time you do this, you break it down a bit more and continue to build the wiring for a more resilient brain.

Changing our mental and behavioral habits can be enough to significantly shift the entire depression loop, but to make more lasting change and uncover happiness, we have to start nurturing our natural antidepressants, and this is exactly what you're about to do.

On the road to change, whenever you fall prey to bad habits, you can expect the brain to default to voices of inadequacy and unworthiness. The best strategy is to forgive yourself for going astray—it's expected. In this space of awareness, investigate and learn from the distraction and then invite yourself to make the choice to start again. Make Forgive and Invite a practice and keep beginning again and again.

PART 2

The Five Natural Antidepressants

STEP 3

Change the Brain
Through Mindfulness

In 2012 my wife, Stefanie Goldstein, PhD, and I created a program called CALM—Connecting Adolescents to Learning Mindfulness. This is an eight-week program, inspired by Mindfulness-Based Stress Reduction (MBSR), that brings teens and tweens through a journey of cultivating presence and emotional and social intelligence. The results have been remarkable.

Early in the program, we give each participant a rock with the word *Breathe* written on it, along with some simple instructions: "Lie down on the ground, put the rock on your belly, and as you breathe, notice it rising and falling. Whenever your mind goes off, thinking about this or worrying about that, just notice what you're thinking and then gently guide your focus back to your breathing." The teens keep the rocks with them and use them as reminders to practice being present.

Andrew was a fourteen-year-old boy in the program. He struggled with bouts of anger and was initially resistant to participating but decided to give it a try. One night Andrew got in a fight with his parents, which was a fairly common occurrence. He fell into a habitual reaction: his body tensed up, he felt a surge of anger, and his mind filled with thoughts about how his parents never listen to him and never will in the future. He was caught in something akin to the depression loop. He ran into his room and slammed the door, with no inclination to respond any differently than he had hundreds of other times that this same scenario played out. But out of the corner of his eye, he noticed the rock. Seeing it opened up a space of awareness. He decided to try lying down and putting it on his stomach. As he did, he expanded the space between *stimulus and response:* a place where choice, perspective, and possibility lie. Within a few minutes, his mind and body calmed, and a new thought arose: "I need to go back and tell them why I got so upset. Maybe we can make this better." To his parents' surprise, Andrew emerged from his room with a calmer and clearer mind, proud of himself for breaking out of this habitual emotional reaction.

What if you could get better and better at noticing when you were caught in a loop and applying a technique that enabled you to access your natural antidepressants? You can: by cultivating mindfulness. In step 3, we're going to delve into what mindfulness means, as well as the neuroscience behind how it turns down the volume on the NUTs in our heads. We'll also look at how we can learn, as Andrew did, to widen the space between stimulus and response enough to begin seeing the choices that nurture our natural antidepressants.

The Case for Mindfulness

You can think of mindfulness as the primary natural antidepressant. The social psychologist Ellen Langer refers to mindfulness as "a flexible state of mind in which we are actively engaged in the present, noticing new things and sensitive to context." Scientists now know that mindfulness trains the more evolved areas of our brains to overcome the impulsive firing of some of our more primitive structures. Mindfulness is fundamental to creating an antidepressant brain, as it opens your eyes to the choices that are in the here and now so that you can engage with the other natural antidepressants that we'll examine later. The example of Andrew and the rock depicts perfectly how this works. He became present, moved beyond his rigid thought of "What's the point?" and was able to see the value of engaging with his parents again. That's the key: we want to train our brains to move naturally beyond rigid thinking, have a more flexible state of mind, and engage healthier mindsets that serve as natural antidepressants.

In many ways, you have already been practicing mindfulness in steps 1 and 2. The moment you become aware of the depression loop is a moment of mindfulness. The same is true of the moment you notice that your head is full of NUTs as well as the moment you opt to name a behavioral bad habit in which you are engaging.

Mindfulness has quantifiable benefits. During the past thirty years, research has shown that when people cultivate mindfulness, they do the following:

- become more flexible in their decision making;
- get better at regulating their bodies in moments of distress;
- are more successful at calming anxious minds that are snowballing with thoughts;
- develop a stronger focus at home and work;
- feel more empathy and compassion toward themselves and others;
- communicate more effectively; and
- become more aware of what is most important in life.

How Does Mindfulness Work?

In my initial years in college, I suffered with insomnia. I just couldn't fall asleep. If you've ever been sleep deprived over a period of time, you know how easy it is to feel anxious and depressed. Just as we see in a depression loop, insomnia filled my head with NUTs, as my mind continuously told me how horrible the next exhausting day was going to be. The more I tried to fall asleep, the more awake I was—and the worse I felt. It wasn't until I became more familiar with mindfulness that I understood how to truly stop the insomnia from gaining momentum.

I became more aware of when my mind was racing with negative thoughts that were fueling the loop. In those moments of awareness, I had the flexibility to access a choice point to decide what was best to do. I didn't put a rock on my belly, but, like Andrew, I concentrated on the natural rhythm of my breath without trying to breathe deeply or control it. I took away the goal of falling asleep and focused instead on training myself to be present more often, stopping the loop. Eventually my experience taught me that simply being aware and curious about what was happening in the present moment allowed my body to do what it wanted to do: rest.

Maybe the greatest gift was my increased confidence that everything was going to be okay. I began to work with certain meditations and also found mindfulness to be a way of life. As time went on, it seemed to arise automatically in a variety of areas beyond just working with my own stress-induced neuroses. Now it comes into my work with clients and my relationships with my wife and kids. It is with me the moment I realize it is best to put down my smartphone and pay attention to what's going on around me. It taps me on the shoulder when I'm at the store and reminds me to see the checker as a person, not just a worker standing behind a register—someone with the same underlying needs as me to feel understood, cared about, accepted. That person is "just like me," and so I look him or her in the eye, smile, and say thank you. In many ways, for me, it has been a lifesaver.

The reality is, the brain is wired to disconnect and check out from life when we're not feeling well. But as you've seen, this often serves to fuel the depression loop. By weaving mindfulness into daily life, we begin to practice connecting to the direct experience of what's here, learn how to trust ourselves, and have the confidence and clarity to choose a healthier response from moment to moment.

It's Not Problem Solving (or Being Versus Doing)

We are hardwired to solve problems. When a problem arises, we want "to do" something about it. That's how we evolved and made the wheel, our first tools, the chairs we sit on, and the houses we live in, and even learned how to read and understand these words. Problem solving is an essential part of life. But contrary to the brain's belief, life itself is not a problem to be solved; it's a constantly evolving experience to be lived.

Here's how problem solving gets us trapped deeper in the depressive loop:

The moment we experience an uncomfortable emotion, the brain sees it as a threat because of its potential to lead to depression. We're supposed to feel well, and when we don't, there is a discrepancy between where we are and where we "should be." This mind thinks, "There is something wrong with me." It perceives a defect, a deficiency, an unworthiness. The brain sees this as something "to fix" and uses self-judgment to tell us that something is wrong with us or maybe conjures up doomsday scenarios to prepare us for possible catastrophes. Then, because of these potential threats, the brain remains on high alert to see if any more signs of relapse arise. The voice inside the mind inquires anxiously, "Is it gone yet? How about now?" This only adds pressure to an already stressful state of being. The more the brain focuses on this gap, the more it highlights it in our minds and strengthens the belief that "something is wrong with me."

This only sinks us deeper into the depression loop, which spurs the brain "to do" something more, continuing to add more fuel to the fire.

But when we're doing this, where are we? We're not in the present—and that's exactly where we need to be to take charge of our brains and see the choices available, and to make a change by using mindfulness.

Mindfulness is about balancing the brain's implicit agenda by training it "to be" with what's there instead of needing "to do" something about it. In using mindfulness to learn how to be with our feelings, we send a message internally that we're worthy enough to pay attention to, closing the gap of unworthiness and disrupting the depression loop.

Right now you can choose to stop what you're "doing" (reading this book) for thirty seconds and practice this state of "being." Just take a breath and acknowledge how you are. Is your mind racing, or is it calm? Is your body tense anywhere, or is it relaxed? Are you feeling anxious, bored, restless, excited, tired, or any number of other emotions?

Breathe in, breathe out. You have arrived.

Contrary to the brain's belief, life itself is not a problem to be solved, it's a constantly evolving experience to be lived.

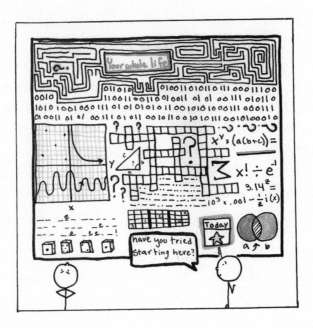

Learning How to "*Be*" in One Minute

Here's an opportunity to stop reading and begin working on developing mindfulness. It's a short exercise that you can immediately start using to help move away from the conditioned loop of depression and into a space of hope and possibility.

Learning how to be is a one-minute practice that can be done anywhere and anytime as a barometer of how you're doing. As best you can, treat this as an experiment in your life. Try it out at first in the moments when you aren't sinking and see what you notice. Like any habit, the more you integrate this into your day, the stronger it becomes in your short-term memory, and the more likely it is to be retrieved during the difficult moments.

Note: first, see if you can set aside any judgments of whether this practice will or will not work for you. Engage this just with the goal of being aware of your experience.

- *Breathe*: Take a few deep breaths. Notice your breath as you breathe in and out. You might even want to say the word *in* as you inhale and *out* as you exhale. This is meant to pop you out of autopilot and steady your mind.

- *Expand*: This is the process of expanding your attention throughout the body and just feeling your body as it is. You can start by noticing the positioning of your body. Then you can move to being curious about how your body is feeling. Imagine that this is the very first time you've ever felt your body. You may feel warmth or coolness, achiness, itchiness, tension, tightness, heaviness, lightness, or a whole host of sensations. Or perhaps you notice no sensation at all in other areas. When you're here, also be aware of how emotions are being expressed in the body. Calm may be experienced as looseness in the back or face. You might also notice painful feelings. Maybe this comes up as tension in the chest or shoulders. If there is physical pain, see what happens if you get curious about the sensation of it and allow it to be as it is. If it gets too intense, use this as a choice point to become aware of what matters in the moment or what you need. Maybe you need to get up, move around, and roll your shoulders. Awareness is the springboard to getting in touch with what matters.

That's it! It may sound too simple to be impactful, but, again, set aside your judgments and let your experience be your teacher.

Just practice being, breathing and expanding into the body in minimoments throughout the day to train your brain to be in that space of awareness and choice that will lead you to a more balanced and mindful life.

To help you remember, you might consider posting signs in your environment that say "Just Be," knowing that means to engage in the "Be" practice. Just as signs on the road remind us to slow down or watch for children crossing, signs around the house or office can remind us to be how we want to BE. Or maybe put a note in your digital calendar to pop up a couple times per day as a reminder. Or the best way to remember may be to share the idea with a friend to remind each other from time to time.

The benefits are enormous—it just takes intention and practice.

Move Your Brain Toward Mindfulness

Most of the time, we're on autopilot, and the brain is making rapid decisions for us. It references our history, mood, and environment to come up with the most adaptive response. However, when we're trying to cultivate an antidepressant brain—being more mindful, for example—we can make some simple changes to set up our environmental cues in ways that support our success.

One way to do this is to expand on the recently recommended use of signs.

(Keep in mind that the entire time you're reading this book is an opportunity to widen your awareness. Do you notice any judgmental voices arising right now? For example, "Short verses? Is he nuts? How could that ever help me?" or "What is this, an affirmation? Those never work." Or "Why am I even continuing to read this? I've already tried stuff like this before." If anything like this arises, don't worry—it's normal. Just take a moment to notice the automatic judgment, let it be, take a breath to help ground yourself in the here and now, and then gently continue on with the next paragraph.)

I use these short phrases all the time to support myself in being more present, grounded, and aware in daily life. I have taught this practice to patients, medical professionals, business people, psychologists, and students for many years now to calm distressed minds and be more present to everyday life.

I suggest reading these examples below and creating little signs in your environment at work and home that serve as reminders for you to automatically drop into more mindful moments throughout the day.

SHORT VERSES

- Take three steps while breathing in and say, "Breathing in, I am here," and then with the following three steps, "Breathing out, I am alive." You can then shorten this to saying "here" as you breathe in, and "alive" as you breathe out.

- If you're walking outside, you can practice "Breathing in, I notice the colors all around me; breathing out, I smile." Then shorten to "Breathing in, colors; breathing out, smile." Even if you don't feel like smiling, science shows that the simple act of doing a half smile can help you ease the tension in your face, recover more quickly from stress, and improve your mood.

- "Breathing in, I have arrived; breathing out, I am home." This is a short verse from Vietnamese Buddhist monk and author Thich Nhat Hanh. You can shorten it to "Breathing in, arrived; breathing out, home." Have you ever had the experience where you were rushing home to relax? It doesn't make sense, and isn't effective in calming the nervous system. Sometimes reminding ourselves that we have arrived at the present moment already and that we *are* home can help calm an anxious mind.

We can then slow down and get home a few minutes later in a more collected and relaxed state.

- "Breathing in, I wash my hands; breathing out, gratitude for these hands." Shorten to "Breathing in, washing; breathing out, gratitude." This practice can not only bring appreciation to one of the unsung heroes of our bodies, our hands, but also reinforce the idea of being aware of all they do during the day and being more mindful of them. This cultivation of appreciation and gratitude can support us in feeling well.

These are just some examples, and as you get the hang of it, you can make up your own that fit for you. You can do this while

HOW MINDFULNESS WORKS IN THE BRAIN

Science has shown that a steady practice of mindfulness induces real changes in the brain. For example, in one study, when two groups were shown extremely sad forty-five-second movie clips from *Terms of Endearment* and *The Champ* (arguably two of the greatest cinematic tearjerkers ever), fMRI scans showed the group that practiced mindfulness for eight weeks exhibited decreased activity in an area of the brain involved in negative rumination and increased activity in other areas known for awareness. The mindfulness group also scored significantly lower on assessments measuring depression. Other studies demonstrated the ability to reduce activity in areas of the brain that light up when we feel pain, and increased activity in areas that are active when we feel happy. This neural activity is the opposite of what we see in depressed brains.

The practice of mindfulness can train our brains to have a new default. Instead of automatically falling into the stream of past or future rumination that ignites the depression loop, mindfulness draws our attention to the present moment. As we practice mindfulness, we actually start wiring neurons that balance the brain in a way that is naturally an antidepressant.

walking or just sitting and breathing. And, of course, most important of all, don't take my word for it, try it for yourself.

If it's not for you, cast it aside—but do give it a shot. Pay attention to how you are feeling physically, emotionally, and mentally before doing it and then again after you practice it for a few breaths.

Turn Up the Volume on Resiliency

Mindfulness also influences brain activity that makes us stronger in the face of difficulty. In a 2003 study, Richie Davidson, director of the Lab for Affective Neuroscience at the University of Wisconsin–Madison, joined with Jon Kabat-Zinn, author and founder of Mindfulness-Based Stress Reduction (MBSR), to provide mindfulness training to workers in a high-stress biotech firm. Prior to any training, they measured their brains with an electroencephalography (EEG) machine to study brain waves and also inoculated the participants with a flu vaccine in order to measure whether or not this had any effect on their immune systems.

After they went through two months of learning and applying a handful of mindfulness practices in their lives, the study showed that the subjects who underwent mindfulness training experienced a decrease in negative emotions and an increase in positive emotions. Four months later, the EEG results revealed significantly increased activity in the left prefrontal cortex. The more significant the activity in the left prefrontal cortex, the more participants reported experiencing positive emotions. This suggests a parallel between the left prefrontal activity and feeling well. They also found that the meditation group responded better to the flu vaccine, suggesting that this practice contributed to a stronger immune system.

What does this have to do with depression?

If you were feeling good while walking down the street and someone gave you a dirty look, you might not even notice it, or you might think, "What was that about? What's wrong with them?" If you weren't feeling well and that same thing happened, you might blame yourself and wonder, "What's wrong with me" or "What did I do wrong?" Same event, but when you're living in the right prefrontal cortex of negative emotions, the NUTs are stirring, ready to be unleashed. The depressive loop needs these negative stories to maintain itself. If mindfulness can facilitate a left prefrontal shift, then we're more likely to be in a positive frame of mind, leading to a greater chance of resiliency.

If we know that nerve cells that fire together wire together, we want to create neurons firing in the left prefrontal cortex, so that can become more of a default response. When it comes to gaining freedom from the conditioned negative voices in our minds and opening up to our natural antidepressants, mindfulness is the fundamental ingredient.

Turn Down the Volume on Emotional Pain

While we can learn to influence brain activity that turns up the volume on resiliency, we can also turn down the volume on our brains' perceptions of emotional pain. How the brain reacts to pain is what makes all the difference in either interrupting the depressive loop or maintaining it. When we train our brains to perceive emotional pain as less unpleasant and less intense, that can change the degree to which the amygdala, or "fear circuit," fires. This affects the frequency and intensity of our NUTs, and this reduces the energy of the depressive loop.

In 2012, Dr. Fadel Zeiden, a postdoctoral researcher at Wake

Forest University School of Medicine, in Winston-Salem, North Carolina, wondered if people could take a crash course in mindfulness to learn to modulate their pain. For this experiment, he enlisted fifteen mildly burned men and women. He asked them to rate a 120-degree heat stimulus on their calves, while fMRI machines measured their brain activity. After that, the participants were instructed to practice meditating for twenty minutes a day for only four days. When he brought them back to his lab and performed the same procedure, he saw a reduction in pain-related activation in the brain. The participants also reported the same 120-degree stimulus to be 57 percent less unpleasant and 40 percent less intense than just four days earlier.

How could this be, and what does this have to do with creating a more resilient brain?

When our bodies experience any given injury, blood flow is sent over to that area as white blood cells rush to fight off any foreign bodies. This is inflammation and it is a necessary component of healing. You've likely noticed it if you have ever cut yourself or sprained an ankle. However, science is now showing us that chronic stress changes the gene activity of our immune cells to fight off a trauma that's not really there. This leads to unnecessary inflammation, which is associated with a host of ills including heart disease, cancer, and depression. The good news is that no matter our genetic predisposition to emotional pain, we can learn how to modulate it. A study out of Richie Davidson's lab examined the effects of a single day of intensive mindfulness practice. The meditators, compared to a control group who were engaged in quiet non-meditative activities, showed reduced levels of pro-inflammatory genes that were also connected to greater physical resiliency in the midst of a stressful situation. This is a direct example of how we can use our minds to change the inflammatory biology of depression.

BRINGING MINDFULNESS TO PAIN

If you notice any emotional or physical pain, see what happens when you bring a beginner's mind to the physical sensation. For a few moments, notice the sensation as if for the first time. Get a sense of where it is in the body, how intense it is, what the contours of it are. Is there a color that comes up in your mind? What happens when you place your hand there? Say to yourself, "Breathing in, opening up to what's here; breathing out, letting it be." As we approach the pain with more mindfulness, the voices that overreact to it, sending an inflammatory response, exacerbating your discomfort, begin to die down. In this space of awareness, we understand that this is temporary and can open up to a clearer choice on what is best to do in the moment.

Consider what life would be like in the days, weeks, and months ahead if you perceived your emotional pain as much less unpleasant and intense. Again, when the threat is minimized, the amygdala doesn't need to get so activated, and we become less likely to be propelled into the depression loop. In the coming chapters, you'll learn how you can train your brain not only to modulate pain but also to turn pain into a cue that fosters a key natural antidepressant for healing.

Research suggests that we can all train our brains to break free from rumination, turn down the volume on fear, and become less reactive to startling and even painful experiences of life, including negative thoughts and difficult emotions.

Build Emotional Intelligence

One of the simplest and least threatening ways of bringing mindfulness to your emotions is simply taking time to discover how you experience them. The reality is that most of us didn't grow up learning about emotions, so we may not recognize them or understand them very well. But, if you recall, when you're able to name it, you can tame it. Bringing a mindful attention to emotions as they arise is a way to shift the activity of our brains, turn down our NUTs, impact the depression loop, and create a sense of acceptance, freedom, and connection that is key to uncovering happiness.

Right now is an opportunity to expand your emotional intelligence. Below are a few categories of emotions and other feelings that are associated with them. Look at each emotion and see if

I'm learning to hold my emotions lightly.

you can match it with a sensation in the body. For me, fear arises as a tingling constriction in the chest, while sadness is a heaviness that I feel mostly in my face and chest. When feeling joy, I feel light on my feet, with an openness across my back, face, and chest. You may resonate with this or have a different experience. Just this practice alone primes your brain to be drawn away from the NUTs and to the sensations when they arise.

Look at the emotion below and think about or write in any bodily sensations that you experience when they're present.

Fear: apprehension, anxiety, distress, edginess, jumpiness, nervousness, panic, tenseness, uneasiness, worry, fright, feeling overwhelmed

_____

_____

_____

_____

Confusion: feeling bewildered, uncertain, puzzled, mystified, perplexed, chaotic, foggy, or unaware

_____

_____

_____

_____

Anger: aggravation, agitation, annoyance, destructiveness, disgust, envy, frustration, irritation, grouchiness, grumpiness, rage

_____

_____

_____

_____

Sadness: alienation, anguish, despair, disappointment, gloom, grief, hopelessness, insecurity, loneliness, misery, unhappiness, rejection

_____

_____

_____

_____

Shame: guilt, embarrassment, humiliation, invalidation, regret, remorse, mortification

_____

_____

_____

_____

Love: affection, arousal, attraction, caring, compassion, desire, fondness, infatuation, kindness, liking, longing, warmth, sympathy, sentimentality

_____

_____

_____

_____

Joy: amusement, bliss, contentment, eagerness, elation, enjoyment, enthusiasm, excitement, exhilaration, hope, optimism, pleasure, satisfaction

_____

_____

_____

_____

Healing Your Emotional Pain

Years ago, when I was in graduate school and living in Mountain View, California, I used to take weekly walks at Shoreline Park. During one walk, I had just learned that someone close to me had passed away, and I was feeling great sadness and grief. My energy was sapped from the heavy emotions, and so I chose to sit down by a lake. As the sadness grew louder within my being, it seemed almost like a child yelling for my attention.

Because mindfulness had become a habit in my life, I was reminded that I didn't have to resist the feeling and had the choice to bring a kind attention to it and allow it to be. I noticed it as heaviness in my face and chest, and it had a certain depth and width to it. The image entered my mind of a dark cloud right there in my body. Another picture came to me of a little boy crying from the loss of his own family as his parents got divorced. That little boy was me. What did that little boy need? I had the insight to put my hand on my heart, acknowledging and connecting to the sadness as if I were putting my arm around that little boy. As I stayed with the feeling of the emotion and my hand on my heart, the dark thoughts began to diminish, and I felt a sense of caring toward myself. The alchemy of this caring and sadness together turned it into a sweet sadness. It was a sense of peace in that moment. I consider that an aha! moment of clarity, one that I discussed in more detail in my previous book, *The Now Effect*.

Any experience of depression poses the possibility of becoming crushed by the severity of the event. However, mindfulness brings to the dark events of life a new lens that provides an opportunity for healing and growth. In his book *The Miracle of Being Awake*, Thich Nhat Hanh says:

The sadness or anxiety, hatred, or passion, under the gaze of our concentration and meditation, reveals its own nature. That revelation leads naturally to healing and emancipation. The sadness, or whatever, having been the cause of pain, can be used as a means of liberation from torment and suffering. We call this using a thorn to remove a thorn. We should treat our anxiety, our pain, our hatred, and passion gently, respectfully, not resisting it, but living with it, making peace with it, penetrating into its nature by the meditation on interdependence.

We all have emotional thorns that we try to avoid in life. We make strategic decisions to guard against these thorns, putting a protective box over them, making sure to steer clear of them. But we can never remove a thorn unless we approach it. Loneliness is a thorn that many of us feel, and we arrange our lives carefully to avoid it. Maybe we enter into relationships in order to stave off the feeling of loneliness, only to find it creeping back in when the person is away or when the relationship ends. At other times, we make sure to fill our environment with always being on the phone, obsessively checking our social media, or filling any alone space with some distraction. Meanwhile, what we experience is the classic adage "what we resist persists."

The only way to ultimately remove this thorn that drives the depression loop is to practice a 180-degree shift of approaching it with curiosity rather than with avoidance. In one of my classes, I led the students through a meditation where you become aware of any emotional pain that arises in the body and see what happens when you "breathe in and open to the feeling, and breathe out and let it be." After we ended, one woman commented that she felt that was a very sweet practice. I asked her to tell us more. She said that while she experienced a host of emotions, many of which were unpleasant, she felt like there was plenty of space in which they could occur. While in other moments she may have been fighting or felt trapped by these unpleasant feelings, with mindfulness she experienced a freedom from the emotions, and that's what was so sweet.

Ultimately you are not the loneliness that is there; it is a temporary feeling that under the spotlight of awareness reveals its nature of impermanence. Stepping into this awareness affords us an opportunity that might appear like a miracle, breaking free from its clutches and experiencing a freedom we may not have known existed before. This is using a thorn to remove a thorn.

Inevitably, even the dark parts of us want to feel understood and cared about; when in the presence of mindfulness, a kind of posttraumatic growth arises naturally. We begin to experience an essential healing element to depression that I'll introduce you to in step 4: self-compassion.

While we may spend a lot of effort protecting or avoiding our emotional thorns, this merely keeps the thorn in place. Only through approaching them can we see how to pull them out and care for the wound they caused. This is called using a thorn to remove a thorn.

STEP 4

Nurture Self-Compassion and Its Wonderful Side Effects

Claudia had a lifelong passion for shoes. Shopping for them and dressing up in them were great sources of joy for her. To Claudia, shoes were art to the point where she kept a one-of-a-kind pair of shoes in a case on her bookshelf; she never wore them. But at thirty-eight, Claudia suffered the greatest tragedy of her life—one that would change all of this. An unfortunate collision with a drunk driver left her permanently disabled, with one leg shorter than the other. Although she was rushed to the hospital, due to the severity of her injuries there was only so much the doctors could immediately do. After recovering from an infection, too much scar tissue had built up and it was too late for the reconstructive surgery she had hoped for. She became flooded with pain, disbelief, sadness, grief, and anger. When the doctor came to her and told her that she would never be able to wear her shoes again, this loss compounded the trauma.

Years later, when she came to see me, she said, "It's been years since the accident, and I can't force myself to look at my mangled ankle. Whenever I think about it, a rush of anxiety and anger washes over me, and I can't get the self-judgments out of my head. What is wrong with me?"

I asked her to come down from her thoughts for a moment and see if she could sense where anxiety and anger lived in her body. "My anxiety is like a pit in my stomach, and my anger is in my clenched fists," she said. I suggested that she bring her awareness to the sensations in these areas of the body and then asked her what would happen if she just let it be. After a few moments, she answered, "It seems to be turning into sadness." I told her to continue to stay with the feeling but to put her hand on her heart while visualizing the accident. As she did this, I added one extra instruction: "Now silently repeat loving phrases such as 'May I be free from this suffering,' 'May I be healthy in body and mind,' 'May I feel safe and protected,' 'May I be at peace.'"

After a few minutes, she opened her tear-filled eyes and looked down at her ankle for the first time in years.

"What are you noticing?" I asked.

With her hand remaining on her heart, she said, "What I went through was terrible. This is the first time I think I've experienced what I've been reading about for so long. This is the first time since the accident that I have felt compassion toward myself."

That was a critical moment.

"Tell me, Claudia," I asked, "what would the days, weeks, and months ahead look like for you if you experienced this feeling of self-compassion more often?"

She looked up, and with tears brimming over her eyelids and her lips trembling, said, "I think I'd really feel that things are going to be okay."

Here is where Claudia found the vein of gold experienced

as self-compassion. And it's an important illustration of how self-compassion can help you as you work to break free from depression.

Self-compassion is the experience of acknowledging pain and then supporting ourselves as we feel that pain. Self-compassion has the power not only to completely shift our emotional experience but also to change the activity in our brains, giving a turbo boost to interrupting the depression loop. It is a key element to uncovering real happiness.

The Power of Negativity

Self-compassion doesn't come naturally to us, and there's an evolutionary reason for this: the brain is wired to cling like Velcro to our negative voices and to act like Teflon when it comes to the positive ones. Think of our ancestors who lived in the wild having to hunt and gather for survival. The ancestors who would sit in a circle or alone marveling at the wonders of the blades of grass and not keenly aware of the dangers around them likely didn't last long. The ones who were on guard and focused on any danger lurking around any corner survived. Our brains have been highly refined and sculpted to be aware of the dangers and negative possibilities of life in order to protect ourselves. This is the foundation for what researchers call the *automatic negativity bias.*

Is there a neurobiological basis for this negativity bias? John Cacioppo, PhD, put this question to the test when he was a faculty member of the Department of Psychology at Ohio State University. In a study published in 1998, he and his colleagues placed EEG electrodes on the scalps of thirty-three participants to measure the electrical activity of their brains. While sitting in comfortable reclining chairs, they viewed a set of three pictures on a computer. One picture was meant to arouse positive feelings (a Ferrari or a smiling person), another was meant to arouse negative feelings (a beaten face or a dead cat), and the third was meant to be neutral (an empty plate or a hair dryer). After viewing each picture, the participants were asked to press a set of keys on the keyboard indicating whether they experienced the image as positive, negative, or neutral. The brain scans revealed that when the people looked at positive and neutral pictures, their brains showed some electrical activity; but when they were exposed to the negative pictures, their brains really lit up, indicating that the brain responds more strongly to things we perceive as negative than to those that are neutral or positive.

Other studies have found that negative events affect the brain *more* than positive events do. Barbara Fredrickson, PhD, of the University of North Carolina, Chapel Hill, has studied human flourishing (how well people do in life) for years. In one study, she asked individuals, married couples, and business teams to fill out a "positivity test." According to Dr. Fredrickson, the experience of flourishing, or "doing remarkably well," has a positive-event to negative-event ratio of 3 to 1. This means that people who feel good in life have at least three positive events to every negative event, which suggests the power of a negative event on our minds.

John Gottman, PhD, one of the leading researchers in the field of relationships, found an even steeper ratio. He has developed a very keen system to conclude quickly whether or not a relationship will work. For years he has videotaped the interactions between couples in his lab. As he and his team review the video, they track the number of times couples fight and the number of times they interact positively. He has found that relationships that have an equal amount of negative and positive interactions are likely to fail. To succeed, a relationship needs five positive interactions for every negative interaction.

When it comes to depression, this effect is amplified. When we're falling into the depression loop, the brain locks in on what's negative externally and especially internally with a focus on "something is wrong with me," igniting a shame spiral that contributes to the depressive loop. Making matters worse, research shows us that people who have experienced depression in the past have lower levels of self-compassion that would help nurture resiliency in the face of self-judgment.

Like Claudia, however, we can learn how to turn this bias into a great teacher. When the negative thoughts and emotions arise in life, we have an opportunity to learn self-compassion, opening us up to a new perspective that "things are going to be okay." With practice, we can train our brains to default to a left prefrontal shift, recognize the humanness in suffering—both others' and our own—and apply an understanding and caring attitude. This inevitably mediates our perception of personal suffering and opens us up to a wiser heart.

In the same way that we trained ourselves to walk and talk, we can train our brains to respond automatically to difficult emotions with a 180-degree shift of self-compassion.

Relax, We're All Imperfect

One of the most important elements of self-compassion is the recognition that to be flawed is to be human. We all share this. Sadly, when it comes to depression, the negativity bias skews reality, and the notion that imperfection is a human experience is lost on us. Instead of connecting us, the experience of fallibility sends us in the direction of disconnection and isolation. When we're caught in the depression loop, we're stuck in a cycle of self-absorbed self-loathing. But this sense of aloneness is another lie that depression tells us.

In an excerpt from an article published in the *New York Post* on November 28, 1972, Albert Einstein, in 1950, wrote:

> A human being is part of the whole, called by us "universe," a part limited in time and space. He experiences himself, his thoughts and feelings, as something separate from the rest—a kind of optical delusion of consciousness. This delusion is a kind of prison for us, restricting us to our personal desires and to affection for a few persons nearest to us. Our task must be to free ourselves from this prison by widening our circle of compassion to embrace all living creatures and the whole of nature in its beauty.

Understanding that our struggles are tied into being human isn't just a theory, it's grounded in science. Kristin Neff, PhD, a researcher at the University of Texas at Austin, has been studying self-compassion for over a decade. She even wrote the book *Self-Compassion: The Proven Power of Being Kind to Yourself*, and says this about it: "Seeing one's experiences as part of the larger human experience rather than as separating and isolating" is an essential aspect of this healing mindset.

In a recent session, a client of mine was struggling with repeated bouts of anxiety but felt too ashamed to share this with her partner, for fear that he would leave her. I asked her if she thought there were other people in the world right now who also struggled with the shame around anxiety and depression. She took a few moments and said, "Yes, I'm sure of it." I continued, "Take a moment to close your eyes and imagine all of those people together with you. What do you wish for all of them? What do you wish for yourself?" She paused and then let out a deep breath. I asked her, "What happened?" She replied, "I imagined us all holding hands on the beach, understanding each other and wishing ourselves to have more ease, to be happy, and to feel safe." And then a smile broke across her face.

"How does that feel?" I asked. She replied, "I feel good."

Learning how to hold the wider perspective that to be imperfect is to be human, allows us to relax a little in the face of imperfection. We start to take our perceived failings less personally and become more understanding and caring with ourselves in those difficult moments. This is the experience of self-compassion. We can eventually begin to understand that the vulnerability of our imperfections is the gateway to self-acceptance, self-love, and healing.

Try this experiment: think of all the people in the world right now who lack self-compassion and get stuck in a depression loop. Take a moment to picture them in your mind. Place your hand on your heart and, as authentically as you can, say, "May we all

TAKE A SELF-COMPASSION INVENTORY

Here are a few questions to help you gauge the strength of your self-compassion muscle. (Note: if you find it's low, don't worry, just like a muscle, it can be strengthened.)

1. Where does the inner critic pop up? At work? When you walk past the mirror? In relationships? In relation to parenting? And so on.
2. What are the repercussions of being so hard on yourself? Does it add to the depression loop?
3. When something difficult arises in life and you fall under stress, where are you on the "to-do" list of people to take care of? Do you apply caring to your suffering or try to avoid it?
4. When things are tough, do you tend to compare yourself with others, thinking that they have it together? Or do you have a balanced perspective, knowing that all humans struggle?
5. What would the days, weeks, and months ahead be like if your stress and inner struggles were met with more understanding and caring?

feel safe, may we all feel healthy in body and mind, may we all be free from fear, may we all accept ourselves exactly as we are." By doing this, you connect with them and enliven the experience of self-compassion.

If you feel like your self-compassion muscle is a bit atrophied, notice if the inner critic pops up around this too. It's tough to be imperfect in a society that emphasizes perfection. Allow this to be a moment of awareness; a choice point to do something different.

Shining the spotlight on our shame or imperfections can bring light to those shadows that have been unwanted and unseen for quite some time. In embracing all parts of ourselves, we feed the voice of self-acceptance that kindles healing and freedom.

The Biology of Soothing

One of the main antidepressant elements of self-compassion is the power to soothe ourselves in the face of suffering. This isn't just a feel-good psychobabble idea; there's a biological basis to it that relates to the hormone oxytocin, which is known as the hormone of love and bonding. Oxytocin is released into the bloodstream during pregnancy, delivery, and breast feeding, among other times—blood levels of oxytocin go up even when you have a good hug. Research has found that increased levels of oxytocin are associated with feelings of trust, safety, calm, and connectedness.

Numerous research studies suggest that the act of self-compassion stimulates oxytocin release in our bodies. You can think of this biochemical response as the opposite of what happens when we're caught in the depression loop. Depression thrives on fear. When fear is aroused, the nervous system kicks into gear to keep us safe and get us ready to fight, flee, or freeze. This releases the hormone cortisol, and as it continues to surge, certain areas of our brains become impaired—including the hippocampus, which, as you may remember, is responsible for learning, memory, and putting life events in context. As the brain and body become impacted, depression often follows.

Engaging self-compassion changes our brain chemistry. One hypothesis based on the research is that oxytocin is released instead of cortisol, and the amygdala calms down as activity shifts to the left prefrontal cortex.

Let It Linger . . .

If we know that neurons that fire together wire together, one thing we want to keep in mind when doing any soothing activity is to let the experience linger, even if just for a few seconds.

Take in the moment fully and sense how it feels in your body. Be curious about the experience knowing that engaging novelty is one of the best drivers of neuroplastic change. As you do this, you're also stamping a memory of the experience that the brain can reference the next time this difficulty arises. As you linger in self-compassion, the firing continues for a longer period of time, giving the brain a better opportunity to wire in the natural anti-depressant of self-compassion.

The Payoff of a Hug

My friend Stan Tatkin, author of *Wired for Love: How Understanding Your Partner's Brain and Attachment Style Can Help You Defuse Conflict and Build a Secure Relationship*, once suggested that when I come home after a long day, I hug my wife and linger in it until both of our bodies relax. He explained that this not only releases oxytocin, which sets us up to feel more balanced and soothed, but it also allows us to feel more connected, as our nervous systems are aligned. He was right! This works even if you don't have someone at home. Studies show that imagining actions stimulates the same parts of the brain as actually doing them. If you don't have someone to hug at home, imagine hugging another person, hug yourself, or perhaps set the intention to hug others more often. The point here is to practice nurturing the release of this natural antidepressant.

The Stick, the Cake, and the Carrot

We can nurture self-compassion in the way that we speak to ourselves. When it comes to depression, our NUTs constantly kick us when we're down as a way to try to motivate us to change. But this always backfires, making it even harder for us to feel motivated or inspired to do anything. The reality is, self-compassion is far more motivating than whipping ourselves with a mental stick. Imagine that you are a child and your parents just received your report card and learned that you had done pretty well in most subjects, but you received a D in math. I'm going to bring you through three scenarios of how this could play out—notice how you feel as you read them.

Scenario 1: The Stick
Your parents come into the room and say,

"What is this D? We do not work as hard as we do for you to come home with grades like this. What the hell is wrong with you? With grades like this, you'll never amount to anything. We've had it up to here. We don't think anyone can help you, and you certainly can't help yourself. What do you have to say for yourself?"

Scenario 2: The Cake
Your parents come into the room and say,

"Wow, this must have been a stressful experience. You know, if you look at all the rest of your grades, you've done pretty well. This is only one class among many; you'll get 'em next time. Is there anything you need from us?"

Scenario 3: The Carrot
Your parents come into the room and say,

"We've just got your report card. It looks like you've done pretty well in most of your classes. An A in English, a B in science, and another A in social studies. Great job! We hope you're able to congratulate yourself; your work in those classes has paid off! We also noticed that in math you got a D. If that grade stays the same, they may make you take that class over again next year, and we know you don't want to do that. Let's look at what happened and find out the best way we can support you in getting that grade up."

Now, which voice would be more motivating to you?

While layering on self-criticism can be motivating, our minds more often than not take it too far, and it has the opposite effect. That's what happened in a study in which students were asked to list a variety of goals related to health, academics, and friends, and then report later on their progress. Those who rated as higher in self-criticism achieved significantly less progress toward those goals. One reason for this may be that it causes greater stress to the nervous system rather than helping to soothe it. The more stress we have, the more fear we have. When the brain experiences fear, it finds ways to avoid the source, whatever that is. This leads to procrastination in an effort to stay away from the perceived threat—or maybe to an impulsive action, saying and doing things that we regret later. At the same time, the stress hormone cortisol gets kicked up. As you might recall, cortisol damages the hippocampus, which is responsible for learning and memory, and is often associated with feeling depressed.

On the flip side, the cake example is like treating someone with kindness but bypassing his or her responsibility. This is self-indulgent and doesn't motivate us to do any better. The carrot example is self-compassion, as it acknowledges the difficulty, and then engages with kindness with an inclination to truly help. A number of studies point to the positive effects of integrating self-compassion into our daily lives as a natural antidepressant.

Paul Gilbert, a professor of psychology at the University of Derby in the United Kingdom, is the founder of compassion-focused therapy (CFT), which was designed to build self-compassion and is currently being used as a therapy for depression, bipolar disorder, eating disorders, and other psychological conditions. He brings people through a process of changing the way they relate to themselves with a warmer emotional responsiveness through visualizations, kinder self-talk, and developing more self-compassionate habits. Another goal is to raise awareness of how the self-attacking voices operate in the mind and to understand that these voices are a way of coping. This often isn't easy.

We know that the thoughts and images in our minds have a powerful effect on our neurochemistry and our bodies in general. Research shows that even just imagining food or sexually appealing images has this same effect on the brain. Think about a time when you were hungry, and a delicious meal was placed before you; your brain reacted and began producing saliva in the mouth. Or think about a time you saw someone you found sexually attractive—in that moment, your brain was stimulated, and your body became aroused. But even if you just imagined the food or the sexually appealing person, your brain would respond. When our NUTs get stirred up in the mind and are relentlessly attacking us, our bodies feel beaten down as well.

We can use this power of thoughts and images to nurture the natural antidepressant of self-compassion. When researchers asked participants to consider a nurturing and soothing image that inspired, warmth, understanding, and compassion, some people thought of a person such as the Dalai Lama, Jesus, the Buddha, or their therapist. Others thought of the sea, a tree, the sky, or an animal. The key here is that images have the power to inspire qualities such as wisdom, strength, warmth, nonjudgment, and acceptance.

In 2006 Dr. Gilbert published a study in which hospital day-treatment patients "with major/severe complex long-term difficulties" who rated high on shame and self-criticism engaged in compassionate mind training (CMT). Participants attended a weekly two-hour class for twelve weeks. The study concluded, "When patients find it difficult to generate alternative thoughts or feelings to their self-attacking thoughts, they can focus on their compassionate image and consider 'what would my compassionate image/perfect nurturer say to me?'" The patients alternated between thinking of the difficult self-attacking experience and then moving to the soothing image. As this is practiced and repeated, eventually the self-attacking reaction arises in concert with the self-compassionate response. This becomes a natural antidepressant and a source of resiliency. The results after twelve weeks showed that participants experienced a decrease in depressive symptoms, shame, and feelings of inferiority. You can do the same.

Whipping ourselves with a stick as a means of motivation can have negative consequences that we can avoid.

Discover Your Self-Compassion Image (or Hero)

Consider for a moment if there is an image of a person or a place that comes to mind that holds for you soothing and compassionate qualities of wisdom, strength, warmth, understanding, nonjudgment, and acceptance. This could be someone close to you in your life, or an animal, or a spiritual figure as mentioned in the study, such as the Dalai Lama, Jesus, or the Buddha. Or maybe it's a place like the sea, the sky, or a wise old tree. When the self-attacking NUTs arise, see if you can imagine that compassionate nurturing person or place and ask, "What would he say to me?" If you like, write it out below to come back to again and again. There is no perfection to this practice; play with it as a way to connect with the wisdom inside of you.

_____

_____

_____

_____

_____

But I Need the Stick!

It's common to experience resistance to turning down the volume on your self-judgment and turning up the volume on self-compassion. This stems from a fear that it will lead you to states

SELF-COMPASSION OR SELF-INDULGENCE?

There's a critical nuance that we need to be clear about when practicing self-compassion. It doesn't mean just being nice to ourselves in order to soothe a difficult feeling. If that were the case, we might use it in foolish ways and just have another drink when we hear the negative voices arising. There's danger in confusing self-compassion with self-indulgence as a form of avoidance, which can turn it into another bad habit.

You'll notice in the "carrot" scenario earlier that the parents didn't let the child off the hook. Nor did they coddle the child by saying, "That's okay, you'll get 'em next time." Instead, they recognized that there was an issue that, if not dealt with, could have more negative consequences. At the same time, the mother and father offered soothing and support to make the necessary changes. True self-compassion takes courage at times to recognize the fact that the way we are going about our lives is not working, but that the most skillful thing to do is to love ourselves and make the necessary changes to move us in the direction of health and well-being.

of laziness, complacency, and attachment to your own suffering. The belief is that if you don't ride yourself hard, you'll fall apart completely. But think of it this way: If you had a friend who needed some motivation, would you say mean things to him? Not if you wanted to keep the friendship. We're often much harder on ourselves than we would ever be to anyone else—and we accept self-talk from ourselves that we would never take from a friend. Kristin Neff's research on self-compassion shows that "the biggest reason people aren't more self-compassionate is that they are afraid they'll become self-indulgent. They believe self-criticism is what keeps them in line. Most people have gotten it wrong because our culture says being hard on yourself is the way to be."

But the logic is flawed. Psychological research demonstrates that we are more effective in the face of support and have greater coping capacities when we make the left prefrontal shift that is associated with approach-related responses, positive emotions, and resiliency. The truth is that it takes courage to begin loving ourselves and to work actively on letting go of our self-judgments. Gandhi said, "Whenever you are confronted with an opponent, conquer them with love." Recognize that right now is a choice point to make a commitment to let go of the stick and play with the practice of self-compassion. You will start to notice that the latter is far more effective.

Uncover What You Really Need

In nourishing self-compassion, a fundamental practice is to simply acknowledge the difficult moment when it's there and ask yourself "What do I need right now?" When all our needs are fulfilled, the brain doesn't need to focus on survival tasks and feels safe enough to open up to our natural presence and uncover happiness. There are feelings of comfort, contentment, gratitude, hope, trust, and energy. When our needs are not met, we feel uncomfortable, hopeless, frustrated, embarrassed, lonely, confused, and the list goes on. As you start pairing the difficult moment with what you need, you begin conditioning a self-compassionate response to emotional pain. At times you'll find it is easier to access the voice within that knows what you need. But more often than not when we're feeling down, we literally don't have the brain power to think of what we need in that moment, much less take action to attain it.

Below you'll find a needs inventory to help raise your awareness of what you may be lacking in difficult moments either with yourself or when you're with others. This list can help identify your needs when your brain isn't working so well. Understanding your needs is a first step to being able to apply self-compassion.

CONNECTION	CONNECTION	PHYSICAL	HONESTY
Acceptance	Companionship	To breathe	Authenticity
Affection	Compassion	To eat	Integrity
Appreciation	Empathy	Movement/ exercise	Presence
Belonging	Intimacy	Rest/sleep	
Communication	Love	Sexual expression	
Community	Nurturing	Safety	
	Respect/Self-respect	Touch	
		Water	

PLAY	PEACE	AUTONOMY	MEANING
Joy	Beauty	Choice	Awareness
Humor	Ease	Freedom	Celebration of life
	Harmony	Independence	Clarity
	Inspiration	Space	Creativity
	Order	Spontaneity	Effectiveness
			Growth
			Hope
			Learning
			Mourning
			Purpose
			Self-expression
			Stimulation
			To matter
			Understanding

One way to get some practice with uncovering your needs is to simply reflect on a recent experience. Start by thinking back to a recent difficult moment. This may have been a stressful time at work, a difficult interaction with a friend, or an onslaught of your NUTs. The more vivid you can make the visualization, the more you'll get in touch with the experience of it.

Once you identify the experience, pause for a moment and acknowledge the difficulty of the situation, maybe saying "That was difficult." Then ask, "What was I feeling?" and "What did I need then?" Look over the list and see if any of these match what it was that you needed in that moment. Or, if you are noticing the emotion of the experience right now, you can ask, "What do I need right now?" Acknowledging the difficulty is a moment of mindfulness, and, as you've learned, this pause alone changes the

THE NERVE OF COMPASSION

The reason we can cultivate compassion as a skill is because there is an underlying biology to it. Science is now discovering that we have a critical bundle of fibers, called the *vagus nerve*, which links our brains with our hearts. While we can't measure vagal tone directly, researchers can gauge subtle variations in heart rate to show the strength of this brain-heart connection, and this reveals what's called your vagal tone. In general, the higher your vagal tone, the better. When your vagal tone is higher, this slows down the heart rate and is indicative of calmness, rest, and relaxation. In this state, the body is better able to regulate the internal systems that keep you healthy, such as cardiovascular response and immune response. When your vagal tone is lower, you experience more symptoms associated with depression—difficulty regulating our emotional state, a flatness of emotion, low voice tone, and imbalanced heart rates. The vagus nerve is also entwined with our oxytocin network, a hormone that is involved in trust, safety, and caring. It helps facilitate feeling connected to others as it helps us tune into facial expressions and tone of voice, nurturing our capacity for connection, friendship, and empathy.

The US Food and Drug Administration (FDA) has approved a surgically implanted device that emits electrical impulses to stimulate the vagus nerve and help relieve depressive symptoms. But there are other, less invasive ways to activate this nerve. The vagus nerve is also active when we feel compassion, witness the good of another, or even just hear a score of beautiful music. It's the feeling of openness and expansion in the body where we are less reactive to depressive cues, better able to self-soothe, and engage socially. This suggests that self-compassion may be a powerful cue for good vagal tone and a natural antidepressant.

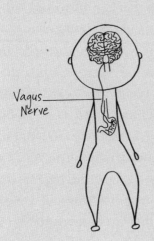

Vagus Nerve

You can think of the vagus nerve as the direct link between your heart and your brain. Compassion increases vagal tone, which has been shown to decrease depressive symptoms, acting as a natural antidepressant.

cycle. When you're able to take it a step further and access what you need, you can open up to choice, learn how to self-soothe, and move toward healing.

Take Self-Compassion Breaks

After identifying what our needs are at challenging times, we can work to come up with ways to meet those needs or take self-compassion breaks. If we need peace, a self-compassion break may be to lie down on the bed and listen to some gentle music. If we need humor, we may be able to open a book or watch a show that makes us smile. If we need community, we can call a friend or go somewhere that gives us a sense of social support.

Two basic things that we often need in difficult moments are understanding and self-love. These are the two pillars of acceptance. One of the quickest ways that I've found to foster self-understanding and self-love is by simply putting my hand on my heart. This gesture of caring connects us with self-care. I often use this strategy during my kids' bedtime routine. Putting my kids to bed is one of those experiences that can turn frustrating very easily. Like most children, they usually don't want to go to sleep, and at that time of the evening, my wife and I are tired from the day. It can be a struggle to get them into their pajamas, their teeth brushed, and to stay in bed. Sometimes all I want in those moments is to crawl under their covers and go to sleep myself. But because of the work I've been doing, I become aware, put my hand on my heart, and acknowledge the struggle. This tends to start a soothing process. I then think of all the other parents that have struggles with their kids at bedtime and wish us all to be at ease. This dispels the tension and at times even opens me up to the perspective that I have beautiful little boys lying beside me.

unbinding the heart

The practice of placing your hand on your heart acknowledges the difficulty, but also physically makes contact with yourself on the area of the body that is most associated with love. People often find this simple gesture to be a powerful way to not only stop the depressive loop but also to experience a homecoming to the heart. If you want to try this out, but your heart doesn't feel right in the moment, you can also place your hand on your abdomen, which is often considered the grounding area of the body. Just placing your hand on the center of your abdomen throughout the day can be a wonderful centering practice.

If all you do is put your hand on your heart and wish yourself well, your time will be well spent.

Four Self-Compassion Breaks
1. Practice Daily Friendliness (to Yourself)

There are multiple opportunities to befriend yourself throughout the day. Perhaps in difficult moments when you ask what you need, you might hear a voice that says, I want to be healthy, or I want to feel safe, or I want to feel at ease. A self-compassion break may be to place your hand on your heart and repeat the phrase of what you need to yourself. For example, if you need to be more at ease, you can take a few deep breaths and say in your mind, "May I be at ease." This is not an affirmation. You're not saying you *are* at ease; you simply wish it for yourself, which is an act of caring and self-compassion.

You can also use a self-compassion break to send the difficult people in your life these same friendly wishes. You can picture them in your mind and practice saying, "May you be happy, be healthy, be more at ease, and be free from fear." Difficult people in life trigger stress and tension in us. But when they do, the one who suffers is us, not them. Wishing these people to be more at ease, to be happier, to be healthy, or to be free from fear can help us release the negative feelings that live inside of us. If you're having trouble seeing the logic in this, consider that if a difficult person in your life felt more at ease, happy, safe, and healthy, he or she might not be as irritating. Slide beneath the judgments about whether this will or won't be effective for you and let your experience be your teacher.

2. Pretend to Laugh a Little

Sometimes we just need to laugh. Plenty of studies point to the stress-reducing and antidepressant qualities of humor and laughter. If depression is an experience of closing down, laughter is a physical experience of opening up that releases endorphins—substances in the brain that are associated with feeling good. This also activates the body, which is often more dormant when depressed and can be a good, gentle aerobic exercise. It promotes the left prefrontal cortex shift that is associated with positive emotions and resiliency. Laughter also helps bring us to the present moment, disengaging from an active depressive loop.

Laughter is also prone to emotional contagion perhaps because we have *mirror neurons* in our brains that mimic the experience of others that we see. Some scientists believe that mirror neurons are why we may yawn after seeing another person yawn or even how we experience empathy. The same goes for laughing. When we see others laughing, we tend to laugh ourselves. In fact, you can just pretend to laugh for a while, and you might notice that you start laughing naturally.

This is the basis behind a large, growing movement called laughter yoga. Laughter yoga was started in the mid-1990s by Indian physician Madan Kataria. He believed that laughter was a form of physical exercise that has tremendous psychological and physiological benefits that counter anxiety and depression. It starts with just beginning to laugh, making eye contact, and being playful, and eventually erupts into real laughter. The underlying philosophy is that the body can't tell the difference between fake laughter and real laughter, and the same psychological benefits follow. It has become so popular that it now has over six thousand social laughter clubs in over sixty countries.

Try the following experiment: watch the three-minute video *Benefits of Laughter Yoga with John Cleese* on YouTube, and see how long it takes before you crack a smile or even laugh. When we smile and have more laughter in our lives, you can imagine that left prefrontal shift countering depressive symptoms and fostering resiliency.

Of course, you can choose other forms of humor, such as your favorite comic strip or the funny antics of animals. Laughter yoga just makes it social, because there are other people involved, even if it's just watching a group of people doing it. When the mind gets a bit too serious, adding laughter to our day as a physical exercise can be a wonderful self-compassion break.

3. **Optimize Your Social Network**

The fact is that some people in our lives are nourishing and some are depleting. With whom do you spend most of your time? Who is most nourishing, and who is most depleting? Are you spending more hours with depleting people or nourishing people? How can you make more contact with those who support your health and well-being? These days we have so many options, whether in person or by way of online social networks, text, chat, email, or phone. A self-compassion break might entail reaching out to someone who nourishes your spirit.

There are also times when we have no choice but to engage with people or activities that are depleting. The question then becomes, what ways might we relate differently to these people or activities to make them less draining? For example, rather than spending your mental energy hating a difficult person, you can make a shift and try to engage in an informal loving-kindness practice. This is where you take those friendly wishes I mentioned earlier and silently wish them for a series of people, including yourself. Most of us spend enough time focusing on what we don't like about ourselves, other people, or the world. This creates an imbalance and feeds the depression loop. Practicing a more compassionate awareness not only brings balance, but, as you've learned, science shows that it also serves as a natural antidepressant. You don't have to like someone to wish him or her well, and we can all get better at realizing the common humanity that ties us together.

Lovingkindness Practice

At any point that you feel comfortable, sit or lie down and picture a living person or animal that you care about. Consider what it is that you love about him or her. Is it her smile, how kind he might be, the way she supports you or is generous in the world? Then imagine that person looking into your eyes and say to him, "May you be happy. May you be healthy in body and mind. May you feel safe and protected from inner and outer harm. May you be free from fear." You can also shorten this to "May you be happy, healthy, safe, and free from fear." While in some mindfulness practices your breath is the object of your attention, here it is these phrases. As you do this, your mind will likely wander onto other thoughts, memories, or some outside distraction. That is fine; just note it. That, too, is a moment of mindfulness, and a choice point to return to your intention.

Then take these same phrases and send these inwardly: "May I be happy. May I be healthy in body and mind. May I feel safe and protected from inner and outer harm. May I be free from fear—the fear that keeps me stuck." If being kind to yourself is challenging, know that this is very common. You can pause here, acknowledging the difficulty, and place both hands on your heart as a gesture of caring; a self-compassion break.

Continue this same process with a neutral person, such as a checkout clerk or a neighbor. Although you don't know much about this person, you do know that he wants to be happy, healthy, at ease, and free from fear. Don't worry about it if the phrases don't fit at this point, just use them as a vehicle to nurture your heart.

Move on to a difficult person: not someone who is related to any real trauma but someone who has been irritating, annoying, or a pain. Picture him and sense his presence. Send him the same wishes that you sent the person you care about: "May you be happy, healthy, safe, and free from fear." If this is too difficult, you can always go back to sending lovingkindness to yourself. Or just place your hands on your heart, acknowledge the difficulty of the moment—knowing that difficult moments are a part of life—and give a gesture of caring to yourself.

Expand this to encompass all people, animals, and, if it feels right, to all beings everywhere. Finally, take a moment to acknowledge yourself for making the effort to engage in this practice for your own health and well-being. This is an act of self-care.

Sometimes it takes darkness and the sweet confinement of your aloneness to learn anything or anyone that does not bring you alive is too small for you.

—BRITISH POET DAVID WHYTE

---

4. Practice Being SAFE

Our brains love acronyms because they're easy to remember. SAFE is a short self-compassion practice that can pop us out of autopilot during a difficult moment, change our relationship to the feelings that are there, create insight into what we need in that moment, and connect us to the common humanity behind our struggles. It has become a core practice in my life and in the lives of all the people I've taught this to. It integrates all the essential components of self-compassion, including mindfulness, kindness, and connection to our shared humanity. Begin practicing this during less turbulent times to get the hang of it. Then practice bringing it into more difficult moments as a self-compassion break. It can calm your racing mind, soothe your nervous system, and open your eyes to a wiser heart.

Here are the four steps:

S—Soften into the feeling.
A—Allow it to be as it is, without resisting or clinging to it.
F—Feel into the sensation of the emotion and uncover your need.
E—Expand awareness to all people struggling with this.

Soften into the feeling.

Whether it's a feeling of stress, anxiety, shame, tension, anger, or fear, the first step is to take a minute and gently acknowledge the feeling that is there. You might say to yourself, "Ah, this is anger," "This is shame," or if an emotional name doesn't come to mind, "This is that dull, heavy feeling in my chest." This allows you to step into the space between stimulus and response where choice, flexibility, and possibility lie. One way of softening into the feeling is to combine it with your breath. You may say to yourself, "Breathing in, opening to the vulnerability that is here; breathing out, softening into it."

Allow it to be as it is, without resisting or clinging to it.

Often what feeds the roadblock with any emotion is the brain's need to resist, get away from it, or hold on to it. As we soften into the feeling, the next step is to simply ask ourselves, "Can I just allow this to be as it is?" This is a 180-degree shift and is pure mindfulness. The process of allowing or "being with" what's here widens that space of awareness in which choice and insight lie. Some people find it easier to combine it with the breath, saying to themselves, "Breathing in, allowing; breathing out, letting be."

Feel into the emotion that is there with a kind attention.

After allowing the emotion, there is space to engage the emotion. Choose to "feel into" it a bit more with a curious and friendly awareness. This shifts you from an avoidant state that is associated with depression to an approach state associated more with feeling well. You might notice where it is in your body, how big it is, the contours of it, or even it if has a color. In doing this, you can still drop in the questions "What does this feeling believe?" Is it that you're unlovable, that things will never change, or that you're deficient in some way? Then follow with the question "What do I need right now?" Maybe it's to be loved, to be at ease, or to feel safe. As you discover what you need, take a moment to wish that for yourself. For example, if you sense that you need to feel loved and to feel safe, you might say, "May I feel loved. May I feel safe." And so on.

It is possible that during this part of the practice you may encounter resistance or maybe one of your NUTS, such as "There's no point in doing this." When this happens, see if you can recognize it as resistance and include that as part of the feeling that is there, feeling into the sensation of resistance with that same curiosity and caring. As you begin to relate to the feeling, you loosen the identification with it, gaining perspective and freedom from it.

Expand awareness to all people who also experience this vulnerability.

The fact is that the feeling of vulnerability is a deeply human experience. Understanding this shared experience of humanity is a core component of self-compassion. Expanding awareness to all the other people who struggle with this same vulnerability takes you out of that self-absorbed state, impersonalizing it more and cultivating a sense of connection that is also a natural antidepressant. Here is where we understand that we are not alone and that in this very moment there are thousands if not millions of people who are experiencing this same feeling. The *E* in SAFE is where we inspire connection with the rest of humanity. In this practice, we can also take what we learned from the *F* in SAFE and send it outward, saying, "May we all feel loved. May we all feel safe." And so forth.

Self-compassion doesn't exist in a vacuum. It's possible only in relation to a moment of suffering. SAFE is a complete self-compassion break that serves as an antidote during difficult moments. You can practice gaining freedom, insights, and self-compassion from what's vulnerable or difficult, while also inspiring a sense of connectedness outside of yourself that is ultimately healing.

Write a Letter of Encouragement

If you want to practice self-compassion, you have to work on letting go of that part of you that says that to do so is self-indulgent, a waste of time, or that you don't deserve it. This is the part that believes there's no reason to love yourself. We need to encourage the part of ourselves that believes we have the same right as anyone else to be happy, to feel safe and protected, to be free from fear, and to be at ease. One way we can do that is to write a letter of encouragement to ourselves when we're feeling well. This helps us to tap into that wise voice that has always been there, so that as time goes on, we get better and better at trusting ourselves. The letter can go something like this:

Dear [Me],

Being depressed is tough. I get it; I've been there. I want to remind you that this feeling doesn't last, and here are a few things to know about you when you're not depressed. When you wake up in the morning, that feeling of dread is not there. You're able to look in the mirror and believe that the day will be good. When the NUTs visit you, they aren't as distracting and are easier to crack. You can shift your attention to other tasks that need to get done. You laugh a lot more and are able to pay attention longer. There are little pleasures that you notice throughout the day. You're kinder and more loving. As the evening winds down, you can relax and go to sleep without much issue.

    This is within you, remember this.

With love,
[Me]

Now take a few minutes, and if you feel up to it, write your own letter. (Note: if you don't feel up to it, perhaps a good friend can write the letter for you, reminding you how you are when you're feeling well.)

_____

_____

_____

_____

_____

_____

After you finish, put this letter in a special place to look at from time to time and pick up when life gets tough. Sometimes you might be able to predict when you'll be more vulnerable, whether it's a season, an anniversary, or an upcoming event. Consider going to the website FutureMe.org (www.futureme.org), where you can paste the letter into a draft and program it to email it to you at times you think your relapse signs might be visiting. If you have a significant other or someone close to you, you can give her this letter and ask her to bring it out during difficult times. This gives that person a way to support you when you feel stuck and is also a good strategy to help hold you up when you feel like you're falling.

Natural Side Effects

Nourishing the antidepressant of self-compassion stimulates positive side effects that begin to fill your needs naturally. Prime your mind to be on the lookout for experiences of hope, gratitude, joy, patience, forgiveness, connection, wisdom, and more compassion for others. When you notice them, see if you can linger in them for a short period of time. For many people, the benefits are robust enough to bring about what Barbara Fredrickson calls an "upward spiral" to happiness and resiliency. The following paragraphs discuss some of those positive effects and how you can harness them to promote a more resilient brain and uncover happiness.

Hope

When we begin to feel supported with a kinder hand, the thought might arise, "I can make it." Hope isn't only a thought; it appears to be a synthesis of emotions and thoughts that allows us to believe we can reach certain goals. Hope isn't a trait that some people have and others don't. It's a skill that we can encourage and cultivate. The late Rick Snyder, PhD, was an eminent psychologist who said that hope is fostered when we have (1) a goal in mind, (2) a determination that a goal can be reached, and (3) a plan for how to reach that goal. In that sense, we can hope for big things (getting the promotion), or we can hope for small things (getting the dishes done). At this point, what you want to do is simply be aware whenever hope arises. With an awareness of it, you stamp it into your memory and make it more likely to come up in the future.

Gratitude

When you're able to experience self-compassion, you are likely to become grateful for the relief and peace that come with it. In 2003, psychologists Robert Emmons and Michael McCollough conducted a study called "Counting Blessings versus Burdens." They split up the participants into three groups. One group counted five blessings per day, one group counted five burdens per day, and one group wrote only about neutral events. The ones who counted blessings experienced less stress and enhanced well-being. Counting our blessings is not meant to be a miracle cure. Instead, we can think of it as laying down new tracks toward the antidepressant brain each time we do it.

One way to nurture this side effect is to pause a few moments a day and intentionally think of what you're grateful for, encouraging an antidepressant shift in the brain. To support yourself through this you can access a free online gratitude journal with grateful160 (www.grateful160.com), where a daily email will prompt you to reply with what you're grateful for in life. At the end of the week, you'll get an email sent back to you with a journal of your week's gratitude. It's amazing to see it all at once. In the Tool Kit in part 3, you'll find a Compassionate Body Scan to play with that integrates mindfulness with an appreciative awareness, strengthening the muscle of gratitude.

What do you have to be grateful for in your life right now, just as it is?

What would the days, weeks, and months ahead be like if your brain automatically inclined toward things for which you are grateful?

Joy

Self-compassion naturally ignites joy, a feeling of openness, lightness, and well-being.

Sometimes in the morning, my mind begins to swim with all the work I have to do that day. However, I can't jump into work immediately, as it's often my job to make breakfast for my family. When thinking about the mountain of work I have, I can get frustrated while preparing the food. When I notice this, I know that it's a choice point, and I come back to placing a hand on my heart, acknowledging the frustration, and then focusing on doing one thing at a time and remembering that I am nourishing myself and my family so we can be well in this world and pass that wellness on to others. Sometimes I imbue the moment with love by repeating in my mind, "May this food support us all in being healthy in body and mind." This begins to kindle the joy of caring for my family.

Your work is simply to be on the lookout for this side effect and note it when you see it. If possible, allow yourself to linger in the experience of it for a few seconds, encouraging that extra firing and wiring. You can also make a list of all the things that bring you joy. If there is anybody else in your life that you know wants to experience joy, how about making a plan to connect and do things together that are on your joy list?

Patience

As I noted earlier, part of the fuel that gets added to the depression loop is an instant reaction of impatient problem solving or fixing any warning sign that depression is here or looming. Applying self-compassion appeases the part of the mind that wants to take action and slows down the process, allowing for a sense of patience to unfold.

Patience slows down the depression loop and widens the space between stimulus and response to help us make a more skillful decision on how best to support ourselves. When we're patient, we also get the sense that we are in the driver's seat and can begin to trust ourselves that we will be okay. Deepen your practice with patience. You can say, "Breathing in, calming my body; breathing out, relaxing into the moment just as it is."

Forgiveness

After twenty-seven years in Robben Island prison, Nelson Mandela said, "As I walked out the door toward the gate that would lead to my freedom, I knew if I didn't leave my bitterness and hatred behind, I'd still be in prison." Mandela knew that although he'd suffered a great deal, the way to support himself was through this self-compassionate act of practicing forgiveness and releasing the burden. Self-compassion is the gateway to forgiveness.

There are many times that we hurt or wrong ourselves or others knowingly or unknowingly. If you have a burden or grudge you're carrying about yourself or another, take a moment to feel this burden that lives inside when you hold so tightly to past hurts. Now ask yourself, "Have I carried this burden long enough? Do I recognize forgiveness as an act of self-compassion? Am I willing to forgive?"

If not, that is okay; but maybe it's worth looking at why you're holding on. What is keeping you attached to the pain? Whatever answer arises, trust that the time will come when you're ready. If you are ready to maintain or deepen this side effect of self-forgiveness practice, you can try "Breathing in, I acknowledge the pain; breathing out, forgiving and releasing this burden from my heart and mind."

Continue this as long as it feels supportive to you.

Connection

Self-compassion ignites a feeling of connection, which is at the center of resiliency: for example, the self-compassion break of putting your hand on your chest is a form of caring touch in the face of a difficult moment. Jim Coan, PhD, the director of the Virginia Affective Neuroscience Laboratory at the University of Virginia, has studied how a loving touch affects the body's secretion of stress hormones. In a study he conducted, he administered mild electrical shocks to sixteen married women while studying their brains with functional MRI brain scans. During the procedures, each woman held her husband's hand, and then a stranger's hand, and then no hand at all. The women reported feeling less stressed when holding the stranger's hand and the least stressed when holding their husband's hand. When the scientists looked at the brain scans they found that when the women held the stranger's hands there was a reduction in activity in the amygdala, the fear circuit, and there was an even greater impact when holding their husbands' hands. Not surprisingly, the brain scans also confirmed that the women whose relationships scored highest in loving connection also experienced the greatest reductions in stress hormone secretion.

Depression thrives on stress, and Coan's research suggests a neurobiology of why a loving connection turns down the stress in the brain. While this loving touch was with another person, my personal experience and the experiences of many of my students, clients, friends, and colleagues suggest that there's a similar effect when we give this warm caring touch to ourselves either physically or mentally with friendly wishes.

Wisdom

One of the beautiful things that comes from working mindfulness and self-compassion into our lives is the cultivation of a balanced mind, where there is a natural state of benevolence toward ourselves and others. What comes with that is a more accepting attitude toward ourselves and toward the changing conditions in life. Opening your heart with this lovingkindness and acceptance transforms even the worst NUT into wise awareness. To encourage this effect, simply close your eyes from time to time, take a few deep breaths, and imagine a smile in your heart and that your awareness is as wide as the sky. Use your breath as an anchor as you sequentially open up to the appearing and disappearing sounds, and then thoughts, and then sensations. Just rest in this seat of awareness and watch the world unfold, feeling into the natural balance that is there.

Practicing self-compassion is about making the decision here and now to love yourself for the rest of your life, for better or worse. We don't do this work to "save" ourselves but rather to "serve" ourselves and ultimately the people around us. In some ways, the mere fact that you've picked up this book is an act of understanding the suffering you've experienced with an inclination to help yourself. This very moment of reading this sentence is an act of self-compassion.

STEP 5

Live with Purpose—
Know Why You Matter and
What You Can Do About It

*If you don't figure out where you are going, you
are bound to end up where you are headed.*
—CHINESE PROVERB

Viktor Frankl, an Austrian neurologist and psychiatrist, em-
bodied the spirit of purposeful living completely. Between 1942
and 1945, during the Holocaust, Frankl was imprisoned in four
different concentration camps. When he arrived at the first camp,
his German captors took away all of his belongings, stripped him
of his clothes and wedding ring, and even confiscated the man-
uscript he was writing. They subjected him to horrible torture,
and he lost his father, mother, brother, and wife. Only his sister
survived. During his internment in the camps, Frankl discovered
something that would save his life: the prisoners who had lost
their sense of meaning and purpose fell into hopeless despair and

were more likely to die than those who didn't. Under the worst conditions that drove so many men to hopelessness, Frankl realized that while the Nazis could take away his freedom, they could not take away his greatest freedom of all: the freedom to choose his attitude and sense of purpose.

In his acclaimed book *Man's Search for Meaning*, Frankl wrote, "The one thing you can't take away from me is the way I choose to respond to what you do to me. The last of one's freedoms is to choose one's attitude in any given circumstance." His choice to focus on meaning and purpose saved not only his life but also the lives of countless others.

What was his purpose? Frankl was determined to use his skills as a psychiatrist to keep other prisoners from giving up or committing suicide. He did this by helping others discover their own meaning and purpose in life. He would tell one man that he must live to be there for his daughter, who was safe in another country. He advised another man that he had to live so he could complete the important book that he'd left unfinished. He counseled others on the purpose of nourishing a rich inner life. In the midst of adversity, they would focus on the beauty of the surroundings, the rich color of the mountains, and the preciousness of a sunrise. They would imagine life after imprisonment and visualize the possibility of seeing their loved ones again. They stayed connected to their spiritual lives and to one another in prayer meetings.

Frankl's work has meaning for all of us, because purpose is a natural antidepressant that we can develop in our own minds. A sense of purpose grows when we become dedicated to a cause or person beyond our own selves. When you have a sense of purpose, you are less likely to need the artificial boosts you get from bad habits, because you get a natural boost by connecting to the world in a meaningful way. The most deeply motivated and resilient people are those who have been able to balance the previous step of self-compassion with purpose for others, opening their minds and hearts to causes greater than themselves.

In this chapter, I'll help you to understand the importance of purpose and show you how to cultivate it in your life. I'll guide you as you search to uncover what matters to you and to learn how to begin nurturing this key natural antidepressant.

What Matters to You?

At some point in most people's lives, they hit a major life moment that forces them to decide what really matters to them. For me, it was in the back of that broken-down limousine when I faced the fact that I had a serious drug problem. Frankl faced it in the midst of the most difficult period of his life. For many people, it happens during what is typically called a midlife crisis; experiencing depression during this time is fairly typical. This is when we wake up and wonder how much life we have left, and what the life we've already lived means. In the United States alone, seventy-eight million baby boomers are at an existential breaking point. But the questions "Why am I here? What am I here for? And where am I going?" aren't set aside for a certain age, ethnicity, or culture. They're questions that every human being asks at different stages of life.

In order to realize what truly mattered to me, I had to think about what I valued in this life. As I held this thought in mind during the days that followed my darkest hour, I had small moments of insight in which I realized that what I valued most was being honest with myself and others, spending time with my friends and family, and taking care of my body by exercising and eating right. Eventually I also realized that I valued what would turn out to be a drastic change in my life: helping others open their eyes to their potential to break free from unhealthy habitual tendencies and open up to a life worth living.

It was straight out of the mouth of a thirteenth-century Sufi poet, Jalāl ad-Dīn ar-Rūmī:

Sometimes you hear a voice through the door
    Calling you,
As a fish out of water
Hears the waves . . .
Come back, Come back
This turning toward what you deeply love
    Saves you.

In those moments, I could feel my heart opening as I started to get in touch with what mattered. I truly cared about myself and others, and this caring moved me back to a choice point. I could choose to begin again—and I did. I began reconnecting with the nourishing, supportive people in my life and spending less time with those who were associated with my unhealthy habits. I set my intention to, as Rūmī wrote, "make regular visits to myself," remembering to pause throughout the day and open my eyes to what mattered. This gave me the strength to shake off my golden handcuffs from the business world, apply to graduate school, and start living the life I wanted to live.

The words you're reading right now are physical proof that it is possible to figure out what you value in life and live alongside it. It's also proof of how connected we are even across space and time by the fact that I am communicating and connecting to you in the present moment from the past.

Being aware of what really matters to you in this world is a key component to living a purposeful life and in turn a key compo-

when I follow what I love,
what I love follows me.

nent to uncovering happiness. If you don't know what you value, or if you are not committed to your values, you suffer. If you value being a true friend, but in little pockets of your life you find yourself gossiping about some of your friends, you'll eventually feel some dis-ease that feeds the depressive loop. If you value the relationship with your partner, but you find yourself flirting with others, you may feel excited initially, but eventually you'll experience emotional consequences of dissatisfaction because your actions are not aligned with your values.

On the other hand, if you value engaging a compassionate life and find yourself in activities of service, you are likely to feel a stable sense of life satisfaction, meaning, and even resiliency that helps prevent downward spirals. That's what happened in a 2009 study of physicians at the Mayo Clinic who said they felt burned out by their jobs. When the doctors were given one day a week to focus on the part of their job that felt most meaningful—whether it was community service, patient care, or research—they reported only half as much burnout as those who didn't. Engaging in purposeful and meaningful activities not only makes us feel good but also helps protect us from entering the depression loop.

Studies show that people who have a strong sense of purpose have stronger immune systems and experience less inflammation, two signs of health. As a group, they're less likely to suffer depression, cardiovascular disease, diabetes, and certain kinds of cancers.

COMPASSION'S SURPRISING BENEFITS FOR YOUR HEALTH (ALL BASED IN SCIENCE)

- Makes us happier
- Speeds up recovery from disease
- Activates the pleasure centers of the brain
- Serves as a buffer against stress
- Reduces cellular inflammation
- Increases our sense of connection with others*
- May lengthen our life spans

---

* Lack of social connection is a greater health risk than obesity, smoking, and chronic high blood pressure.

Making a Stand for Purpose

Carla was a thirty-year-old executive assistant for a well-known health care provider. She'd struggled off and on with anxiety and depression since she was a teenager, and when she first met with me, Carla told me that she had a nagging feeling that if she disappeared, the world wouldn't miss her. One morning when she came into my office, I asked her to imagine herself many years from now lying on her death-bed and looking back at the present moment. "What would

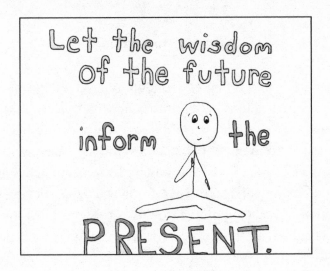

that woman with all the years of experience see that you might not be seeing?"

While that question can ignite an understanding of what matters for some people, Carla struggled with it. So I took a different approach. I asked her to close her eyes and said, "Imagine yourself at your own retirement party. Imagine a few people who knew you well stepping up to express their reflections. What would you like these people to say?"

She took a few moments to think and then answered, "I guess I'd want them to talk about what a good friend I am, how generous I've been, and how I often brightened the office with my humor." In that moment, she was connecting with some of her values. I reflected back, "So you value being a good person, being someone who gives and brings humor into life?" She nodded, smiled, and said, "Yeah, I guess so." Taking an inventory of what you value is an important strategy to uncovering the natural antidepressant of purpose.

What Do You Value?

When we fall into a depression loop, our values can provide a North Star that guides us back to a healthier place. Take a few moments to close your eyes and visualize what you'd like people to say at *your* retirement party. When you are ready, write them on the lines below. Maybe you want to be remembered as loving, caring, determined, or creative. Maybe you value sticking up for the underdog or being present to life, pausing to smell the roses. As you begin to jot these down, you're planting seeds for purpose to grow.

_____

_____

_____

_____

_____

Values as Verbs

When most of us first think of what we value in life, we often come up with adjectives and nouns such as a healthy body, good relationships, and the respect of others. But I want you to start thinking of values more in terms of verbs than nouns—actions instead of finished products.

Here's how I explained this to Carla: "From thoughts come actions, and from actions come consequences. The action of turning values into verbs can make them come alive and have the antidepressant effect of leading to more purpose and meaning." Carla and I looked at what being a good friend meant to her. I said, "If you value good relationships, you might change that to 'I value acting in a kind and loving manner with my friends and family,' and 'I value listening.' If you value being a giving person, you might change that to 'I value practicing compassion and being of service to those who are less fortunate.'" All of a sudden, vague values became something she could actually visualize practicing in her daily life.

When you translate values into verbs, it inclines your mind from just thinking to taking action. "I value inner harmony" goes from being a nebulous goal to a doable action: "I value practicing daily meditation or yoga." That makes it more likely to be real in your life. If you value a healthy body, you might say, "I value exercising on a regular basis and eating healthfully." The results of your values aren't as important, and they are never guaranteed. What matters are your intention and your actions.

Take sixty seconds to make this real for you. Ask yourself, "What's important to me? What does this look like in my daily life?" Below are some examples of values as nouns. Take a look at these to inspire your top five values. Write them on the lines below and then translate them into actionable verbs.

World peace	Equality
Freedom	Compassion
Strong family	Pleasure
Close friendships	Accomplishment
Inner harmony	Sexual or spiritual intimacy
Self-respect	Spontaneity
Happiness	Respect from others
Wisdom	Mindfulness

MY TOP FIVE VALUES

Examples

Mindfulness   Paying attention, on purpose, to life just
                     as it is on a daily basis.

Inner harmony   Placing my hand on my heart in a
                     moment of difficulty.

World peace   Volunteer or give money to [pick your
                     organization].

_____

_____

_____

_____

_____

The Dalai Lama said, "It's not enough to be compassionate, you must act." Phrasing values as verbs allows them to come alive and makes us more likely to turn them into action.

_____

The Power of Connection

We are social beings, and connection to something greater than ourselves, even if we're simply thinking about it, gives us resilience and makes us feel safe, protected, and at peace. Psychologist Dennis Proffitt at the University of Virginia and his colleagues conducted an experiment to see what effect social connection would have on perception. They had some participants stand alone and estimate the slant of a hill, while others stood next to a friend or visualized a friend next to them. What he found was that when people were accompanied by a friend (or even just visualized being with a friend), they perceived the hill as being less steep. Inclining our minds in a *prosocial* direction creates connection and helps us to perceive our mountains as molehills—or at least small mountains instead of big mountains.

When we can bring attention to being of service to something greater than ourselves, we feel connected to others and to what really matters in life—and this is often a good feeling. At this point, your subconscious voice might be saying, "I should focus on helping other people? But I can barely help myself." This may be the case if caregiving has contributed to your depressed mood. (I'll speak specifically to caregivers later in this chapter.) But if that's not the trigger, it would be good to examine whether that voice is a mind trap or NUT that encourages avoidance.

> **A GENTLE SELF-EXAMINATION**
>
> Take a prosocial checkup right now.
>
> Are you involved with a cause other than your own? Do you make donations, ladle out soup in a homeless shelter, read to the blind, arrange flowers in a nursing home gift shop, or even just offer smiles to people who seem to be having a tough day?
>
> Cultivating the ability to branch outside of ourselves, feel into the lives of others, and even take action to support them (for them, not for us) can have wonderful effects on our mood, self-esteem, and pure joy in this world.

In order to discover the natural antidepressant of purpose, it's helpful to shift our lens from an antisocial direction (ourselves) to a prosocial direction (others). Prosocial direction leads to a feeling of connection, the exact opposite experience of being depressed.

Know What You *Can* Do

Do you find that your mind has a tendency to focus on what you *can't* do instead of what you *can* do? This mental habit can get in the way of living with purpose. Here's a question I often ask my clients and students to help them understand what strengths they have to contribute to compassionate acts: What have you been given in terms of freedom, education, opportunities, wealth, networks, identity, and creativity, and what purposes can they serve in relationship to what you have found matters?

Carla happened to have a natural gift for humor, and she eventually created a blog to allow her humor to reach more people, brightening moments of their days with a little laughter. John, another client of mine, held the value of compassion. He happened to be endowed with a large income and thought that one way to turn this value into a verb was to use his money to positively impact the field of mental health. We identified specific organizations to which he could donate funds, as well as serve. What *can* you do with what you have to support one of your values?

Dr. Martin Luther King Jr. recognized that he had the constitutional right of freedom of speech and took this to speak for those who felt they could not and inspired the civil rights movement in

America. Can you use your freedom to speak up for those who cannot? Philip Burguieres became one of the youngest Fortune 500 CEOs in the 1960s. He suffered greatly with major depression and eventually used his fame and credibility to speak up about depression in corporate America, giving thousands of others permission to open up about it and seek help. If you have a gift of some kind, in what way can you compassionately use your influence to better the world?

Bringing awareness to what you *can* do reminds you that there is an internal locus of control: a belief that while we can't control what happens in any given moment, we can control how we prepare for what might happen and how we respond to things when they do. In contrast, an external locus of control is the belief that we are a victim; it focuses on what we can't do and leads us to blame others for things that happen to us. Having an internal locus of control works against the learned helplessness that accompanies depression. Right now is a choice point. Your gifts can be a pathway toward more compassionate action—and a natural antidepressant as well. Make it concrete and jot down a few ideas of what you have that can be a vehicle to manifest your values.

_____

_____

_____

_____

_____

_____

Consider for a moment that meaning and significance are found in giving away what you have.

Ask yourself, "What *can* I do?" instead of "What *can't* I do?"

Optimize Your Motivation

One thing we know about the brain is that it needs encouragement. You've already taken the step of uncovering your values and translating them into verbs to make them more practical and real. The next step is to make the connection in your mind as to *why* you would live these actionable values. When I first asked Carla this question, she said, "Because I'm tired of feeling so disconnected and being depressed." While this can provide some motivation, notice how the default reason was to avoid some feared reaction. Doing things to avoid consequences is a common motivator in many areas of our lives. We're supposed to go to the dentist to prevent cavities, not because we care about our teeth. Maybe we exercise every day to prevent a heart attack instead of nurturing a healthy heart. But this kind of reasoning does *not* truly empower people, and when it comes to depression, it's a trap.

From the brain's perspective, acting from fear fires up the amygdala, which we're trying to reduce. Activity in the amygdala ignites negative thinking, slipping us into bad habits and greasing the tracks toward a depression loop. What we want to do is connect our values with reasons that bring meaning and purpose into our lives. One of my clients had a heart attack a few years back and was told by his doctor that if he didn't take his medication and exercise seriously, he was at risk for another heart attack.

"That didn't get me to do it," he said. "What got me to stick to it was when my daughter asked me, 'Do you want to live to see the smiling faces of your grandchildren?' That did it." Another client of mine had wanted to practice yoga consistently for years because she heard it would help ease her stress. But it wasn't until she thought about how she wants to be flexible on the dance floor with her husband in her old age that her behavior shifted.

As for Carla, she realized that acting kindly and listening to friends and family strengthened relationships that she wanted to have later in life—and, of course, it made her feel good. Making other people laugh lifted her up. When she engaged in being of service to others who were more disadvantaged, she felt like there was a reason for her existence. She saw these—rightfully—as habits for happiness and resiliency.

When you look at your top five values, think of some specific *positive* reasons that you would maintain them. If the value is exercising three times a week, you might write, "To be able to hike with friends later in life." If you value close friendships, you might write, "To feel a sense of belonging and also to build in support and resilience for future difficult times." If you value compassion, it could be, "To make the world a better place for the next generation." On the lines below, list positive reasons why you want to live these values. This is far more motivating to our brains.

_____

_____

_____

_____

_____

_____

When Money *Can't* Buy Happiness

When I was young, my family used to jokingly call me Alex P. Keaton, after the Michael J. Fox character from the TV show *Family Ties,* because I was so focused on money. In fact, I remember tying my purpose in life to making lots of money. I used to think that when I was thirty, I was going to be a millionaire. Later on in my midtwenties, I was making good money in sales and management, but I wasn't truly happy. It's common for us to look outside of ourselves for things such as money, fame, and power when searching for a sense of purpose and happiness.

"Money can't buy happiness" is a saying, but research suggests that it's also a scientific fact.

Edward Deci, Richard Ryan, and Christopher Niemiec are some of the leading researchers in the field of motivation. They study what motivates people, and their discoveries are quite surprising. In one study, they asked graduates from the University of Rochester, in New York, about their life goals and happiness levels. Some grads said they were looking forward to becoming wealthy or achieving fame—what are known as *extrinsic goals.* Others had more purposeful aspirations such as helping people somehow, or what are known as *intrinsic goals.*

Almost two years later, the researchers asked the same group of students how happy they were. They found that the students who were living in line with their intrinsic goals were happier than those chasing extrinsic goals. Even more interesting was that this latter group exhibited increased stress, anxiety, and depression.

In our culture, the understanding is that if you like something and you get it, your life will improve. But this study shows that when you focus on valuing outside stuff too much, you may be *worse* off. In a 2009 published report, the researchers write, "The findings are rather striking, as they suggest that attainment of a particular set of goals has no impact on well-being and actually contributes to ill-being." The researchers also supported the importance of focusing on prosocial attention versus antisocial attention. They write that one of the reasons that the participants who attained their extrinsic goals experienced higher anxiety and depression is that their extrinsic drives "crowd out" a focus on good relationships. When you're focused on making money and attending to all the things on the outside, you spend less attention on the things that really matter, such as love, relationships, and feeling at peace.

It's important to note that taking action on more purposeful, intrinsic goals is not a panacea or depression cure, but it is a source of resiliency. Mother Teresa had plenty of purpose, and yet she spoke of having had many dark experiences. However, she also spoke about the natural sustaining power of her intrinsic goal of being a compassionate hand of God to those who were suffering. She was able to ride out the darkest hours with more grace and inevitably be more resilient. In this same way, your intrinsic motivators can give you the fuel to continue overcoming depression and uncovering happiness.

Happiness researchers identify two different types of happiness: hedonic and eudaimonic. Hedonic is the notion that increased pleasure and decreased pain bring happiness. Eudaimonic is based on the idea that people feel happy when they experience purpose, meaning, and growth. At a cellular level, we respond to stress better with eudaimonic well-being.

When Money *Can* Buy Happiness

Years ago, I collected some of my writings, along with interviews that I had conducted with leaders in the field of mindfulness and psychotherapy such as Jack Kornfield, Dan Siegel, Jon Kabat-Zinn, Tara Brach, and Sharon Salzberg, among others. I paid to have it edited and decided to offer it as a book called *A Mindful Dialogue: A Path Toward Working with Stress, Pain and Difficult Emotions*, with 100 percent of the proceeds going to a relief effort to help victims of the 2010 earthquake that devastated Haiti. The act of putting that together filled me with a sense of elevation. Every month, I would give hundreds of dollars to these relief organizations, and each time, it had a positive impact on my mood. I felt really good thinking about how my contribution could change lives. Money can't always buy a sense of purpose and happiness, but sometimes it can support your meaningful actions. As it turns out, there's a scientific explanation for this too.

On a routine morning in Vancouver, British Columbia, Michael Norton, a professor at Harvard Business School, along with some of his colleagues, asked people on the campus of the University of British Columbia if they would like to take part in an experiment. If people said yes, he first asked them how happy they were. Then he handed them an envelope containing anywhere from $5 to $20, along with a slip of paper that said either "By five o'clock today, spend this money on yourself," or "By five o'clock today, spend this money on someone else."

Later that evening, the researchers called the participants and asked them what they spent the money on and how happy they felt. They found that those who spent their money on other people were happier at the end of the day, while those who spent it on themselves remained at the same happiness level. The researchers also discovered that the denomination didn't matter—the results were the same whether the volunteers spent $5 or $20.

Of course, the moral of the story here isn't to give away all your money, but it suggests that when we tap into the prosocial purpose that involves giving to others in one manner or another, it actually makes us happier and even more successful at what we do—which is a mediating factor in resiliency during difficult times. Even if you don't have a lot to give, giving something to others can make a difference in how you feel and is a natural antidepressant. Can you think of a person or organization to which you'd like to give even a small amount of time or money? Making some time to investigate this and take action with it serves to make someone's life a little bit better and nurtures a sense of purpose.

When we give time or money to a cause we find meaningful, it can ignite our own sense of meaning and purpose—and serve as a natural antidepressant.

PURPOSE AS A PRACTICE

One way of instilling more purpose in your life if to ask yourself three daily questions:

1. What prosocial purpose am I focused on?
2. What action can I take today that is in line with this purpose?
3. What is this action in service of that is greater than myself?

Try this out as an experiment.

You'll find a Twenty-One Days of Purpose practice in the Tool Kit at the end of the book.

Is There Such a Thing as Too Much Compassion?

Sara was a client of mine who was called overseas to spend a year caring for her sick aunt. She became so exhausted caring for another person that she slipped into a depression. She scheduled a Skype session with me and said, "It's as if I've completely forgotten about myself. I am consumed with her and her needs. I don't matter. I also fall into fits of despair getting overwhelmed with fear that this will never get better and angry that it's happening."

Sara's story is a common one. Although caring for others can be a natural antidepressant that lifts our spirits and gives our lives purpose, too much can have the opposite effect. When, like Sara, we are so focused on someone else that we neglect to take care of ourselves, compassion can turn on itself in the form of "compassion fatigue." An array of studies has shown that people who care for elderly, abused, or traumatized patients eventually became desensitized and less compassionate toward the people they were caring for. Caregivers were at risk of losing access to their natural antidepressant of purpose and also became depressed.

During our sessions, we talked about and worked on experiencing the quality of equanimity, or balance. Equanimity, the perfect partner to compassion, brings stability, spaciousness, and balance to our hearts and minds. It's the ability to remain deeply present and open to what is here. It's allowing ourselves to know our pain or the pain of another without getting lost in it or overwhelmed by it. Sara and I worked with a few things to help her taste the quality of equanimity. First, we did a mountain meditation to feel this sense of balance and mental stability. I asked her to sit in a comfortable sitting position, close her eyes, and begin by taking a few deep breaths from her abdomen. I specifically suggested the abdomen because this is a central grounding post for our bodies.

I then told her to imagine a mountain with all its foliage. As she did this, I brought her through all the seasons of fall, winter, spring, and summer, and told her to visualize how those seasons affected the mountain. She told me about the beautiful colors of fall, how the leaves fell off many of the trees as the snow fell and covered the peak of the mountains. Soon the snow melted, and the leaves began to grow again. I asked her, "Tell me how the ground of the mountain changed." She said, "It didn't change, it remained the same." I followed, "Beneath all the emotions that come with taking care of your aunt, the moments of frustration, exhaustion, anger, sadness, and feeling overwhelmed, under all of that, you are this mountain: solid, rooted, and stable."

I also gave her a practice to deepen her sense of feeling grounded while caring about herself. I said, "Placing one hand on your heart and the other on your abdomen, imagine that you are this mountain, solid and unshakable. Now, breathing from your belly, say to yourself, 'Breathing in, I imagine myself as a solid mountain; breathing out, I meet my vulnerability with love.' As you do this, shorten it to 'Breathing in, mountain; breathing out, love.'"

After practicing this for a minute, Sara opened her eyes and said she felt calmer, more relaxed, and more accepting of her vulnerability. I told her to practice this a few times a day to balance the caregiving and see if she could bring it to her aunt's bedside table during the difficult moments.

I also reminded her to take a step back at times, acknowledge her suffering, and remember to take a self-compassion break, opening with the question "What do I need right now?" and allowing the answer to be her guide. As Sara practiced this, she noticed at times that she needed more moments of pausing, stepping outside, and appreciating the beauty of the landscape. Other times she needed to get out and socialize with a few people she knew in the area. Her ability to pause and check in allowed her to eventually hire a nurse part-time to give her a few hours off here and there.

Planting seeds of self-care helps us ride the waves of compassion without drowning. In part 3, "The Natural Antidepressant Tool Kit," you'll find another practice called Sky of Awareness that you can play with to give you the experience of equanimity. This can help give you a sense of spaciousness within, so while storms of compassion fatigue may come, they don't overtake you.

Ultimately this experience gave Sara a gift. She came to understand the need for balance in the face of tremendous compassionate responsibility. From a place of compassion fatigue, she reexperienced the power of self-compassion. With time away and the opportunity to begin paying attention to her own needs, Sara bounced back and began to reconnect with the purpose of her being there: to help her aunt heal.

In the midst of sweeping emotions, be the mountain. "Breathing in, I imagine myself as this mountain; breathing out, I am grounded and solid." Feel into the balance that's there.

For me, engaging purpose in my life allows me to feel more connected and engaged, and raises my awareness that I actually matter. This is all contrary to the depression loop. It's not always easy, but as we turn our values into actions, we begin to realize our own value as human beings on this planet. Naturally, this lifts us up. In the following pages, get ready to discover the new science and practice of one of my favorite natural antidepressants: play!

STEP 6

Go Out and Play— Rediscovering the Joy of Life

W hen Eve was twenty-eight years old, she came to see me because she was struggling with what she called being "generally unhappy." Although she was working to become a designer, she really wasn't sure whether that was what she wanted to do with her life. After a few sessions, I discovered that she'd basically been depressed off and on since she was thirteen years old. As puberty began, Eve felt uncomfortable in her developing body and would give in to peer pressure around drugs and alcohol in order to fit in. She eventually became dependent on the powerful painkiller Vicodin and surrounded herself with fellow addicts. She wanted to change, but didn't know how.

Whenever I meet anyone, I always want to get a sense of (1) who they surround themselves with and (2) what they do during the day. This gives me a good picture of whether their environment is enriching or depleting. We went through an inventory of who she spent her time with, and agreed that she needed to spend more time with nourishing people who supported her change and less time with depleting people who promoted the status quo. The next step was for her to describe what her days looked like. As she brought me through her day, it seemed like she was bringing me down an assembly line: everything was routine; there was a real lack of joy. When it comes to our bad habits, we often seek artificial boosts through eating, drinking, and checking our smartphones, among other things, not only to avoid what's uncomfortable but also because we lack the natural boosts that come from contentment, a sense of calm, and self-confidence. But if we encourage the natural boosts, we have less need for the artificial ones.

I asked Eve to close her eyes and think about what images came into her mind in connection with the word *play*. She said she hadn't played in a long time, so I asked her to think back to her childhood. She remembered her parents bringing her to a ranch and her being in awe of the horses. She also recalled a time during her teen years when she worked on a ranch, grooming and riding horses. On the ranch, Eve said, she felt free.

"Then we gotta get you back to a ranch," I said.

That may seem like a simplistic response, but it seemed to be exactly what Eve needed.

As it turned out, Eve had known a woman who owned a ranch. However, I knew that Eve was still caught in the depression loop, and one of the detrimental habits that is a part of that, aside from all the NUTs, is procrastination. I sensed that she needed a little nudge, so I took a risk and asked her if she was open to calling the woman at that moment during the session. She hesitated, but went ahead and did it. The owner was happy to hear her voice and accepted her request to come help out on the ranch.

The first time Eve arrived at the ranch, she was nervous—she had a whole lot of voices in her head shouting their bad advice, telling her to sneak out and leave. But she stuck with it, and in a short time, she began to regain that feeling of just loving being there. Eve was playing again, grooming the horses, riding them, and even helping out as an equine assistant.

It wasn't long before she began to feel better and decided that she wanted to take a big next step in her life and start on the path of becoming a psychotherapist herself. She uncovered a buried purpose of wanting to help others who were suffering and combined that with her love of animals. Today Eve is an equine psychotherapy assistant. This is a rapidly growing field of psychotherapy in which a client is led through interactions with a therapist, an assistant, and horses for emotional and therapeutic growth. All of this continues to lift her and weave a web of resiliency. The day may come when Eve will get hooked by the depression loop again, but this new, nourishing environment builds up her natural immune response, supporting greater resiliency

As Eve's story shows, play is not just for kids. It's actually an essential ingredient of a happy adult life and a natural antidepressant. Recent science shows that the absence of play in adults contributes to depression, and adding it back into our lives not only helps make us happier and more resilient but also positively impacts our brains.

In the following pages, I'll show you what play is and why it's such a powerful antidepressant. I'll help you to see why having toys and playmates can build a more resilient brain, and I'll explain ways to bring more play into your life starting now.

What Is Play?

Children play. Nobody has to show them how to do it; they're just born knowing. But as adults, we become so disconnected from it that we forget what it is and how to do it. So let's start by looking at what play is and what it means for adults to engage in play.

Psychiatrist and clinical researcher Stuart Brown, who founded the nonprofit organization National Institute of Play in Carmel Valley California, says "Play is an ancient, voluntary, inherently pleasurable, apparently purposeless activity or process that is undertaken for its own sake, and that strengthens our muscles and our social skills, fertilizes brain activity, tempers and deepens our emotions, take us out of time, and enables a state of balance and poise." Play is happening when you are so engrossed in something you enjoy that you lose all sense of time and don't want it to end. It's where that inner critic finally shuts up, self-consciousness fades away, and we can open up to new possibilities. Mihaly Csikszentmihalyi, a Hungarian-born psychologist and researcher, calls the experience of play a state of "flow." In flow, while there may be a goal, the activity is its own reward. The degree of difficulty is just enough to keep you interested but not so difficult that you're tempted to give up. This balance of play is a feeling of engagement and satisfaction—the opposite of depression.

When we're depressed, play can seem like a foreign concept. Sometimes when I ask my depressed clients what they envision when I say the word *play*, they look at me with a blank stare. So I decided to conduct an experiment about play with a number of people I worked with, as well as some family and friends. It was simple: I asked them all what play meant to them. I found that many people I spoke with had a hard time conceiving what play is for grown-ups, because it's different from child's play, which was the only kind of play they knew. In fact, in a culture that prizes productivity, adult play seems to be defined as a negative, unproductive, self-indulgent activity—or even something X-rated. I believe that we need to update our definition of play.

My questioning led me to believe that play means different things to different people. For example, after my kids go to bed, I enjoy playing around in the kitchen making homemade granola—but my wife would see this as a decidedly unplayful chore. I enjoy being creative and engaging in the process of playing with different ingredients. For one of my clients, play means getting lost in the book *Fifty Shades of Grey*, while that would be torture to her boyfriend. Another client revealed that one of her "guilty pleasures" was lying down in her pajamas and immersing herself in the TV show *Game of Thrones*, a purposeless yet pleasurable activity. She was surprised to identify that as a moment of play for her, and she no longer felt guilty about it. She had redefined what play was, and soon you will too. But first, let's talk about how the absence of play can feed a depressive loop.

I am the source of my own happiness.

Play is different for different people. One of my clients discovered that creating origami brought her joy, while for others that may be the last thing on earth they'd want to do.

All Work + No Play = Depression

You've probably heard the proverb "All work and no play makes Jack a dull boy." It turns out that this old saw is pretty accurate, for a life without play can be not just dull but depressing. In the 1970s, Mihaly Csikszentmihalyi, the researcher who defines play as "flow," ran a study in which he asked the subjects not to do anything enjoyable, or "noninstrumental" for forty-eight hours, such

PLAY REVERSES THE DEPRESSION LOOP

The depression loop is fueled by negative emotions, self-judgments, disengagement, helplessness, and isolation. Play inspires the exact opposite qualities and takes away this fuel. The act of play is filled with positive emotions, is engaging, satisfying, connecting, and social, while the depression loop narrows what is possible, making us rigid in our thoughts and actions. Play opens up a more flexible mind, beckoning us to seek out novel thoughts and actions in response to the task at hand. Play builds physical, emotional, social, and intellectual development. As we continue to play, we become more flexible and creative in the way that we approach things—even the depression loop—fostering a resilient brain.

In *The Ambiguity of Play*, Brian Sutton-Smith, one of the foremost play scholars in the last hundred years argues that the opposite of play is not work, it's depression.

as taking walks with friends or reading for pleasure. The study's results revealed an essential truth in our human experience.

After just a single day, participants "noticed an increased sluggishness about their behavior." Many people had difficulty concentrating, felt sleepy, or were too restless to sleep. Csizkszentmihalyi wrote that after only forty-eight hours, "the general deterioration in mood was so advanced that prolonging the experiment would have been unadvisable."

Do these symptoms sound familiar? His study shows us that the absence of play in our lives lends itself to depression. This is backed up by Stuart Brown's research. After intensively studying violent criminals for many years, he discovered a stunning common thread that changed the course of his career forever: a lack of play in their lives. Since then, Brown has spent decades collecting more than six thousand "play histories" from a vast array of subjects, including business people, artists, and even Nobel Prize winners. He was interested in seeing the role of play from childhood to adulthood. Brown found confirming evidence that lack of play was an important factor in predicting mood instability and even criminal behavior. In all these thousands of play histories, he also found that the presence of play is a key natural antidepressant. It can reverse the depression loop, pulling us out of melancholic states, rekindling disconnected relationships, enhancing emotional intimacy, and even creating connection and healing between strangers.

Diego's Play History

When Diego first came to see me, he was a sixty-two-year-old upper-echelon executive who hadn't experienced pleasure in life for quite some time. "Every morning I say a prayer," Diego told me: "God, please let me find the joy in my life, to be happy, and to find purpose." Diego had come to this country from Spain in the 1970s and had dreamed of success in the film industry. But when he first came to see me, he found himself at a transition point in life. Although he had achieved success working for a well-respected entertainment company, he wasn't happy. When I asked him what play was like for him while growing up, he told me that as a child he had to be careful with play because showing signs of joy in his house was met with criticism and judgment from his mother. It was as if the very idea of playing was tied to being vulnerable and that guarding against vulnerability was key to his survival. Unfortunately, this carried over into his adult life.

As I inquired more into his play history, it turned out that Diego loved art. As a kid, he would collect pictures of his favorite cartoon character. I asked him to tell me about it, so that he could inhabit that experience of playfulness. On a couple of occasions, I caught him smiling as he reflected on these memories, which brought the experience alive again for him in the present moment. As an adult, this translated into a love for film and art. While he collected art books, he never ever opened them—so I suggested that he take a couple of hours a week to just get lost in his art books. When I said this, I saw that his body immediately tensed up because of his deep-seated belief that he didn't deserve play or that play was dangerous in some way. It was hard for Diego at first, but he pushed himself to peruse his art books, and he began to feel good. Eventually he admitted to feeling joy. "I felt my chest expanding, I felt lighter, and I was smiling a lot," he said.

This was only the beginning of his journey into play. Little by little, he began getting out more, going to galleries and buying art. He started listening to the yearnings of his heart rather than the critical voices in his head. He began to bring play into his relationships, challenging himself to be vulnerable with others and sensing a greater intimacy and connection with them when he did. One day he told me, "Something is really changing in me, I feel more open, I'm happier." At that moment, his prayer was answered. When I asked his permission to use his story in this book, Diego smiled, laughed a little, and said, "Of course, but only if you reference me as 'the Studly Spaniard.'" Playfulness was clearly alive in him.

In order to rediscover play in your life, it's helpful to look back in your past and see how you played and what gave you joy. Your experiences from childhood are stored as encoded memories that inform your perceptions today. Recalling them can provide clues to what gives you joy now, as an adult.

Take a moment to think about how you played as a kid. Was it alone or with friends? What did you enjoy most? Maybe you engaged in imaginary play with dolls or invisible friends. Or perhaps your most pleasurable time was spent building sandcastles on the beach or making intricate beaded necklaces. You may have spent hours building Lego castles or cities. Or maybe life felt most enjoyable when you were outside playing tag, kickball, or some other sport. Your most playful memories may be of the rain, dancing around, making mud pies, and feeling happy to be as wet as you could be. I think of my young children and how they can just get lost in a drawing with their crayons. In my teenage years, I spent hours doing rough-and-tumble play with my friends, collaborating to beat video games, or shooting baskets.

Of course, what was enjoyable to you as a kid may not be fun for you as an adult. The board game Sorry! may have been a laugh for you in fourth grade but might drive you up a wall today. That's okay. In the next section, you'll get clearer on how this translates into your adult life. For now, just going through the exercise of reminding yourself of what play was like is part of the process of priming the mind, and soon you'll be updating it into a more current "playbook."

If you like, write down some thoughts and examples of what play was like for you as a kid. Notice if at any point during the reflection of past moments of play a smile arises and the corners of your eyes turn up. This is a natural smile; give yourself permission to linger in it for a few moments.

_____

_____

_____

_____

_____

In order to rediscover play in your life, it's helpful to take a "play history," looking back in your past and seeing how you played and what gave you joy.

_____

Toys and Playmates

Numerous recent studies have shown that when it comes to play, two elements are both needed to make it a natural antidepressant: toys and playmates. In the 1960s Marian Diamond, a professor of neuroscience and anatomy at the University of California at Berkeley and one of the world's top researchers on neuroplasticity, pioneered research to see what effects "enriched" environments had on the brains of rats. It turns out that the neural development of rodents is similar to that of humans. Diamond and her col-

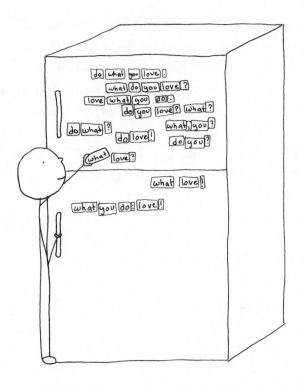

leagues took thirty-six rats and split them up into three different groups based on environment: (1) enriched, (2) standard, and (3) impoverished. All the cages had the basics of food, water, and lighting. The enriched environment was the play space with friends and toys. The standard environment was a cage less than half the size with friends but no toys. The impoverished environment was a single rat alone with no toys.

After the experiment ended, scientists examined the rats' brains. The rats who had toys to play with *and* other rats to socialize with had thicker *cerebral cortexes* with more neural connections than the other rats. The cortex is a critical area of the brain responsible for cognitive processing, attention, and awareness. They also found that the greatest neural change happened in the first thirty to sixty days, cluing us in to the importance of novelty in neuroplasticity. Engaging in novel things in life has also been shown to increase levels of dopamine, the motivational brain chemical, or *neurotransmitter*, that many studies suggest is low when feeling depressed. Diamond's research proved a fundamental breakthrough, showing us that the environment—the toys and playmates—can actually change neural architecture for the better. What's more, the impoverished rats actually showed *decreased* cortical thickness—implying reduced cognitive processing.

To give you an example of why thicker is better, psychologists have shown that rats living in enriched environments with thicker cortexes ran mazes faster and more efficiently. The takeaway here is that more neural connections—or a thicker cortex—means a greater ability to discern what is best quicker. Not only that, some studies suggest that play may cause the brain to process energy better. The brain, like the rest of the body, depends on the simple sugar known as glucose for energy. The synapses in our brains use glucose to supply their energy. Researchers have found that rats living in enriched environments needed less glucose to function. This suggests the brain is actually more efficient when exposed to more enriching environments. Still other studies found that exposing rats to cognitive, physical, and social play increased survival of nerve cells in the hippocampus, allowing this critical part of the brain to thrive. With respect to depression, when we can reduce the amount of energy the brain needs to function well and can grow parts that are responsible for learning, memory, and better discernment of optimal choices, we are nurturing a more resilient brain.

Of course, you and I aren't rats. You can't just throw us in a cage together with the same toys and expect positive effects. In crafting an enriching environment for ourselves and uncovering the natural antidepressant of play, you can draw on your play history to take stock of your personal play preferences. What are your toys? How do you create novelty in your life? Who are the playful people you can surround yourself with, and how can you create a more nourishing social environment?

That's what we're going to do right now.

When thinking about an enriched environment of play, you need to consider what your toys are *and* who your playmates are.

What Are Your Toys?

Years ago, when I was living in San Francisco, I gathered a few people together, and we began a twelve-week expedition into play. We used Julia Cameron's book *The Artist's Way: A Spiritual Path to Higher Creativity,* which instructs you to take two-hour time-outs for yourself once a week and again once a month for an entire day to reflect and engage in things that you find creative. This doesn't have to be anything stereotypically artistic, such as painting or drawing, just something playful. Some people in my group chose to walk around neighborhoods they always wanted to visit, others opted to paint, and others played musical instruments. I noticed that this permission opened up possibilities to things I'd long thought I might like to do but had always thought I didn't have the time to do or weren't important enough. During one of the "Artist Dates," I went on a reflective walk in the woods, brought along a poetry book by e. e. cummings, laid under a tree, and read this poem:

somewhere i have never travelled, gladly beyond
any experience, your eyes have their silence:
in your most frail gesture are things which enclose me,
or which i cannot touch because they are too near
your slightest look easily will unclose me
though i have closed myself as fingers,
you open always petal by petal myself as Spring opens
(touching skillfully, mysteriously) her first rose
or if your wish be to close me, i and
my life will shut very beautifully, suddenly,
as when the heart of this flower imagines
the snow carefully everywhere descending;
nothing which we are to perceive in this world equals
the power of your intense fragility: whose texture
compels me with the colour of its countries,
rendering death and forever with each breathing
(i do not know what it is about you that closes
and opens; only something in me understands
the voice of your eyes is deeper than all roses)
nobody, not even the rain, has such small hands

I spent the day under a tree reading this and other poems over and over again until I had them memorized so that I could always have them with me. The process was fairly purposeless and deeply enjoyable. I was playing, and the poetry was my toy. Today, having a couple of rambunctious kids makes taking a day to myself to read poetry under a tree seem a remote possibility. But I can access that memory of play by keeping books next to me on my nightstand and spending a few minutes with them here and there.

Getting back in touch with what your toys are and reengaging with play can seem difficult to do, especially if you're not feeling well. That is why I'm going to start you off with "Fifty-two Ways to Play" to spark creative ideas for your mind. There is a continuum of options here, from activities that take very little effort, to others that take more effort. After reading them, see if any of these seem like toys to you. How can you begin integrating them into your life and even switching them up from time to time? As you read the following list, you don't need to just stick to what's familiar as a form of play; keep an eye out for novel ways to play, too. Remember, novelty is essential to enhancing neuroplasticity; it provides challenges that force your brain to grow and adapt in order to process the new information.

Fifty-two Ways to Play

1. Riding horses
2. Playing video games
3. Making a new dessert
4. Lying under a tree
5. Watching a favorite TV show
6. Having a long dinner with friends
7. Looking at art books
8. Reading poetry
9. Soaking in the bathtub
10. Collecting things (shells, art, coins)
11. Going on a date
12. Going to a movie
13. Listening to music
14. Lying in the sun
15. Doing laughter yoga
16. Reading magazines
17. Spending an evening with good friends
18. Meeting new people
19. Eating good food
20. Cooking new foods
21. Doing yoga
22. Having a quiet evening
23. Having sex
24. Wearing sexy clothes
25. Playing sports
26. Flying kites
27. Taking care of houseplants
28. Camping
29. Hiking
30. Arranging flowers
31. Singing around the house
32. Repairing things in the house
33. Having a day without a to-do list
34. Going to the beach
35. Painting
36. Playing a musical instrument
37. Putting on a dinner party
38. Taking a nap
39. Planning a trip
40. Travelling abroad or within your area
41. Visiting a trendy neighborhood
42. Gardening
43. Going to a park and watching children play
44. Taking a scenic bike ride
45. Kissing
46. Buying new clothes
47. Thinking about what's going well
48. Attending a play, musical, concert, or sports event
49. Dressing up
50. Taking up knitting
51. Going swimming
52. Writing poetry

Who Are Your Playmates?

Having toys can be helpful in facilitating a sense of pleasure in life. And as we saw in Marian Diamond's study, having playmates and toys creates the optimal enriching environment for facilitating a resilient brain. The greatest way to cue us to do anything is if there are other people around engaging in that same activity. This isn't news: every wisdom tradition focuses on the importance of community because it's the most effective way to keep us connected to what matters. Throughout this book, there's been an emphasis on connecting with others. The truth is that play helps us cultivate connection with other people, which is the opposite of feeling alone and isolated. Playful interactions and communication makes for easy connection and deeper intimacy. When we feel more connected, we often feel less depressed.

It's important to take a look at who inspires play in you or who you would like to play with in an activity of *healthy* pleasure as opposed to *unhealthy* pleasure. I had a client who enjoyed playfully going out, getting drunk, and sleeping with strangers, but those kinds of playmates increased her shame and fueled her depression loop. When we looked at her play history, we discovered that as a kid she enjoyed riding her bike with friends and exploring new areas of her rural town. This led to the idea of reengaging with old friends who'd be interested in exploring unfamiliar areas of Los Angeles, including the array of hiking trails. Much to her surprise, she really enjoyed herself. This gave her hope that she could rediscover joy in life. Hope is a fundamental natural antidepressant.

In the self-compassion chapter, we looked at how you might optimize your social network: Who is a nourishing source of compassion for you and worth spending more time with, and, conversely, who depletes you, and, therefore, perhaps should be kept at a distance? In the same way, we can review our social network again and see who we're spending most of our time with and if they are healthy or unhealthy playmates. The idea here is to create more space for people who spark that sense of healthy play in you.

I credit a big part of my recovery from the days when I was lost in my addictive behaviors to surrounding myself with a new set of people who were not only nourishing but also inspired me to play with my artistic side and explore new worlds of philosophy, spirituality, and meditation. I found them through joining creative improv classes, forming The Artist's Way group, and eventually going back to school with many others who were interested in growing creatively. Consider right now, who are your playmates, and from the list of your playful activities, who might join you in them? Take a moment to make it real and write this out below.

PLAYMATES   **TOYS**

_____

_____

_____

_____

Now take a look at the list. Is there a way to make more frequent connections with more of these people? Nowadays there are so many ways to connect: online, on the phone, in person. You can even form a group of these people to meet on a more frequent basis supporting the mindset of play. Pick one or more of those people and set an intention today to make contact with them. You will thank yourself later.

FINDING PLAYMATES

It may be that you've come up with some toys but don't have people in your life you consider playmates. That doesn't mean there aren't people out there who are interested in doing the things you find playful. There are often more ways than we think to find playmates. If you have a dog, you might meet kindred spirits at a dog park. If you like sports, perhaps you can join an intramural sports team in your area. If you are part of an organized religion, you can participate in events or services at a local church, synagogue, temple, or mosque. Most towns and cities offer community education classes in photography, cooking, meditation, art, and a host of other enjoyable activities. A downloadable phone app called Insight Timer (www.insighttimer.com) not only helps you track your meditation practice but also connects you to people in your area or online who are doing the same. You can also check out websites such as Meetup (www.meetup.com) to find people gathering to explore common interests. This site also has listings for where you can find an Artist's Way group. Put aside your judgments about whether or not these would work for you, and let your experience be your teacher. What would life be like with a few more playmates?

Make Your Playdates

As adults, play can be so foreign to us, or we're so out of practice with it, that we actually need to create recurring playdates with ourselves and others, or else we may let them slide. Starting now, set a goal of taking a minimum of one hour a week to spend in intentional play. Schedule it in your calendar as an important appointment that you won't miss. Take a look at the activities that represent play to you and see where you can put them into your calendar. You can either play alone or with playmates. Either way, you have to give yourself permission to play—not as an indulgent activity, but more with the understanding that it is a key natural antidepressant that engages novelty, helps shape a more resilient brain, and uncovers happiness. If during any of the playdates, you notice that you're enjoying yourself, try these three steps to savor it, allowing the neurons to fire together and wire together:

THREE STEPS TO SAVORING

Say to yourself:
1. "This is a good moment."
2. "In life there are good moments [or joyful moments]."
3. "Can I bring gratitude into this moment?"

Notice what happens when you begin to savor more play in your life.

Working with Resistance to Play

For many of us, the idea of engaging in a more playful life is a direct cue for our mind traps and NUTs to arise, leading to resistance. Maybe you hear, "I don't have time," or "This just seems silly; it won't work for me." Or maybe there's the thought that "I don't deserve to play." Why do these voices arise so often in the face of play? Maybe it's because we've grown up in a culture or family that reinforces work and sees play as something trivial— something just for kids. But probably the single greatest reason your brain would automatically resist engaging play is to guard against vulnerability. Having had depression in the past means that you've suffered a trauma, and your brain is on guard not to take that fall again. If you allow yourself to experience the joy of play, then you might be caught off guard and take a deeper fall. Your brain says, "You're not going to catch *me* being vulnerable!" and so it squashes the potential joy. Sometimes that's the only cue you need to start feeling bummed out, heavy, and unmotivated—an open door to the depression loop.

Brené Brown, PhD, a leading researcher at the University of Houston, spent over a decade interviewing thousands of men and women to study the science of vulnerability. She found that some of the most resilient people allow themselves to be vulnerable. On the flip side, she has also observed that the experience of resisting joy is incredibly common in our culture and has coined the term "foreboding joy." A pivotal moment for my client Diego was when he chose to go on a trip to visit a number of art galleries. While he was enjoying himself walking through the galleries, within a half hour, he started to feel shaky, lightheaded, and nauseous. He thought, "Maybe I should leave and go home." He decided to apply mindfulness to the moment, acknowledging the feeling and placing his hand on his heart to engage self-compassion. Because of the work we had done, he was primed to understand that the distress was meant to distract him from his joy. The picture of himself being vulnerable as a child in the face of play shot through his mind, and he understood that he was experiencing foreboding joy. He started to cry, but he described it as a sweet sadness because he finally understood that this was his brain trying to protect him like it did as a child. Diego also realized that he must open up to being vulnerable in order to truly experience joy and freedom.

You may also experience resistance to play. If so, check in to see if this might be a guard against experiencing joy. Is there something initially uncomfortable about the thought of play? Does the idea of experiencing joy in your life leave you open to being vulnerable? If so, take a moment to visualize what might be good about engaging play?

If you did engage some of your toys and playmates, what do you think you'd look back on and be grateful for? Allow this to be the motivation to start creating your weekly playdates. The science is clear that a lack of play in our lives sets in motion a depressed state. While the brain may have its reasons to resist play, taking a play history can inspire an enriching environment of new toys and playmates today that can not only buffer against the depression loop but also begin to awaken a more joyful and vibrant life.

In the following pages of *Uncovering Happiness*, you're going to take the final step: learning how to get better and better at integrating all the previous steps into your life to wire your brain toward maximum resilience and well-being.

STEP 7

Learn to Get Better and Better

*Do not worry about immediate results. More
and more you must concentrate on the value,
the rightness, the truth of the work itself.*
—THOMAS MERTON (1915–1968),
TRAPPIST MONK AND AUTHOR

When anyone asks me why I got involved in the work I do, I always say it was because I felt an underlying need to help others live the lives they want to live. But the full story is that although I love helping others, my work actually saved *my* life. After I had reached rock bottom in my personal life years ago, I tried very hard to get back to some kind of stability; some way to *achieve* a more balanced life. But life is a good teacher, and as I continued to fall back into the old patterns of false refuges through abusing drugs and alcohol, I kept coming to the conclusion that I was a failure and that maybe I couldn't change. Over time I came to understand that the best way to get continually better at cultivating a more resilient brain was by shifting my focus from my achievements—which were not necessarily in my control—to the process of learning, which was in my control. Once I started seeing life as a classroom where the emphasis was on learning, rather than a stage where the goal was to perform flawlessly and successfully at all times, my entire perspective changed.

Eventually I began to see vulnerability—the deep sadness, the feeling of hopelessness, the uncertainty, and the desire to escape again—as a teacher rather than as a foe. When I fell into these emotionally exposed states, instead of seeing them as moments of defeat or that I was "back to square one," I started to see them as friends waking me up to a choice point and an opportunity to engage life differently. I learned that if I had any goal, it wasn't to achieve happiness, it was to get better and better at getting out of my own way and understanding how my mind and body worked for better and worse. Ultimately I found that through dropping my performance-based mindset and stepping into a learning mindset, I could catalyze all the previous steps to make cultivating an antidepressant brain a reality for myself. And you can too.

The final step is about learning how to move toward mastering all the previous steps. Mastery is not some achieved state of being but rather the *process* of growing and learning how to get continuously better at something. This mindset is what creates the most dramatic changes in the brain. Achieving self-compassion is a *performance* goal. Being able to practice self-compassion is a *learning* goal. We use both types of goals, and both can indeed lead to achievement. But only one leads to mastery and uncovers real happiness.

In the following pages, you'll discover the science and practice behind the essential mindset that is going to give you the best chance at embedding all the previous natural antidepressants.

You'll begin to weave together everything you've learned and practiced into a cohesive approach to bolster your natural anti-depressants, and to change the activities in your life in order to flourish. If the dogs in Martin Seligman's studies on learned help-lessness knew what you're about to learn, they would have broken out of their cages and marched out into a life of doggy bones and freedom.

Getting Better Is Not About Performing Well

At the end of leading a daylong seminar on uncovering happiness, I was approached by Lisa, a woman in her late fifties who had just lost her husband of twenty-eight years to a yearlong battle with cancer. "Elisha," she said, "I have no idea how to live without him." Lisa was dealing with the greatest loss of her life, hopeless that anything could change. She had done everything in her power to save him, even taking out a second mortgage on her house to pay for an experimental treatment that didn't work.

"Lisa, you've been taking care of him intensely for so long," I told her. "You did everything you possibly could. But that time is over, and now it's time to learn how to take care of yourself." After falling into tears for a few minutes, she looked up and said, "I'm afraid I don't have the ability to do that. I will never be happy again." She felt helpless and was slipping from grief to depression. It's common for someone who has lost a loved one to feel helpless. I paused and said, "Of course, and right now the grieving process isn't about *achieving* happiness or independence, it's simply about taking all that we have talked about today and *learning* how to get better and better at applying all of this to your life and healing." As I looked into her eyes, Lisa seemed to be taking this in, but she said, "I just don't think I have the ability to do it."

Lisa was operating from what's referred to as a fixed mind-set. She felt her ability to handle the grief she was experiencing couldn't change. But I wanted her to understand that she was more resilient than she realized, so I told her about the research of Carol Dweck, who discovered the key attitude that can help us all get better and better at cultivating all of the natural antidepressants.

Dweck is a psychology professor at Stanford University who has been studying the field of motivation and mastery for over forty years. She's found that there are two different types of mindset people hold when it comes to motivation and change. Some people believe that they have finite abilities that they cannot increase. This is called a *fixed mindset*. Others believe that different people hold varying abilities and that ultimately with strategy and effort, we can increase these abilities. This is called a *growth mindset,* a more flexible state of mind where you believe with understanding, application, and effort that you can increase your abilities. If you believe that the ability to gain mastery over depression is fixed, then every encounter with the depression loop becomes a measure of how much ability you have. If you believe your ability is something you can learn to increase, like pumping iron increases muscles, then the same encounter becomes an opportunity for growth. One mindset says that your ability to cultivate an antidepressant brain is something you exhibit, while the other is something you can nurture and develop.

Dweck wanted to figure out what makes a capable person give up in the face of obstacles, when others get motivated by those same obstacles. Her initial experiment was simple. The participants were schoolchildren who had been recognized by their teachers as being helpless. These were kids who would give up in the face of a difficult math problem and not even try other problems they had previously been able to complete. The children in the study were randomized into two groups. Half were given what's called *learning goals*. These children were trained to see difficult problems as a process of learning and were encouraged to give more effort when facing a challenge. The other half was given *performance goals*. These children were encouraged, as our culture does, to get a high grade on the test. It turns out that the students with the learning goals not only scored much higher but also worked harder on the challenging problems.

In her book *Self-Theories: Their Role in Motivation, Personality, and Development,* Dweck writes, "With a learning goal, students don't have to feel that they're already good at something in order to hang in and keep trying. After all, their goal is to learn, not to prove they're smart."

In a later study, Dweck enlisted college students who exhibited depression, assessed their mindset, and asked them to track their moods, activities, and coping strategies. She discovered that certain students kept rehashing their setbacks and attributed them to their fixed trait of being deficient and unworthy. One student said, "It just kept circulating in my head: 'You're a dope.'" They felt helpless, less motivated to get things done, less able to move through their difficulties. They were stuck. But other students who also felt miserable showed completely different behavior. The more depressed they were, the more actively they confronted it. They reached out for help, kept up with the responsibilities of school, and were more resilient. What was the difference between these two groups?

The members of the first group clearly had a fixed mindset, where they weren't performing well and identified themselves as failures. It became part of who they were and led to a sense of helplessness. The students in the second group had a growth mindset: they believed that they could learn to get better and better; setbacks were painful for them but didn't define them—and could even be opportunities for growth.

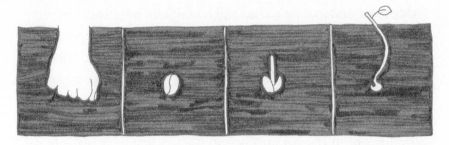

"Seeds plunge all the way into the dark and somehow they know which way to grow to find the light." -Pavi mehta

You can think of shifting from a fixed mindset to a growth mindset in the same way that you think of nurturing a garden:

1. Open up your fixed mindset.
2. Plant the seeds of growth.
3. Water the seeds of growth.

As long as you are human, your abilities are not fixed. You can learn to get better and better at all the steps in cultivating a more resilient brain and uncovering happiness.

Open Up Your Fixed Mindset

To begin training your brain to uproot a fixed mindset, start recognizing when it's happening. This mindset is reflected in the voices of doubt that say, "This might work for other people, but it won't for me." Or if you experience yet another relapse, the voice may come up, "I've tried this before, I'm just not capable; I'm clearly going to disappoint myself again." In this space of awareness, recognize that you're awake and in a choice point to relate to this moment differently. Is there another way to look at this?

After our initial conversation at the seminar, Lisa came to see me in my private practice. Here's how that played out. In our initial session, I asked her, "What mindset do you think you're identifying with when it comes to working with depression?" With a knowing smile, she said, "Clearly the fixed one. I suck at this." She understood, but then she immediately got caught in it again. I asked her, "Do you see how the end of that statement where you said, 'I suck at this,' was showcasing a fixed mindset? It's as if your brain is saying you're not performing well at this." Lisa's beliefs were rigid, and she saw her abilities as unchangeable. The fact is that when it comes to doing any of this work, a performance-based mindset creates a formula in the brain to see perceived failure around whether you're performing adequately with mindfulness, self-compassion, purpose, play, or even mastery. It sets you up to feel that something is wrong with you or that you're falling short in some way. The brain is ripe to sense deficiency that can leave you vulnerable to the depression loop with an onslaught of mind traps.

Lisa and I worked on mapping out her personal depression loop, and she made it a learning goal to notice it and all its associative elements as they arose. She also set the intention to experiment with mindful and self-compassionate responses when experiencing bouts of grief. She remembered that she valued her friendships and began calling old friends and making playdates, exploring new parts of her city that she never had with her late husband. She even started a course called "Drawing from the Right Side of Your Brain" to nurture her creative mind. Life wasn't a ball of joy by any means, but she got increasingly better at seeing "failures" as part of the learning process rather than as poor performance. Her goal shifted from achieving happiness to developing an entirely new way of relating to life and learning how to build true resiliency.

After a few months, she walked into my office looking very proud of herself. "Last night something profound happened," she explained. "I was lying in bed looking at my husband's picture, and I noticed a surge of anger come up in me." As her face shifted into an angrier expression, she began to choke up. "I said, 'Why did you leave me? Why did you leave me? I'm so pissed at you for leaving me!' In that moment, I remembered all the work that we've been doing, I saw the loop I was in, fell onto my bed, and became aware of the anger inside my body. I was in so much pain and was aware of my own suffering. I knew I needed to be cradled, and so I put my hand on my heart and tried to be with this with a loving attention." In that moment, she was challenging a fixed mindset that said she couldn't handle her pain. Instead, she opened up her heart to learning what might happen if she tried something new.

She looked at me, now smiling, and said, "In the past, this might have set me back for days. But this time it felt good to be angry, and it felt good to care for myself, too. I remembered how much I love my husband, and in that moment, I knew I was going to be okay. I felt the love that was there between us. It was so healing." I was so proud of her for moving from this fixed mindset and being open to learning a new way of relating to her pain.

"Did this surprise you?" I asked. Without hesitation, she replied, "Absolutely. I guess I just never thought I was capable of having an experience like this until now. I think I believe in myself a bit more." To this, I smiled and said, "You're learning—and growing."

Plant the Seeds of Growth

After practicing uprooting the voices of your fixed mindset, you can begin planting the seeds for a growth mindset. There is always an emotion that is behind the voice of a fixed mindset. Notice the choice to dip beneath the voice and go directly to the source: the emotion. Oftentimes it's some form of fear, shame, sadness, or anger. Play with meeting the feeling with a tender attention; some self-compassion. Try putting your hand on your heart or abdomen and saying, "Breathing in, I am aware of my own suffering; breathing out, may I be at ease." Regardless of the immediate outcome, this is now an opportunity to water the seeds of self-compassion and mindfulness. This sets the stage for opening up to new possibilities, nurturing growth, and cultivating mastery.

Understanding that her journey through grief was a continual process of planting seeds of growth was a great help to Lisa. She was now free to fail, as it was no longer seen as something that was bad but as something to be curious about and learn from. Not too long after her moment of insight around getting angry with her late husband, she told me, "I love my husband, and I know I'll always miss him. But I know that things always change, nothing stays the same. At some points, I feel stronger, and at others, not so strong. I'm getting better at noticing that in the moments when the grief washes over me that it's not forever; it doesn't need to turn into depression. And even this process has given me the gift of loving myself in a way that I never have before in my life. For that, I am grateful. I know I'll continue to struggle, but I feel confident now that I can rely on myself to get through it.

"Who knows," she said with a slight smile and a twinkle in her eye, "maybe there's even someone else out there for me."

As you continue to move forward on this path with the intent of learning to get better and better, instead of performing to some unrealistic standard, you'll plant seeds of growth and also have more motivation to practice. Neuroscience gives us the physical proof that the brain has the ability to grow and change throughout the life span. You can gain mastery with your natural antidepressants with a learning mindset and intentional effortful practice.

Water the Seeds of Growth

The final step in cultivating a growth mindset is to regularly look back and notice what you've learned in relationship to nurturing any of the natural antidepressants. Think about challenges that you've learned from and improved through. Maybe you were able to notice a choice point to apply self-compassion, or have had moments of being more playful. You can even water the seeds of growth by looking at past challenges that didn't work out. With what you know now, how might you have approached it differently? In the days that follow, be on the lookout for the growth mindset voices, the ones that are looking for things to learn in the moments of life. Just like a flower in a garden, whatever you shower with attention is going to grow.

Now, let's take a look at what your mindset is and learn how to apply all we've learned into a cohesive strategy to get better and better at growing our natural antidepressants.

What Is Your Mindset?

It's time to figure out your mindset. Which of the following statements do you identify with?

1. When it comes to cultivating your natural antidepressants, you have an idea of what you can and can't do, and there's not much you can do to change that.

2. No matter what your upbringing is or genetic predisposition, there is always opportunity for change.

3. While you can change your actions, you have a natural set point that you'll always come back to with regard to depression.

4. There is always the possibility to change certain things about what you believe you can and can't do in the world.

Answer: You can see here that questions 1 and 3 focus on performance and are born out of fixed mindsets, while questions 2 and 4 imply the ability to learn and are born out of growth mindsets. Which do you find yourself more drawn to? If it's the fixed mindset, you may notice a lot of resistance to taking action with any of the steps in uncovering happiness. Ask yourself, "What would be different if I saw it from a learning perspective?"

Let me make this more real.

Imagine that you are walking down the street, and five people walk by you. Four of them greet you with some form of salutation and a compliment such as "Hey, how you doing, you're looking good." Then the other person walks by and says, "You're a jerk, and your hair looks terrible today."

Now, allow yourself to be in a fixed mindset. Your social acceptance is being challenged. Can you see all the other people around you who might be looking at you? Can you hear the voices in your head worrying if it's true? Feel the tensing in your muscles, notice the hole punched in your ego. What else do you notice?

Now brush that off.

Imagine the same scenario, but put yourself in a growth mindset. Every opportunity is an experience to learn. So what are you learning? This person is providing you an opportunity to notice how easy it is for your NUTs to be activated. Despite all the positive comments, this one cues a flurry of NUTs. Do you notice the depressive loop in action? Are there any mental or behavioral bad habits being triggered? In this space of awareness, what happens when you acknowledge your emotional reaction and drop in the question "What is it that I need most right now?" The answer might be taking a few deep breaths or practicing mindfulness— maybe the "Be" practice? Or perhaps you hear a voice inside needing some self-compassion or maybe even compassion for the negative person who was likely imbalanced, saying something like that.

As you begin identifying when your mind is in a fixed mindset, you step into a choice point, to refocus the growth mindset. Ask yourself, "Is there anything for me to learn from this right now?" Understanding the importance of identifying and shifting these mindsets is the essential ingredient that makes the strategy and effort behind cultivating an antidepressant brain work. Up to this point, you've been learning about and putting into practice recognizing the depressive loop, breaking bad habits, and cultivating mindfulness, self-compassion, purpose, and play. You now know that encouraging the growth mindset is the central thread that weaves all the previous steps together and is the key to motivation

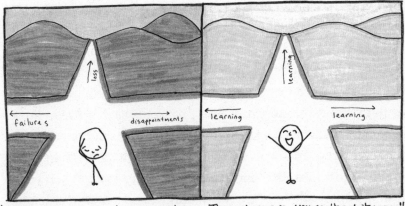

"The bad news is; you can't get it right... The good news is, you can't get it wrong"

and mastery. Now we're going to learn a cohesive strategy that will help you effectively integrate all the natural antidepressants with a growth mindset into daily life.

From Disengagement to Engagement

The essential thread to mastery is nurturing a growth mindset with learning goals, but when we're slipping into a depression loop, the fuel of effort is what seems to go first. The more we try to motivate but fall short, the stronger the depression loop grows and the deeper the grooves of learned helplessness. That is why a key goal for nurturing the natural antidepressant of mastery is learning how to employ the right *strategy* that moves us from disengagement to engagement, incorporating all the previous steps for bouncing back and healing depression.

When I met Joey, he was in his early twenties and had just finished an inpatient rehab program for addiction to marijuana. He had a job in retail that he was dragging himself to, was attending some Marijuana Anonymous twelve-step groups, but that's about it. "I feel so alone here, and I just can't seem to get motivated to do anything," he said. "I know exercise would be good for me, and I should get up early in the morning to meditate, but sometimes it's even difficult to fix myself a meal. I spend most of my days off just watching hour after hour of television." Having all of the activities he "should" do swimming around in his head only made him want to disengage more; this was all part of the depression loop.

I told Joey that disengaging from active life is not only a symptom of depression but also a key contributor to depression. I also told him that his lack of motivation wasn't his fault. When you're feeling depressed, your brain is literally depleted of neurochemicals such as dopamine, which is a neurotransmitter for motivation. When this happens, the strategy of "Just Do It" doesn't work very well. The more you think you "should" just do it, the more defeated you feel.

He turned toward me and gave me a smile of recognition. "That's exactly how it feels. I get to the place where I'm either saying 'What's the point?' or beating myself up for not having done something."

I continued, "It's not about trying, it's about creating a strategy that bypasses the brain's snap judgments and gives you a better chance at turning the tide." In fact, studies show that being strategic about increasing activity alone can significantly reduce depression and foster resiliency during relapse. In doing the practice you're about to learn, Joey discovered the one thing that helps him when he senses a relapse coming on. Although from time to time the depression loop knocks him down, with this new strategy, he is learning to get continuously better at picking himself up.

The strategy is called *activity scheduling*. Thousands of therapists and millions of clients have practiced it as a fundamental intervention, and we'll be adapting it to incorporate all the previous steps you have learned into a cohesive action plan. As you engage this practice, you'll learn new ways to be active and begin experiencing a sense of accomplishment with all the previous steps. As you continue to apply a growth mindset, you'll strengthen the feeling of personal control (mastery) and the belief that "I care about myself, and I can make it." Ultimately these experiences feel good and foster the invaluable strength of hope.

Activity scheduling has three steps:

1. Build awareness of the activities that currently fill your day.
2. Extend that list with activities that enhance your natural antidepressants.

3. Gradually begin swapping out optional neutral or depleting activities with your natural antidepressants. If you can't replace one with a natural antidepressant, see if you can infuse it with one. For example, if finding yourself stuck in traffic is depleting, what happens when we bring mindfulness, self-compassion, or play to it?

Ultimately these three steps are about you taking more control over your life, bringing the locus of control inside and experiencing more confidence. As you do this, you'll begin to not only experience mastery with your natural antidepressants, but also open the window for uncovering happiness.

Before entering into this practice, set aside your fixed mindset that's filled with the mind trap of self-doubt that you can achieve this or not. Now embrace a growth mindset as we enter into building this antidepressant activity list. Remember, obstacles are inevitable, but they are challenges from which to learn.

Let's jump right in.

With a growth mindset, you can begin to create a plan to move from disengagement to engagement. The main strategy to strengthen personal control, mastery, and hope is through a gradual step-by-step process called activity scheduling.

Build It

To illustrate how to put activity scheduling into practice, I'll show you how Joey used it.

In our second session, I gave Joey a piece of paper and asked him to make a list of all his daily activities from the time he woke up to the time he went to sleep. I asked him to be as specific as possible. After he created his list, I told him to put a notation next to each activity: an *N* for "nourishing," a *D* for "depleting," or a dash next to anything neutral. Then I told him to think about how he could increase the nourishing activities in his day and either decrease the depleting activities or figure out how to make them less draining.

He looked at one of the first items on his list: waking up in the morning and checking his cell phone. Joey realized this made him anxious, so he decided to eliminate that practice by putting it in a different room. One of the next items on his list was driving to work. He said he felt depleted by constant traffic and wondered what he could do to make sitting in traffic less agitating. I turned the question back to him so he could have the experience of listening to his own wisdom and trusting it. He said, "I guess I could see it as a time to slow down, maybe turn off the news and play some tunes I don't usually give myself a chance to listen to." Then he followed with a slight laugh. "Or I guess I could use it as a time to be mindful of my frustration."

Although that last comment was meant to be a joke, there was some truth to it. I said, "While that's funny, it's a chance to train your brain in using what you've learned about working with difficult emotions. How might you do that?" He thought for a moment and replied, "I guess I can do what we've practiced. I can recognize it as a difficult moment [mindfulness]. I can note where the feeling is in my body and ask myself what I need [self-compassion]. I think I'll need a few deep breaths and then refocus on my tunes [play]." That was a great response, and I told Joey to play with it like an experiment. It's just about learning to try on new things and see what comes up.

Another depleting item on his list was interacting with a particular coworker. "Just seeing him makes me tense," he explained. "He's competing with me for a promotion, and he is always judging the way I interact with customers." Most of us have difficult people in our lives, but we don't have to take on their energy. I told Joey that underlying judgment is often a simmering fear or anger, and it doesn't feel good to the person doing the judging, either. I asked Joey if he could take a moment to imagine his coworker as a child on a playground who, out of his own insecurity, is judgmental and bullying other kids.

"What does it seem that that kid needs?" I asked. Insightfully, he answered, "I guess to feel secure?"

"Exactly. Try to see this coworker this way and practice with intention and heart saying to him in your mind, 'May you feel secure, may you feel safe and protected from inner and outer harm, may you be happy [compassion].'" I told Joey to fake it till he makes it, if necessary. This was a good start.

For Joey, taking this high-level view of his daily life was, in his words, "one of the most helpful things I have ever done in my life. Because in just a few minutes, I had perspective on how to reconfigure my life to reinforce what supports me and to lessen or get rid of what is hurting me. I feel more in control."

Now it's your turn. List all of the activities in your day from the time you wake up until you go to sleep. To help you out, here are just a few generic samples of what people in different situations might experience in a day.

WORKING MOM	STAY-AT-HOME MOM	SINGLE MAN/ WOMAN	MARRIED MAN
1. Wake up.	1. Wake up.	1. Wake up.	1. Wake up.
2. Turn on news.	2. Take quick shower.	2. Check phone.	2. Check phone.
3. Nurse baby.	3. Wake up kids.	3. Get up.	3. Get up.
4. Iron clothes.	4. Make all breakfasts.	4. Brush teeth.	4. Exercise.
5. Curl hair.	5. Pack kids' lunches.	5. Take shower.	5. Make coffee.
6. Get dressed.	6. Serve breakfast.	6. Shave.	6. Make breakfast.
7. Play with baby.	7. Get dressed.	7. Get dressed.	7. Talk to wife.
8. Get baby dressed.	8. Get everyone in car.	8. Brush hair.	8. Take shower.
9. Grab breakfast bar, lunch, pump, and diaper bag.	9. Drop off at schools.	9. Put on makeup.	9. Shave.
10. Get in car.	10. Run errands (grocery shopping, post office, bank, and so on).	10. Make breakfast.	10. Get dressed.
11. Sit in traffic.	11. Put away groceries.	11. Eat breakfast.	11. Kiss wife good-bye.
12. Drop baby off at day care.	12. Make lunch for kid.	12. Make coffee/ tea.	12. Traffic.
13. Drive to work.	13. Read kid a book.	13. Travel to work.	13. Get on conference call in car.
14. Log in at computer.	14. Put down for nap.	14. Reply to emails.	14. Get to work.
15. Look over emails.	15. Clean dishes.	15. Work on projects.	15. Client calls.
16. Go get coffee and eat breakfast bar.	16. Make beds.	16. Meetings.	16. Work on projects.

WORKING MOM	STAY-AT-HOME MOM	SINGLE MAN/ WOMAN	MARRIED MAN
17. Go to nursing room to pump.	17. Pick up around house.	17. Travel home.	17. Go to bathroom.
18. Sit in meeting.	18. Play game with kid.	18. Take dog for walk.	18. Go out to lunch with coworkers.
19. Warm up lunch.	19. Pack snacks.	19. Make dinner.	19. Walk back to office.
20. Pump again.	20. Pick up other kids.	20. Eat dinner.	20. More meetings.
21. Call day care to check on baby.	21. Bring kids to park or other activities (dance, gymnastics, karate).	21. Watch TV.	21. Get another coffee.
22. Eat snack.	22. Drive home.	22. Talk to friends.	22. Drive to client site.
23. Tie up loose ends.	23. Start prepping dinner.	23. Read book.	23. Call wife in car.
24. Drive to pick up baby.	24. Serve dinner.	24. Wash face.	24. Meet with clients.
25. Get home.	25. Help kids with homework or clean.	25. Brush teeth.	25. Prepare for next day.
26. Do dishes.	26. Bathe children.	26. Go to sleep.	26. Drive home.
27. Turn on TV.	27. Read to children.		27. Talk to wife.
28. Nurse baby.	28. Put them to bed.		28. TV.
29. Spend family time.			29. Prepare dinner.
30. Eat dinner prepped by Dad.			30. Eat dinner.
31. Give baby a bath.			31. Have wine.

WORKING MOM	STAY-AT-HOME MOM	SINGLE MAN/ WOMAN	MARRIED MAN
32. Nurse again.			32. Maybe make love.
33. Tell baby a story.			33. Go to sleep.
34. Put him to bed.			
35. Make lunches for tomorrow.			
36. Do some laundry.			
37. Turn on TV.			
38. Do dream feed.			
39. Brush teeth.			
40. Wash face.			
41. Apply lotion.			
42. Kiss husband good night.			
43. Pass out.			

Take out a piece of paper or open up a document on your computer and write down your activities. You can also write your activities below right now:

_____

_____

_____

_____

_____

Now, look back at the list and see if any of these activities already fall under the natural antidepressants of mindfulness, self-compassion, purpose, play, and mastery. It's sometimes helpful to bring awareness to the fact that we already are weaving some natural antidepressants into our day. Don't worry if many of your activities don't fall under these categories; we'll get to insert more of them in the next section. Now, next to each item, mark an *N* for "nourishing," a dash for "neutral," or a *D* for "depleting."

Extend It

After you finish, extend this list with additional activities that you would consider falling under the category of any of the previous natural antidepressants. You can bring step 3 into your activity scheduling with a meditation practice, or step 4 with scheduled self-compassion breaks. When you look at step 5, you might consider actions of contribution such as volunteering, making that donation, or doing that favor for your friend. In step 6, you can think of all the ways you'd like to play. You can even integrate the step of mastery by picking a task (cleaning the corner of a room, studying, playing guitar, exercise) that gives you a sense of personal control or accomplishment.

If you're currently not emotionally feeling well, it may be hard for you to think of things that fall under the categories of the natural antidepressants. Whether or not this is the case, the following paragraphs outline an antidepressant list of seven simple science-based actions that are good for an antidepressant brain and can help be your guide. As you read these, remember: this is not about overwhelming your schedule. These are just ideas to help you flesh out which healthy activities may fall under the previous steps and give you a sense of personal control or mastery. If you look closely, they are also all suggestions of healthy behaviors that can be replacements for unhealthy behaviors. Don't worry about implementing these yet; the next section will focus on *how* to bring them into your life in a way that is at your own pace and leads to a healthier brain.

Move Your Body and Feel Better

It's good for the brain. A study carried out at Duke University found that thirty minutes of brisk exercise three days a week was a reliable predictor of reduction in depression relapse. In this study, researchers randomly assigned people to three groups. The first did exercise only, the second did exercise plus antidepressant medication, and the third did medication only. When relapse rates were measured, the study showed how beneficial exercise can be: Only 8 percent of the exercise-only group experienced a relapse, compared with 31 percent of the exercise-and-medication group and 38 percent of the medication group. We can speculate that the reason for this may be that the people doing exercise only bolstered their internal locus of control—which is the opposite of depression, where the control lies outside of us. They were active participants in their health and well-being. This is not to slight medication; it can be a great benefit to many people. But the focus here is on how beneficial exercise can be as a natural antidepressant.

There's a dilemma here, though: depression sufferers are often advised to throw themselves into *vigorous* exercise—jogging, running, swimming, cycling, walking on a treadmill, lifting weights, playing team sports, and so on. But when depression hits, the dopamine levels are low, and the last thing many people feel like doing is exercising. So we have to really ask ourselves, "Out of all the various forms of exercise—even just taking a brisk walk— what do I feel like doing? And for how long?" If the answer is, "A brisk ten-minute walk three days a week," then tell yourself you'll start with "A brisk walk for five minutes a day for three days a week." You want to scale down from whatever you believe you can do. Why? Because the idea is to just get going and experience accomplishments. If you believe that you can do ten minutes, then you're highly likely to be able to do five minutes. It's just a way to trick the brain into success.

Another way to work on your brain's cues is to set out your exercise clothes and shoes right next to your bed so that when you wake up, you're cued to get going. But even the thought of any exercise can seem overwhelming at times. If so, see if you can agree to put on your exercise clothes and shoes with no further commitment. Allow that to be an accomplishment. Sometimes we just need to get the engine running before we can drive.

SEVEN MINUTES OF EXERCISE MAY BE ENOUGH

According to a study published in the *American College of Sports Medicine Health & Fitness Journal*, a seven-minute exercise regimen, with little over thirty seconds for each practice, may give you the benefits of prolonged endurance training. After reading about this, my friends and I designed our own program where, at times throughout the day, we would perform seventy-five jumping jacks, fifty sit-ups, and twenty-five pushups. It took only a few minutes, and after a while, we could all see and feel the effects.

Figure out a few exercises and experiment with what works for you.

Add Brain Food to Your Diet

Supplementing your diet with brain food is not only an act of self-compassion but also quite an accomplishment. You can start by looking at your sugar and *simple-carb* intake. They are the quickest source of energy and also digest rapidly. They are also highly inflammatory to the brain and can edge you toward depression. Make a plan to swap them out at times for *complex carbs* that are more colorful, such as fruits and vegetables, which are rich in fiber and packed with vitamins and *antioxidants,* chemicals that prevent slow cell damage and nurture your brain. Make a plan to eat foods rich in docosahexaenoic acid (*DHA*), an omega-3 fatty acid that combats the blues. Omega-3s are found in certain seafood, cold water fish, and wild game. Studies have shown that a shortage of vitamins B_{12} and B_6, and another B vitamin, folate, are connected to depressed moods. While it's always preferable to get nutrients through the food we eat rather than via supplements, we don't always get them via the food we eat and it may be worthwhile to look into supplements. Do your own research here: go online, ask a doctor, or some friends. Then try it out for yourself as an experiment; it's all a process of learning what works for you.

Get Better Sleep

There is a direct connection between inadequate sleep and feeling physically and emotionally imbalanced. Not sleeping well tricks your brain into emphasizing what's negative in life versus what's positive. The hippocampus processes the positive or neutral memories, while the negative memories get processed through the amygdala. Insufficient sleep affects the hippocampus directly, and so it follows that the brain recalls more actively what's negative. In studies, when sleep-deprived college students tried to memorize words, they recalled 81 percent of the words with negative connotations, such as *cancer* and only 31 percent of positive or neutral words like *flower* or *plate.*

If you struggle to get enough sleep, make a schedule to treat yourself well with a healthy bedtime routine. Experiment with this; learn what works for you. Some suggestions are to take thirty to sixty minutes before bed to make yourself some decaffeinated tea, turn off the electronics, find a book or magazine, and just relax. If you have a partner, you can take this time to connect.

I also highly recommend a Compassionate Body Scan or the meditation called Movie in Your Mind. You'll find step-by-step instructions for both in part 3: "The Natural Antidepressant Tool Kit." This is just sensible sleep hygiene that will be pleasurable as well as give you a sense of personal control and achievement.

Brighten Your Life with Outdoor Light

Many of us are susceptible to seasonal affective disorder (SAD), which gets reinforced by gray skies and hunkering down indoors. Low levels of vitamin D have been associated with weaker immune systems and depressed moods, but you can boost your vitamin D level with exposure to sunshine, which allows your body to manufacture the vitamin. In one study, spending twenty minutes a day outdoors in good weather improved mood, helped people create perspective, and improved working memory. Another study showed that a single twenty-minute exposure to the sun's ultraviolet (UV) rays reduced blood pressure. If there is light outside, make a plan to get out more and walk in it or let it wash over your face for a few minutes. If sunshine isn't available, an artificial light box has been shown to be helpful, although it doesn't have the UV rays to boost Vitamin D.

Get Connected

That's right. Do you remember Dr. Dennis Proffitt's research on predicting the incline of a hill on your own as opposed to having a friend with you? It seemed less steep when someone accompanied the participant. Research shows that a strong connection with family and friends can dramatically reduce depressive relapse.

One of the detrimental behaviors associated with the depression loop is avoiding people, especially at times when being with them might be the healthiest course of action. This makes the slant of life seem steeper. Think of all the people in your life who are nourishing to you and connect with them. This doesn't have to be a prolonged event. It can be something as simple as getting together for a quick coffee, or texting or emailing a few more friends, or messaging some Facebook contacts—anything that reconnects you to the nourishing people in your life.

You might also consider spending less time with people who deplete you. But if that's not possible—perhaps you work with such a person or are in a caregiving situation—look for ways to change your relationship with him or her. One way to do this is through a Just Like Me practice that you'll find in the Natural Antidepressant Tool Kit. The essence of this is to practice seeing the difficult person as a human being who wants essentially the same things as you do. Another way is to see him or her as a teacher to your nervous system's reactivity. Learn how easily the looping gets triggered and accept it as an opportunity to practice breaking the loop and rebalancing your system. As crazy as it seems, you might even eventually discover gratitude for people like that. As you go through these practices, you can soften your inner irritation and open up to a wiser relationship.

Cross Off the To-Do List or Tie Up Loose Ends

Maybe it's a bill that's waiting to be paid or tasks that you've been meaning to do for a long time but just never seem to get around to. Find that space in your day or week that is filled with a neutral or depleting task and swap it out for that long-overdue task. These can often be small, seemingly inconsequential responsibilities, but it feels good when we get to them. It may be cleaning out the closet, buying that picture frame and putting a photo in it, organizing the pile of books on your bedside table or that random drawer or your file cabinet, cleaning out your car, recovering that chair, making the dentist or doctor's appointment, or even just clipping your cat's or dog's claws.

While chores such as paying bills might seem like a depleting activity, once we do it, we feel a sense of achievement. Cleaning that corner of the room that has been staring back at us for weeks or standing in line at the post office—these are all accomplishments that loosen the shoulders. But how do we make the process of the task less depleting? When you approach the job, try doing it slightly slower than normal, put a time limit on it, and treat it like a meditation. The task is the focus. When your mind wanders, you note where it wandered to and gently guide it back. If frustration arises, see if you can allow that to be a learning moment for practicing what you've discovered about the antidepressant of self-compassion. If there are difficult people involved, like a stressed-out postal worker, see if you can see the person behind the uniform and strengthen the antidepressant of compassion, wishing him ease, to be healthy and happy. Consider what other things on your to-do list need to get done? How might you apply what you've learned to make it an opportunity to strengthen any other natural antidepressants? What would the days ahead be like if you could get to these loose ends more often? Use this feeling as a motivator. Ultimately there's just something very satisfying about crossing things off the list.

Use the lines below to begin brainstorming from the list above what actions might fall under the categories of the natural antidepressants of mindfulness, self-compassion, purpose, play, and mastery.

_____

_____

_____

_____

_____

Schedule It

In this final step, you'll use the lists you just built and extended to put mastery into action. Go back and look at your original list of daily activities and see if there are any optional activities that don't fall under any natural antidepressant category. See if you can identify one or two hours a day to either change your relationship to the neutral activity or swap the neutral activity with one from the extended list. Here's a partial sample of Joey's neutral activities on his list, the optional activities that he planned to swap them out for, and the potential natural antidepressants that he was learning:

NEUTRAL ACTIVITIES	EXTENDED LIST ACTIVITIES ACCOMPLISHMENT/PLEASURE	NATURAL ANTIDEPRESSANT
Wake up, check phone.	Take a few deep breaths or the "Be" practice.	Mindfulness
Make breakfast.	Healthy eating: swap frozen waffles for healthier choices such as oatmeal or granola and yogurt. Remind myself this is taking care of me.	Self-compassion, purpose, play
Take shower.	Bring more mindfulness to the shower experience.	Mindfulness
Drive to and from work.	Listen to audio programs I've been wanting to hear.	Purpose, self-compassion, play
Checking email during lunch.	Go out on a twenty-minute walk.	Self-compassion, purpose
Click through TV channels at night.	Either watch specific shows that are fun for me, take a bath, or connect with friends and family.	Play
Check messages before bed.	Listen to relaxing old tunes, do a meditation, read a book I've been meaning to get to.	Play, self-compassion

Set the aspiration to replace some of the neutral or depleting activities that you can with five or so of the activities from the extended list that provide natural antidepressants over the course of this first week. Remember; as you engage with these practices, hold the intention of the growth mindset. For example, you may have written down "Mindfulness practices" as an activity to bring into your day. If you go into that step with the goal of achieving a mindful moment to prove that you can be good at this or just to check it off the to-do list, you set up an expectation, and then you're more likely to get frustrated and give up when they don't occur. If your mindset is about learning, you open up and become more flexible with whatever arises. Not only are you less likely to give up, but you're going to continue progressing en route to mastery.

The more you're able to replace the neutral activities for ones that nourish you with your natural antidepressants, the more you'll uncover happiness and resilience. As you continue to learn, picture your brain creating those new antidepressant connections. Keep doing what you're doing. The bottom line is that it's not important how much of it you get done but that you engage in it and see how you feel, allowing your experience to be your teacher.

Treat activity scheduling like a mindful experiment. When you find yourself off the path, as best you can, without judgment, be curious about what derailed you, learn from it, and gently guide yourself back again and again.

It Requires Effort, but What Else Is New?

Cultivating mastery takes effort, but what else is new? It took us over a year and a lot of effort to learn how to walk, but we kept on going even when we fell down time and time again because we were driven toward mastery. The painter and architect Michelangelo said, "If people knew how hard I worked to get my mastery, it wouldn't seem so wonderful at all." But if you take a moment to consider it, effort means that we care enough about something to engage in it. Walking was purposeful to us as toddlers, and it drove our motivation. The fact is that whatever we want to learn—whether it's talking, driving a car, exercising, playing an instrument, or cultivating an antidepressant brain and uncovering happiness—all take effort.

While famous athletes may have natural talents, their feats that we watch in awe of are the result of practice. Think of something you've been dedicated to, whether it was walking as a child, learning to type, playing an instrument, or getting better and better at your job. When you intentionally practice something with strategy over time, you can become very good at it. While *effort* and *discipline* are words that can come with a serving of eye-watering lethargy, I urge you to try on a new lens and see it in a new, authentic way. Intentional effort is simply the act of watering the seeds of a happier brain.

Uncovering happiness is a lifelong practice fostering many gifts along the way. With a growth mindset and effort, you will be less affected and more forgiving of the inevitable bumps ahead and continue to gain confidence with the steps to your antidepressant brain. If you find yourself off the path, just practice Forgive and Invite: forgive yourself for the time gone by; in this present moment, invite yourself to embrace a growth mindset;

and get back to your intention. Every time that you make the effort toward mastery with any of these steps, remind yourself that this is an act of self-care. If you're bold, you can even call it self-love.

A central idea of this book is that new science is revealing that we have within each of us natural antidepressants that we can nurture to prevent depression from relapsing and even to un-cover happiness. While the engagement of this science can seem difficult when we're not feeling well, there is reason to be hopeful.

The scientists who have studied the role of these natural anti-depressants, many of whom you've read about in this book, offer us psychological and neurobiological explanations for why these internal virtues are so powerful. We know that understanding and naming the depression loop when it occurs can shift the activity in our brains to turn down our fear and turn up our ability to make conscious choices that can facilitate resiliency. The science also shows that there is a way to stop believing everything we think; when we do this, we not only curb our behavioral bad habits but also cut off the fuel for the habitual nature of the depression loop.

The science that has been revealed in this book reinforces what we know already in our hearts: That the practice of learning to be more mindfully present and aware is adaptive, healthy, and full of purpose. That self-compassion is a critical and fundamental as-pect to healing our wounded minds and hearts. That understand-ing our values and beginning to put them into action can give us a sense of purpose that makes us feel good. That developing the skill of compassion and helping others brings about a feeling of support and connection that is the opposite of depression. That play is a highly undervalued asset of our adult lives and is the springboard for experiencing more joy. That beneath it all, having a learning mindset, being curious about life, and engaging this en-tire process for its own sake, rather than for the goal of happiness, is a far better way to live our lives and, paradoxically, can uncover happiness.

The implicit nature of human beings is to feel connected, happy, and free. To go a bit deeper, engaging our natural antidepressants is not an act solely for you. As you begin to practice, your actions and changes inspire other people, and their changes affect others, and the ripple effects are exponential. Think of this playful adventure as something that is for a cause far greater than just yourself: your actions bring these virtues to life to affirm and heal our humanity.

PART 3

The Natural Antidepressant Tool Kit

This tool kit includes tips, strategies, and practices to draw from and bring to life.

You can sift through this section and take what's helpful to you whenever you want. One thing to note is that in the Tool Kit, you'll find a number of shorter and longer audio-led practices that you can access via my website.

Put on your growth mindset, pick and choose what tips to use, and continue coming back to this tool kit. Use it as a companion along this playful adventure of life.

WHAT YOU'LL FIND IN THIS TOOL KIT

Uncover Happiness: Ten Strategies to Make It Come Alive

Five Strategies to Stick to Healthy Habits

Three Yoga Poses for Depression

Five Steps to a Growth Mindset

Twenty-One Days of Purpose

Strengthen Your Natural Antidepressants—Longer
Practices

Recap Chapter by Chapter

Discussion Guide: Twenty Questions to Give Group
Guidance

Find Out More

Uncovering Happiness

Top Ten Strategies to Make It Come Alive

Whatile you already have the seeds to cultivate an antidepressant brain and uncover happiness, here are ten strategies that you can consider as the food to nurture mindfulness, self-compassion, purpose, play, mastery, and all their wonderful side effects.

Strategy 1: Form Your Get Well Team

Throughout the text, I've woven in the importance of surrounding yourself with people whose presence is nurturing, playful, and healing. Philip Burguieres, whom you read about earlier, was the youngest CEO of a Fortune 500 company. Years later, he went public about his lifelong struggle against depression. When he opened up about it to a good friend, he discovered that his friend, too, struggled with depression, and he wasn't so alone. Likewise, his friend said that when Philip confided in him, he also felt relieved not to be so alone. He immediately shifted from the insecurity of disconnection to the security that lies in connection. The two men created a "Get Well Team," supporting each other along the way. Burguieres went on to be one of the leading corporate advocates for opening up about depression.

There's science behind this. After an initial study suggesting that obesity was "contagious" up to three degrees of friends, social scientists Nicholas Christakis, MD, PhD, and James Fowler, PhD, took this investigation further to study the possibility of "emotional contagion," and found that loneliness also spreads three degrees. In the 2009 journal article "Alone in the Crowd: The Structure and Spread of Loneliness in a Large Social Network," coauthored with John Cacioppo, PhD, the authors wrote, "The spread of loneliness was found to be stronger than the spread of perceived social connections, stronger for friends than family members, and stronger for women than for men."

They explained: "The spread of good or bad feelings might be driven partly by 'mirror neurons' in the brain that automatically mimic what we see in the faces of those around us—which is why looking at photographs of smiling people can itself often lift your mood." So if there are people in your network who are having difficulties in their lives, your brains may begin to mimic their mood.

Christakis and Fowler also found that happiness spreads by three degrees of separation, and each additional person in your life who is feeling well boosts your chances of feeling well by 9 percent.

Consider who is in your immediate social network right now. Is there anybody else you know who has struggled with depression? Are there people who are supportive of your work to become more present to your life? If not, is there a way you can get in touch with others who live in accordance with those values? Maybe there are people on the periphery of your life with whom you can reconnect. If you're in Los Angeles, you can look up an *Uncovering Happiness* group or form one in your area. Or maybe you can look up a local in-person mindfulness-based cognitive therapy (MBCT) group or find support online through eMindful (www.emindful.com). eMindful is the leading live-online provider of mindfulness-based progams for healthcare, business and education. If you want to connect through other areas of interest, visit the website Meetup (www.meetup.com). There are many online forums for virtual support. For example, PsychCentral (http://psychcentral.com) gives you the option to ask a therapist a question or interact in a number of self-help support groups.

What would life be like if you surrounded yourself with people who understood and cared about you? How much better would you feel if you had people who were supportive of you living the life you want?

Strategy 2: Start Your Day Right . . .

How we start the morning often sets the stage for the rest of the day. Of course, life throws us curveballs in the middle of the day: maybe you get a stressful email, or your car gets rear-ended, or you lost that deal that you were confident you'd land. Anything can happen in the present moment, but how we start our day can often affect how we greet those challenges.

Here are four tips to start your day that will help you with life's inevitable ups and downs.

1. Mindful Check-in—It's good to begin the day with the following question: "Where am I starting from?" How is your *body*? If you're lying in bed, note whether your body feels comfortable or tense. What *emotions* are present? Are you feeling calm, anx-

ious, annoyed, or maybe neutral? Is your *mind* calm or already racing off to work?

On my website, www.elishagoldstein.com, find the two-minute video of the "Mindful Check-in" from *The Now Effect* and give it a go.

2. Prime Your Mind for Good—After a brief mindful check-in, one way of inclining your mind toward resiliency and even opening up to the good of the day is to consider an intentional gratitude practice. What do you have to be grateful for right now? It could be anything: waking up on the right side of the bed, having a roof over your head, savoring a good morning cup of tea or coffee. Keeping a gratitude journal to read or add to throughout the day could be a wonderful gift for you. It could be a small one that fits in your pocket or a note on your cell phone. As I mentioned earlier, the website grateful160.com sends you an email prompt to reply to and then emails you back your journal at the end of the week. Whichever way you choose, just practice inclining your mind to the good in life.

3. Bring Presence to Morning Activities—When you're in the shower, *be in the shower*, not solving problems at work. When you're making breakfast, bring awareness to the fact that this food nourishes and gives strength to you or your family. Put some love into the food. If there are pets or other family members in the house, before you leave, make sure to say an intentional good-bye, looking into their eyes.

4. Red Light Practice—If you drive to work, use red lights as an opportunity to check in, pressing the reset button if traffic has got you flustered or just using it as an opportunity to get centered and focus on what matters. You can make the choice to

listen to your favorite music, plan the day in your mind, or just have a quiet drive for a change. If you take public transportation, walk, or ride a bike, you can do the same thing every time you reach a stop sign or light. If you work from home, try this before turning on your computer. Exposing yourself to choices and acting on them just feels good and primes your mind for the rest of the day that you have choices in how you want to respond to situations.

Try these four routines each morning as an experiment to see how your life changes.

Strategy 3: . . . And End Your Day Right

Before Thomas Edison invented the light bulb, the average American slept ten hours a night. The National Sleep Foundation reports that today people sleep an average of just six hours and forty minutes per night, when the recommendation is seven to nine hours.

Sleep issues are one of the first things I look for when someone's not feeling well. Barring any medical issues, when it comes to difficulty falling asleep, there is one main culprit: the mind. There are general good tips to consider for a restful night's sleep, such as creating a bedtime ritual that remains as consistent as possible. It's generally a good idea to cut out technology an hour or so before sleep (best to keep it out of the bedroom), minimize caffeine intake, and not snack or exercise too close to bedtime. All of these activities serve to activate the brain when we want it to start calming down.

However, there are a few fundamental things you can do that can also help. The first is to activate your growth mindset when it comes to sleep. This means the goal isn't to *achieve* sleep, but to *learn* what is most supportive to you. As you take this approach, your mind begins to worry less about falling asleep—which is often what keeps you awake.

The next thing is to begin engaging a practice that facilitates disrupting the stress loop. While there are many I recommend, a fundamental practice is a basic body scan. This is the practice that the Compassionate Body Scan in the Tool Kit is based on. Here's how you do it:

Start off by taking a few deep breaths. Now, with a beginner's mind, as if this were the first time you ever felt your body before, bring your attention to your feet, feeling them from the inside out. You'll notice sensations arise: possibly heat, coolness, itchiness, tingling, heaviness, or lightness. At your own pace, move attention up the body to the legs, hips, torso, arms, hands, neck, face, and head. It is natural for your mind to wander. When it does, just note where it went and gently guide it back. On the final exhalation, release any intentional attention on the body and, for a moment, come back to notice how this body just breathes naturally. And always thank yourself for taking the time out to do this; it is an act of self-care.

The purpose here is not to achieve relaxation but to simply become curious about the feelings there, without judgment. In this way, we break the loop between thoughts, emotions, and sensations, and simply get back into our bodies. You can do this on your own or watch a three-minute version of it on my website to help you get a feel for it now. If you'd like to move onto longer practices, you can find that in the "Deepen Your Practice" part of the Tool Kit.

The final thing I recommend for ending the day right is a forgiveness review. As you lie down, look back on your day. If there is anyone who has harmed you—including yourself—knowingly or unknowingly, out of pain, confusion, or ignorance, practice saying silently in your mind: "Breathing in, I acknowledge the pain; breathing out, forgiving and releasing this burden from my heart and mind."

Prepare for a better night's sleep.

Strategy 4: Make Your Antidepressant Cheat Sheet

We all experience personal *relapse signs* such as the desire to sleep more, avoiding socializing with people, increased or decreased appetite, heightened irritability, poor focus, a heaviness in the body, and more automatic negative thoughts. Yet when these signs come on, you don't want the default mode of the brain that's filled with mind traps for coping to be the one making decisions for you.

Instead, having an antidepressant cheat sheet on hand can be immensely helpful. It can remind you of the relapse signs—those sticky negative thoughts that keep you stuck—and specific things that you can do to engage your natural antidepressants. I've adapted the following five steps to creating the antidepressant cheat sheet from an exercise I've taught in mindfulness-based cognitive therapy (MBCT).

Step 1. Get out a single sheet of paper or open up a document on your computer.

Step 2. Write the title at the top: "Antidepressant Cheat Sheet."

Step 3. Underneath that, write "My Relapse Signs," and write out a list of personal signs that often emerge before any relapse.

Step 4. Write: "When I notice these signs, engage in any of these natural antidepressants even if there's a voice inside that says, 'What's the point?' or 'It's not going to matter.'" The second half of that statement is necessary because when the mind is depressed, it will likely filter in a thought that has a bleak or negative outlook about the future. While the thought may appear believable and convincing, it is not a fact.

Step 5. Draw a line underneath that and then list many examples that fall under the categories of mindfulness, self-compassion, purpose, play, and something that gives you a sense of personal control or mastery. You can borrow from the examples you came up with throughout the book in the respective chapters. Make sure that you have a continuum of activities in there, from little effort (petting my dog or cat) to something that takes more effort (cleaning the house).

When you finish, congratulate yourself for making this document, and each time you engage in these activities. Doing this is an active choice and deserves some form of self-acknowledgment.

When you notice the relapse signs coming on, you can have this list close at hand. Pick up the checklist and allow your actions to do the talking for you.

Strategy 5: Prepare with Minimindful Workouts

We can't control what happens to us in any given moment. We can only prepare and respond. Taking time out each day to complete a short mindful exercise can have tremendous results in training our brains to automatically be more aware. This makes sense, as habits are formed when we intentionally practice and repeat things in daily life. Check out the following three two- to three-minute practices on my website, Breath as an Anchor, ACE, and

Just Like Me, which are intended to cultivate your natural antidepressants.

Sprinkle these throughout your day. Activate your growth mindset and learn what the best times are for you to drop into a short practice. Investigate what you notice when you practice. What happens when you engage any of these in the face of relapse signs? Does it widen the space of choice?

Minimindful Workout 1:
The Breath as an Anchor

The breath is always here as an anchor to the present moment. Train mindfulness and mastery as you pay attention to the breath and continue to gently guide your attention back each time it wanders.

Check out Breath as an Anchor on my website.

Minimindful Workout 2: ACE
(Awareness, Collecting, Expanding)

Practice these three steps to break out of autopilot, steady the mind, and ground yourself in the present moment. Train mindfulness, mastery, and self-compassion as you bring awareness to the breath and body, gently guide attention back when it wanders, and be attuned to how you're feeling with a kind attention.

Check out The ACE Practice on my website.

Minimindful Workout 3: Just Like Me

We often default to seeing people as disconnected and separate from us. Train yourself to have mindfulness, mastery, and purpose as you (1) bring awareness to other people, (2) improve at reigning in your judgments, and (3) realize that, fundamentally, there is meaning in our connection.

Check out Just Like Me on my website.

Strategy 6: Your Purpose, The Twitter Version

Why are you here? That's a big question, but the answer needs to be simple. One way to keep it simple is to consider how you want to be remembered by people when you pass. What will be the epitaph, that simple poetic phrase, on your tombstone? Some people might say, "Humanity, Justice, Equality," meaning that this was a person who found value in the rights of all people. Another's might read, "Beloved Sister, Devoted Wife, She Saved the World." This loving tribute implies that she valued family and making the world a better place.

What's the Twitter version of your purpose? Write it below.

_____

_____

When you look at what you wrote, does this match the way you're living your life right now? If not, what are some things you can do that are in line with this purpose? Remember to activate your growth mindset. No single person in music, sports, or humanitarian leadership ever achieved mastery overnight, and when it comes to finding purpose, this is often a lifelong pursuit. Take a breath: there's plenty of space and time.

When you lay your head down on the pillow at night, look back on the day and ask yourself, "Where did I live my purpose today?"

Strategy 7: Three Tips to Mastery

All the research around neuroplasticity says that the change in brain architecture is due to some kind of deliberate practice that has been repeated over time. Practicing mastery with your natural antidepressants can be simple. Here are a few steps to remember:

1. Focus on any single task.
2. When the mind wanders, practice Forgive and Invite, and gently guide it back.
3. Repeat step 2 indefinitely.

Following these three tips will remind you not to spend too much time ruminating on the obstacles but to continue to gently come back to what matters over and over again. It's also a good idea to look at the mental and behavioral bad habits that distract you from your best intentions, so that you can get increasingly better at being aware when they're around. What are they teaching you? Take these three steps with you when trying to cultivate mastery in your life.

Strategy 8: Get Unstuck, Go Play

When it comes to natural antidepressants, we must take time out of our lives for play and self-compassion. Consider what it would be like to make a two-hour date with yourself every week to do something that you might not normally do. Julia Cameron, in *The Artist's Way*, calls this an "artist's date," although, she says, it "need not be overtly 'artistic'—think mischief more than mastery. Artist's dates fire up the imagination. They spark whimsy. They encourage play." Just ask yourself, "What sounds novel and fun?" and let that guide your way.

Strategy 9: You! The Therapist

Whenever it's time to end the course of therapy with someone, I always remind the person that she spent one hour every week in personal investigation and reflection. Just because therapy is ending doesn't mean that gift to herself needs to end. Likewise, making space for yourself once a week to assess how things are going in cultivating an antidepressant brain is a form of *proactive attention*. The problem, though, is that the brain sees this time of self-reflection as important but not critical. In fact, your brain sees your Facebook, Groupon, or text message as more urgent than this, so if we leave it up to the brain, your attention will default there.

When it comes to working the steps, taking this time for yourself each week gives you a significant edge in making it happen. You can see this as a time for building hope. The late psychologist and researcher Rick Snyder wrote that hope is built from having a goal in mind, the determination to reach that goal, and a plan to make it happen. In this proactive space, you can ask yourself, "How did this week go in terms of engaging the steps? Where did I get distracted? What are my intentions and plans for the next week? What's most important for me to be focusing on to really go forward in my work or be more successful and happier in my personal life?"

Engaging in this space of self-awareness will also elicit a number of natural antidepressants. You're being mindful, engaging self-compassion by taking time for yourself, practicing personal control in your life (mastery), trying novel and creative activities (play), and finding a sense purpose in pursuing a meaningful activity. You can plug this time into your activity scheduling and allow it to be a practice in mastery. As you get better at engaging what matters in life, you'll find that you'll be "doing" less because there's less clutter.

Strategy 10: Make It Pocketsize

Sometimes the blues can catch us off guard when we're out and about. What if you had a small wallet- or purse-sized piece of paper that gave you the key elements to helping you in that moment? Fold a square sheet into four sections that can be folded again into a smaller pocket-sized square.

The first section will list your top five reasons why it's worthwhile to work with the steps of *Uncovering Happiness*. These need to be intrinsic, positive reasons in order for your brain to buy them. For example, you might write, "to be a better parent to my kids," "to live with greater ease," or "to be happy."

The next part will list a number of ways to cope when warning signs come. You might grab ideas from the seven steps, such as "See the depression loop," or "Remember, thoughts aren't facts," or "Get out the antidepressant cheat sheet." Having this handy might be just what you need during those times when the brain doesn't seem to be working.

Another square should contain contact information for your Get Well Team. These are people in your life who support you. They may be people you've met who are also reading this book, or maybe they're from some other group, or potentially they're family, friends, or colleagues. It's wonderful if these are people who have experienced depression in the past and can understand what you're experiencing. If not, just having people who are nourishing to you is also good.

The final square is a mindfulness practice that you deem essential to widening the space of awareness in order for you to have a greater chance to access the choice, possibility, and freedom of the moment to engage in what matters. This might be the "Be" practice, a short basic body scan, or maybe ACE.

Here is a sample of the card below:

TOP 5 POSITIVE REASONS FOR STICKING WITH THE PRACTICE	SOME WAYS TO COPE
1. Example: To experience more grace. 2. Example: To be a less reactive father. 3. Example: To experience more joy! 4. 5.	Actions I can take when I notice warning signs coming on: • Recognize the depression loop. • Remember that thoughts aren't facts. • Get present—practice "Be"-ing. • Hand on heart, "What do I need?" • Read antidepressant cheat sheet. • Do an activity on the sheet. • Read letter of encouragement.
GET WELL TEAM MEMBERS (FRIENDS, FAMILY, THERAPIST) 1. Dad 2. Jennifer (friend) 3. Bob (therapist) 4. _____ (your team member)	"BE"-ING SPACE Breathe: take a few deep breaths. Expand awareness throughout body, feeling what's there. (Or fill in your favorite practice.) "What is most important to pay attention to?"

Go ahead and make this square. Have it handy. If you're tech savvy, it's skillful to pair this with something you have with you most of the time, like your cell phone. Plug it into a document that is accessible anywhere, anytime.

Five Strategies to Stick
to Healthy Habits

It's well documented that exercise, diet, and stress reduction are key elements in warding off depression. That's why there's big money in those markets for diet books, exercise workouts, and stress reduction programs that promise significant results. But often when you engage in these prescriptions, you might find that the river flows downhill, and it's hard to make the intended changes stick. The gravity of our everyday lives begins to weigh on us, and we just get pulled back down to the place where we're most comfortable. We can end up isolating ourselves, buying into our mind traps, or reaching for whatever pacifies us.

Here are five steps that underscore any program you choose in making healthy habits stick:

1. Uncover the Purpose (and Play)—Whether it's diet, exercise, or mindfulness, having an awareness of why it's important for you to engage in it is the first step. In his book *Drive: The Surprising Truth About What Motivates Us,* science journalist Daniel Pink highlights the paradigm shift for individuals and businesses: intrinsic motivation is a more powerful driving force than than extrinsic motivation. Exercising to build sculpted abs is not as

motivating as doing it to live a longer life. Practicing mindfulness because it's en vogue and you'll look cool is not as motivating as practicing to be more at ease in life. Find a good intrinsic reason for doing the practice and then play with it, treating it like an experiment, being curious about what you discover.

2. Make a Plan—One of the keys to building motivation is having the belief and hope that you can actually do this. In order to build hope, you need to have a realistic plan that can serve as a map. Whatever program you choose, make sure that you're clear on what your plan is and that it's realistic. Ask yourself, "What do I believe I can do?" and then scale back a bit from there. You want to make sure that the task at hand matches your perceived abilities. If at any point you are feeling particularly low, be kind to yourself and do less that day.

3. Remember the Key to Mastery—When transforming to a healthy lifestyle, embrace a growth mindset. This is not about achieving a certain end goal; it's a learning process toward a healthier life. If and when obstacles arise, rather than seeing them as signs of failure, investigate what happened. What can you learn from this as you continue moving forward?

4. Get a Buddy—Many of us have the rule in our heads that "I can do it on my own." The fact is, you are more likely to actually integrate a new practice if you have others alongside you who are trying to do the same thing. Finding a group of people in your area or on the web that you can connect with is very important to deepening the belief that "I can do this" and sustaining a practice. You can connect through the challenges, learn from others, and feel part of a community. The community also serves as a reminder that people are important in your life.

5. Forgive and Invite—A wise person understands that there will always be obstacles along any road to change. When you notice yourself off the map that you created, congratulate yourself for being present. Stand in that space of awareness and choice to investigate how you got there and to begin again. There's no benefit at all in buying into the NUTty voices. Instead, forgive yourself for straying, and in that space of awareness, invite yourself to begin again. Do this over and over again, each time learning a bit more.

Try out these five steps when integrating a healthier lifestyle. Build them into your routine and have compassion for yourself, as making changes is often a difficult challenge—but one that is entirely attainable.

Three Yoga Poses
for Depression

What we do with our bodies affects our minds and vice versa. Yoga is one of the best practices for giving our bodies the gift they need to cultivate the natural antidepressants of mindfulness, self-compassion, purpose, play, and mastery. Depression is the experience of closing down. Practice the following three very gentle poses, which serve to open us up. As we practice opening our bodies, we also begin to open our hearts and minds.

Sun Breaths

Here is a good pose to start off with that begins a sequence of opening (with a little humor in the name). You can do this sitting or lying down. If you do it outside, you will literally be opening up to the sun. Inhale as you bring the arms straight up over head and reach through the fingertips and exhale as you bring the arms down. Do this five to ten times.

You can also make this a practice where you're connecting with the intentions of uncovering happiness. As the arms go up, you can say, "Breathing in, opening up to more mindfulness in my life," and as the arms go down, say, "Breathing out, letting go negative self-talk." Or "Breathing in, opening to joy" and "Breathing out, letting go of self-loathing."

When you finish, bring mindfulness to the moment, just notice what's there with a warm curiosity. Are you aware of anything that feels more open? Is there more energy circulating in the body? Congratulate yourself for taking this time.

Squat

Our hips often get stiff because of the way we're trained to sit in angular chairs of 90 degrees. Over time the body adapts to this posture, and we lose our natural range of motion. We become less flexible. This is exactly what depression is: a lack of flexibility, but in the mind. One of my good friends and colleagues, Denise Kaufman (of Ace of Cups), is a passionate proponent of teaching us how to squat again. She has started a "squat revolution." She says you can do this anywhere, anytime: while watching TV, talking to a friend, chatting on the phone, reading your iPad, weeding your garden, or when giving someone a shoulder massage. Denise produced a very funny video about it that you can find on YouTube called "The Squat Song." She says that with a simple squatting practice, we can get rid of our back pain, improve circulation, open our hips, stay more limber in life, and help us feel more grounded and connected. The mind will follow.

Squat

If you're ready to move to an unsupported squat, simply aim your buttocks toward the ground and bring your hands together in a prayer position. Enjoy the opening.

Smiling Heart Pose

Many yoga traditions recommend this gentle back bend as a natural antidepressant. The exercise is the perfect self-compassion practice after a difficult day. Amy Weintraub, author of *Yoga for*

Depression: A Compassionate Guide to Relieving Suffering Through Yoga, calls this the Smiling Heart Pose, and you'll need a few props to get started.

1. Grab a pillow, bolster, or folded blanket, and place it right under your back. Adjust it to your body's comfort.
2. Roll a blanket or towel and place it directly under your neck so that your head is positioned in a place of rest.
3. Place a cushion, booster or blanket under your legs, allowing them to be in a relaxed position about hip-width apart.
4. Extend your arms and allow them to rest on the floor, with the palms facing up. If you'd like to play with this, you can also rest your arms overhead.

As you lie here for five minutes or more, understand that this is a time and space where there is nowhere to go, nothing to do, and no problem to solve. You're just here in rest. You can choose just to bring awareness to your body, but if you wish, allow this to be a time to notice your breath as it comes in and goes out. Watch as the whole body naturally expands and contracts. Notice how the body breathes itself without any need for you to control it.

Say to yourself, "Breathing in, [what it is you're wishing for yourself: love, peace, joy]; breathing out, [what you're wanting to let go of: NUTs, stress, judgment]."

Every time you engage in these simple practices, know that you are igniting the natural antidepressants of mindfulness, self-compassion, purpose, play, and mastery. Enjoy!

Five Steps to a
Growth Mindset

The ability to see life as a classroom has enabled me to adopt a growth mindset where my goals are about learning how to apply these principles to my life. In doing this, the setbacks don't hit me so hard, and I can come back sooner to what matters. Over time something must have changed in my brain, because I often notice much of this visiting me as moments of grace. In step 7 I talked about how my client Lisa's willingness to be open to the idea that her abilities weren't fixed allowed her to move with more ease through grief. This growth mindset inevitably helped her notice more choice points to apply what she has learned in the midst of relapse signs to stave off steeper tumbles into depression.

Throughout the days that follow, see if you can apply the following five steps to weave the growth mindset more into your life:

1. Be on the lookout for a fixed mindset. This is the one that says, "Is this the right practice for me" or "Maybe I should be trying something else." Or if you experience yet another relapse, the voice may pipe up, "I've tried this before! I'm just not capable; I'm going to disappoint myself again."

2. In this space of awareness, recognize that you're awake and in a choice point to relate to this moment differently.

3. Feel into the emotion behind the voice. There may be a sense of sadness or fear there. What would it be like to meet it with a tender attention and some self-compassion? Maybe put your hand on your heart and say, "Breathing in, aware of my own suffering; breathing out, may I be at ease."

4. Respond with a growth mindset. If the fixed mindset voice says, "I've tried this before, and I'm just not capable," after recognizing the emotion behind it you can respond with "I have tried something like this before, but this is a new moment, and maybe there is something I can learn from it." If the voice continues to insist that you will fail again, you can counter, "Almost everyone who is effective with their mental health has had setbacks along the way."

5. Take action with the growth mindset. Engage it with the attitude of curiosity and learning. Just like riding a bike, as you continue to do this, your confidence will grow.

Twenty-One Days
of Purpose

You have a purpose in being here, and part of that is remembering that you are part of something much larger than yourself. Science and thousands of years of human experience are showing us that this feeling of connection to something greater than ourselves gives us a heightened sense of well-being and resiliency. In short, it's a natural antidepressant. I want to invite you to an experiment that can help you nurture this positive shift in your brain but also positively impact the world around you. You can try this experiment on your own, or it can be fun to do with friends. Let others know what you're up to and see the ripple effects of a group doing Twenty-One Days of Purpose.

Instructions

Look back on step 5, about what you value, why you would engage these values, and what you *can* do. Choose one of your actionable prosocial values that you've uncovered and commit to Twenty-One Days of Purpose. Below is an example of what this can look like:

THREE DAILY QUESTIONS

1. What prosocial purpose am I focusing on?
2. What action *can* I take today that is in line with this purpose?
3. What is this action in service of that is greater than myself?

THREE DAILY ANSWERS (SAMPLE):

1. What prosocial purpose am I focusing on?
   (a) Compassion
2. What action *can* I take today that is in line with this purpose?
   (a) Money. Every day for twenty-one days, I could give a little money to a cause I care about.
   (b) Time. I can share through friends and social media why this cause matters and what they can do about it. And I can take time to volunteer, alone or with friends.
   (c) Fame. I can set a plan for myself to focus on joining forces with larger organizations and create an event or program and use my notoriety to gain the attention of the masses for important causes.
3. What is this action in service of that is greater than myself? Here are some examples:
   (a) Undernutrition contributes to the deaths of 5.6 million children worldwide each year. My efforts with the organization Save the Children can save the mental and physical lives of a generation of children. Improving their lives is likely to have ripple effects across all the lives that they in turn touch.
   (b) Approximately one hundred million people in the

United States breathe air that is below federal air quality standards. My efforts in organizations that help clean the air improve the quality of life for millions of people.

(c) In the last thirty years, the rate of childhood obesity has tripled among children ages six to eleven. This leads to a broad range of physical and mental health problems. The work I do to raise awareness of this can change the lives of many children and their relationships for years to come.

Take a moment to really think about what this might look like for you. If you want help in finding causes to support or to be a part of something larger, a great place to start is Charity Navigator (www.charitynavigator.org). Once you get some ideas, to help you with carrying out Twenty-One Days of Purpose, go to my website (www.elishagoldstein.com) to set up a free automatic email reminder that will prompt you to stay on task. The email will simply remind you of the questions and give a short inspiration. Here you'll also find access to a community of others who are engaging in this process for ideas, support, and connection to share and be inspired by all the different ideas and experiences of a community doing Twenty-One Days of Purpose. Since I can't be with you in person, this is my way of supporting you beyond this book.

Strengthen Your
Natural Antidepressants:
Longer Practices

Throughout this book, you were introduced to several mindfulness practices. If you're in a moderate-to-severe depressive episode right now, I'd suggest skipping this section until you start to feel a bit better. If you're feeling anywhere from the blues to well, here's an opportunity to deepen your positive experience with the natural antidepressants of mindfulness, self-compassion, purpose/compassion, play, and mastery. The purpose of setting aside longer periods of time for these specific practices is to help prime your mind to drop into those spaces of awareness and clarity more often in your daily life. Studies find that the more intentional attention we give to these practices, the more we see brain change. This helps us reprogram a healthier autopilot in ourselves.

However, creating the space in a busy day for longer periods of practice can seem incredibly difficult sometimes. Yet at the same time, we create space every day with ease. We intentionally set aside time to go to work, drive our car, go out to dinner—even read this book. Probably the number one mind trap that arises in reaction to the notion of creating space for practice is, "I don't have time." What would happen if you were aware of this thought, but instead of grasping onto it, you let it fall away? Ask yourself this question once again: "Where can I create space for five, ten, fifteen or more minutes a day to deepen my practice?" Then see what comes up. Keep letting the thought of "I have no time" come and go until a new thought arises.

Can you wake up ten minutes early? Is there a space and time at your job where you can stop and practice? Maybe even sitting in your car after work and before you enter the house? Oftentimes people like it later in the evening when the lights are out and there is a natural stillness to settle down into one of these practices.

Creating a space for practice in your home, office, or outdoors can help incline you to settle in. In this space, you can clear away any possible distractions such as alarms or cell phones. Some people like to have certain pillows and blankets available to make them comfortable while sitting or lying down. Others have some objects around that carry the meanings of calm, wisdom, effectiveness, balance, or love. These are objects to remind us of our intentions for uncovering happiness.

Again, bring a spirit of playfulness and experiment with this exercise. Each practice has a link to audio or video that you can watch to help you get started. If you have created a Get Well Team, you can support one another to stick to the practices and even get together weekly to practice and discuss your experience with them. See what works for you, and try one out for a week at a time.

Think about when you can clear away five minutes a day to start these practices. If you want to start with more time, all the better. If time goes by, and obstacles arise that prohibit you from practicing, know that as soon as you realize this, you are present and in a space of awareness and choice. In this space, you can once again look at your day and see where you can train your mind to be.

If you have the time right now, let's give it a go.

The Compassionate Body Scan

The body scan is a classic mindfulness practice where you go through each part of the body, from the feet to the head, feeling the sensations from the inside out. Whenever the mind wanders off, you just note where it wandered to and gently guide it back. The Compassionate Body Scan adds in another element. With each body part, you take a moment to appreciate that it's functioning and how it allows to you to be alive in the world. For example, feel into the feet and notice all the sensations there: warmth or coolness, wetness or dryness, achiness or itchness, pulsing, pressure. Or maybe it's just neutral. Then you notice that here are these two feet, relatively small compared with the rest of the body, that allow you to walk, balance, and maybe drive a car. You then spend a moment holding all the sensations of the feet with appreciation.

After leading people through any body scan, I always ask, "How was that different from how you normally pay attention to your body?" The overwhelming response is "That's assuming that I normally pay attention to it." When I add in the layer of appreciative awareness, most people find that concept to be even more foreign. Living a short distance from our bodies and taking them for granted is an epidemic in our culture. Since the body is a barometer that tells us how we're doing from moment to moment, it would behoove us to develop a greater intimacy with it.

The Compassionate Body Scan is focused on doing just that.

The following steps will guide you through preparing for the practice, and then they will take you through a step-by-step guide to deepen your connection to the body and train your mind to use your body as a barometer. It will help you notice physiological relapse signs of depression and allow you to break free from the depressive loop when it arrives.

Preparing for Practice

1. Set aside ten, twenty, or thirty minutes to sit or lie down. Use this time to slowly bring awareness to the sensations in your body. Move your focus progressively from your feet to your head. Sensations may include heat, coolness, tingling, itchiness, wetness, dryness, pressure, heaviness, lightness, and even pain. Use a timer or alarm to remind you when the time is up. You can also use the Insight Timer app previously mentioned in step 6. Don't worry if you haven't made it through your whole body when the time is up. The purpose isn't to complete feeling the sensations of the whole body from head to toe but simply to practice dropping into spaces of awareness and mindfully attending to the direct experience of your body as it is right now.

2. Remember to bring an appreciative awareness to each body part, considering how it enables you to function in the world. For example, if it's the arms, you might consider how they allow you to hug other people, balance, or signal with a wave of communication.

3. Remember to also bring a playful awareness to this practice; when your mind wanders off, think of it as a puppy and practice "*See, touch, go.*" *This is a term from* The Now Effect, *where you "see" where the mind has wandered, "touch," or spend a moment with the thought, and then gently "go" back to paying attention to the body.* Keep the intention to bring a kind and caring attention to your body, allowing and welcoming whatever is there without judgment. You can treat this as a game, starting with a short practice and building up slowly.

4. Be aware of the spaces when you move from one part of your body to the next. Recognize that this space holds a choice: you

can intentionally guide your attention to the next part of your body.

Step-by-Step Instructions

1. Mindful Check-in. Notice the position of your body. What emotions are present? What thoughts are filtering through your mind? Are there any judgments or resistance? Is your mind telling you that there are more important things to do? Whatever is there, see if you can just acknowledge it and let it be.

2. Breath as an Anchor. Begin to gently shift to noticing your body's breathing. Imagine that it's the first time you've ever noticed your breath. Where do you feel it? What is the sensation like? Continue this for about a minute or until it feels right to move on.

3. Your Feet and Ankles. Bring your attention into your feet, and welcome any feelings that are there. As with the rest of this practice, if there are no feelings, notice what it's like to experience an absence of sensations. Consider the function of the feet and ankles and how they allow you to relate to the world. Before moving up your legs, notice that you are in a space of awareness with the choice to move your attention. Now intentionally move your attention.

4. Your Legs. Slowly guide your awareness up either one leg at a time or both legs at once. Dip your awareness into your body, feeling and allowing what is there. Notice sensations in your calves, shins, knees, and upper legs with the hamstring muscles in back and the quadriceps muscles in front. Sense the density of this area of the body. Consider the function of these legs and

what they allow you to do. Can you hold them in appreciation? Before moving on to your hips, notice again the space of awareness between stimulus and response.

5. Your Hips. Become aware of your entire hip region. Notice and be open to any sensations in your buttocks, the sides of your hips, and your genitals. What are the gifts of this region? If for any reason this area of the body triggers an emotional reaction for you due to past trauma, please be sensitive to that and go at your own pace.

6. Your Torso. You can bring your attention to your back and then move to the front or do the whole area at once. If you choose to do them separately, go up the back vertebra by vertebra and sense any feelings that arise with curiosity and without judgment. When you get to the abdominal region, breathe into your abdomen and notice it expand. Then breathe out and notice it fall. The abdomen and chest are often places where people hold emotions such as fear, love, and restlessness, among others. If you come across any emotions there, see them as simply sensations in the body. Name them and let them be. Consider what this part of the body gives you. It holds the ability to digest food and encases two vital systems of circulation in the heart and ventilation in the lungs. Ask yourself, how does the torso allow me to relate to the world around me?

7. Your Shoulders. This is another area that can retain tension. Being present about what's here may prime your mind to be more aware of tension you hold in your shoulders during the day, so if you notice that your shoulders are tight, it may trigger your mind into letting them relax. Can you hold the sensations with appreciation? If your mind has been skipping over the

space between one part of the body and the next, bring back the awareness now.

8. Your Face and Head. As you scan your face, be aware of any points of pressure. This is often a sign of resistance. You can let these points soften or just notice the sensations as they are. Consider that here is an area that holds so many senses from taste and smell to sight and hearing. If you have these senses, can you hold the sensations here with gratitude?

9. Back to the Breath. To end the body scan, spend another minute riding the breath with the awareness, curiosity, and sense of welcoming that you intended throughout the practice.

10. Thank Yourself for Taking This Time. This may seem trivial, but it sends the message internally that you care about your well-being. It also helps sow the seeds of resiliency.

Of course, if you don't want to practice on your own, check out the audio on my website Compassionate Body Scan to guide you.

Movie in Your Mind

Movie in Your Mind is an integrative practice that provides the experience of intentionally bringing your attention to a variety of things, eventually leading to new thoughts. As we practice relating *to* our thoughts instead of *from* our thoughts, the spaces of awareness begin to open up. This allows us to be freer from the mind traps that arise when we get stuck overidentifying with our thoughts.

Preparing for Practice

1. Set aside ten, fifteen, or thirty minutes to sit either in a chair or on the floor. There are six steps to this practice, so depending on the amount of time you allot to it, break up each step equally.

2. If you sit on the floor, you can sit on cushions to help your posture. You'll want to have a straight yet comfortable spine to support being awake. If for any reason you are uncomfortable sitting, you can lie down. Use a timer or alarm to remind you when the time is up.

3. Remember to bring some playfulness to this exercise, so when your mind wanders off, practice what I recommended earlier— think of it as a puppy and practice "*See, touch, go.*" Hold the intention to bring a kind and caring attention to the activity, allowing and welcoming whatever is there to be as it is without judgment. You can treat this as a game, starting with a short practice and building up slowly.

4. As you breathe, notice the space between one breath and the next. Focus on the time between the moment your mind becomes stimulated to shift to the next part of the practice and the moment it is actually shifting. Be aware that it is a choice.

5. If you're doing this on your own, that is perfectly fine. The purpose isn't to get through all the steps but simply to play with what's there.

6. If your mind comes up with a story of how there is no time to do a longer practice such as this or it says that you'll get to it sometime later, without any specific suggestions as to when,

simply see the net effect of that thought. It's the autopilot at work, and it's unlikely that you will make the time to do this in the future. *Now* is the time; it's the *only* time.

Step-by-Step Instructions

1. Mindful Check-in. Begin this practice with a mindful check-in, sensing how you are at the moment.

2. The Breath as an Anchor. Use the breath as a means of beginning to steady your mind. Notice the spaces between inhalation and exhalation.

3. Feel Your Body. Unlike in the body scan, in this practice, we notice the entire field of sensations. There may be some parts of the body that have more sensation than others; there may be moments when you notice a sensation that increases in intensity, and then, as you get curious and play with it, it passes gently, demonstrating the impermanent nature of all things.

4. Hear the Sounds Around You. Just as we can be aware of the breath and sensations in the body, we can be aware of sounds and hearing. Sounds come in the form of pitches, tones, and frequency. A sound also has the quality of coming and going, like sensations and the breath. There are also spaces between sounds. As you pay attention to sounds, you may notice associated images running through your mind. *See, touch, go* with these as you prepare to peer at your thoughts.

5. See Your Thoughts. In the same way that we can be aware of sounds, we can bring attention into the mind to notice our thoughts. This is a bit more abstract, so it helps to use metaphors or images to describe how to do this. Imagine sitting in

a movie theater and looking at the scenes and actors on the screen. We are not in the movie but are watching it unfold. In this same way, watch the appearances and disappearances of thoughts in your mind. As one thought disappears, is there a space before the next one? At times you may notice that you're getting caught up or lost in the story of your thoughts, as often occurs when we watch a movie. When this happens, *see, touch, go.*

6. The Breath as an Anchor. Come back to where you started to end this practice.

7. Create Some Simple Gesture. Do this to acknowledge your effort to take this time out for yourself. This leaves an imprint in your memory of caring for yourself, which makes it easier to recall later on.

Of course, if you don't want to practice on your own, use the audio on my website Movie in Your Mind to guide you.

Lovingkindness Meditation

Lovingkindness practice has been called the healer of fear, and you got to experience some of it in step 4's work with self-compassion. Though many know this process as a *metta* practice from Buddhist philosophy, the idea of lovingkindness has been found among many peoples. The Greeks called it *agape.* The Jews practiced *chesed.* Christians practiced *centering prayer.* Getting in touch with our hearts is something that millions of people have found helpful when cultivating more kindness toward themselves, their community, and the world.

Note: notice if any judgments arise, such as "This can't help me," "I've tried this once in the past or something like it, forget it," or "This sounds woo-woo." These judgments are strong, underlying habits of the mind trying to maintain the status quo. Practice "*See, touch, go,*" and gently return your attention to the practice.

In this practice, we are cultivating intentions, wishes, or aspirations, starting with someone that you care about. Next, we move on to ourselves; after that, to someone who is neutral; then to someone with whom we are having difficulty; and, finally, to our community and the world. This is not an affirmation practice, as we are not telling ourselves something that is not there at the moment; we are simply wishing ourselves and others to be happy, healthy, free from harm, and free from fear.

You can come up with your own wishes for yourself, but they should be things that you can also wish for others.

You may do this for five, ten, fifteen, or even thirty minutes. If you choose a shorter amount of time, you can begin by doing only the first few steps and building up from there as time goes on.

The Phrases

The following are some examples of phrases you can use for yourself and others during this practice.

May I be safe and protected from inner and outer harm.
May I be truly happy and deeply peaceful.
May I live my life with ease.
May I have love and compassion for myself.
May I love myself completely, just the way I am.
May I be free.

Step-by-Step Instructions

1. Mindful Check-in. Take a seat, feel your body, and notice how you are doing in this moment, physically and emotionally.

2. Focus on a Friend. Picture a living person you really care about; someone you are on good terms with and whom it is easy to wish well. You can also choose an animal that you love. With intention, connecting to your heart, repeat the phrases a few times as if you were speaking them to this friend. To prime the heart a bit more, you may want to do this with another friend before bringing the focus on yourself.

3. Focus on You. Continue by wishing the same phrases for yourself. This may be difficult, as you may feel a lot of pent-up unworthiness. At times, a feeling of sadness may arise along with compassion. If this is challenging, you can also imagine the friend you just focused on saying the phrases to you. Take this practice at your own pace, knowing that even experimenting with it is moving you in the direction of greater self-love.

4. Focus on an Acquaintance. Consider someone you don't know too well, maybe a checkout clerk at the store, a friend of a friend, or a person you seem to see everywhere but have never met. Picture that person in front of you and wish him or her the same phrases.

5. Focus on a Difficult Person. When choosing a difficult person, make sure that he or she is not *the most* difficult person in your life or someone with whom you've experienced extreme trauma. Instead, pick someone who frustrates or annoys you. If you're feeling resistance, it may be helpful to reflect upon who actually suffers mentally and physically from resentments

and grudges. With this practice, we can start to neutralize such feelings, unlock the door to forgiveness, and begin to heal. See if you can get in touch with your heart in the same way that you did for your friend earlier, and wish this person well with the phrases. If you continue to struggle, recognize that you are suffering and then turn the lovingkindness back to yourself.

6. Focus on a Community. Some people have a community to which they feel connected. This might be a religious community, a school community, a group of friends, or even your city. Get a sense of the whole community, say, "May we all be well," and then follow with the remaining phrases. You might even consider the connection of all humans on the planet. Imagine: if we all felt well and safe, there likely wouldn't be any need for war. So why not wish wellness for everyone?

7. Mindful Check-in. End this practice with a mindful check-in, thanking yourself for taking the time out of all your daily busyness; this is an act of self-love.

Of course, if you don't want to practice on your own, check out the audio for Lovingkindness Practice on my website to guide you.

Sky of Awareness Meditation

The intention of the Sky of Awareness Meditation is to cultivate a spacious open-mindedness and give you the experience of the reality that underneath all the thoughts, sensations, and emotions is a grounded loving awareness. You'll be opening your attention to an unfolding of sounds, thoughts, body, and breath. The wonderful thing about this practice is that you can do it anywhere and anytime because the environment is the only equipment needed.

Preparing for Practice

1. Set aside ten, fifteen, or thirty minutes to sit, stand, or lie down. There are six steps to this practice, so depending on the amount of time you allot to it, as best you can, allot the same amount of time to each step.

2. Remember to bring a sense of curiosity and playfulness to this practice, treating it as an experiment that includes neither good nor bad. Hold the intention to bring a kind and caring attention to yourself, allowing and welcoming whatever is there to be as it is without judgment. You can treat this as a game, devoting a short time to it and then building up slowly.

3. If you're doing this without audio guidance, that is perfectly fine. As always, the purpose isn't to get through the entire practice but to play with your attention, continuing to bring it back gently to the present moment.

4. If your mind sends this to the bottom of your to-do list, investigate whether that is really what you want to do or if that is your autopilot.

Step-by-Step Instructions

1. Mindful Check-in. As with previous practices, start by acknowledging what's present in this space physically, emotionally, and mentally.

2. Sounds. Whereas with other practices we began with the breath, this is different. Take a moment to imagine that your

awareness is as big as the physical space you are in right now. Notice the sounds rising and fading. Next, allow your awareness to go beyond the borders of the room, spreading throughout the sky. It is infinitely expansive, without boundaries.

3. Thoughts. Within this vast and wide awareness, there are also thoughts that come in the form of talking and images. Proceed by opening and welcoming the thoughts that are there along with the sounds. Just practice allowing what's there to be as it is.

4. Body. Consider for a moment that your body is simply a collection of physical sensations that come and go within this sky of awareness. Allow the image of a physical body with boundaries to dissolve, and the feelings, thoughts and sounds that are there to filter within this awareness. There is plenty of room for all of it, and you are just watching, experiencing, and opening the space. See if you can connect with the feeling of being awareness itself, grounded, spacious, and open.

5. Breath. Now bring in the breath and practice open-mindedness, allowing all of the phenomena to shift, change, appear, and disappear within your sky of awareness.

6. Make a Small Gesture Inward. Thank yourself for taking this time out for practice.

Of course, if you don't want to practice on your own, check out the audio for Sky of Awareness on my website to guide you.

Uncovering Happiness:
The Recap

In this day and age, when our brains have become so accustomed to shorter messages, it's helpful to have a recap of the book that is short, simple, and to the point. That way, when you're out with a friend over coffee or tea, and she asks, "What's all this new stuff you're doing?" you can discuss it easily because you understand. In the following pages, I'm going to give you the coffee-talk version as well as a version you can fit into a status update.

Status Update

When you hear the word *antidepressant*, you think of a pill. Science is now showing us that we all have natural antidepressants within us that can be accessed and cultivated. They can become enduring to prevent relapse, allow us to live with more ease and grace, and let us fundamentally uncover happiness.

ELISHA GOLDSTEIN, PhD

Coffee-Talk Version

When it comes to the field of depression, the most prevalent marketing for healing is pharmaceutical antidepressants. While these can be helpful, thousands of years of experience, now combined with current scientific research, is showing us that we also have natural antidepressants. These can be accessed and cultivated to not only overcome depression but also uncover happiness. This approach has seven steps. The first two are:

1. Understand how the depression loop works, and
2. Know our bad habits that keep us stuck.

From here we can nurture five natural antidepressants:

3. Mindfulness—awareness and also deliberately paying attention to the present moment while putting aside our programmed biases.
4. Self-compassion—the ability to understand that we're suffering with an inclination to help ourselves,
5. Purpose—The sense that you have something to contribute to the world.
6. Play—A flexible state of mind in which you are presently engaged in some freely chosen and potentially purposeless activity that you find interesting, enjoyable, and satisfying.
7. Mastery—a feeling of personal control and confidence that is best developed with the mindset of learning versus achievement.

Finally, a tool kit of tips can help you strengthen the seven steps.

Recap: Chapter by Chapter

Introduction

Research has shown that having experienced depression in the past can induce a sense of learned helplessness, which teaches us to stop trying to help ourselves in the face of future pain and even prevents us from learning new ways to prevent relapse. Depression is more prevalent than we realize, and the World Health Organization predicts it will be the second greatest killer behind heart disease by 2020. Relapse rates are high. Depression doesn't discriminate, and it affects us all differently. Some people function throughout life with a low-grade chronic unhappiness, while others become incapacitated with rolling bouts of self-loathing and a murky maze of feelings that take residence in the mind and body. For the first time, science is ahead of the disease. We now know that we can deactivate the area of the brain that is involved with snowballing automatic negative thoughts. We can grow new neural connections in areas associated with awareness, learning, memory, and even empathy. We know that from here, natural antidepressants emerge and can be strengthened to support resiliency during difficult times—in addition to uncovering a more meaningful and happier life.

Part 1: A Naturally Antidepressant Brain

CHAPTER 1:
UNDERSTAND THE DEPRESSION LOOP

There are four things happening that comprise someone's experience in any given moment: thoughts, emotions, sensations, and behavior. When it comes to depression, these four elements use one another to create a depressive feedback loop. While nobody knows what the causes of depression are, we do know that as this feedback loop repeats over time, it becomes a conditioned habit. A single stimulus or cue such as a negative thought or tiredness in the body can trigger the looping to occur. Yet having had depression in the past doesn't mean you're fated to have it the rest of your life. Understanding how the depressive loop works is the first step to stepping outside of it, gaining perspective, and moving into a space of choice, possibility, and freedom.

CHAPTER 2:
REVERSE BAD HABITS

There are two types of bad habits that sustain a depressive loop: mental bad habits and behavioral bad habits. Mental bad habits include believing that you *are* your thoughts, while typical behavioral bad habits encompass being a couch potato, procrastination, overchecking social networking sites, working, drinking, smoking, shopping, and so forth. To get started in reversing mental bad habits, we have to understand that thoughts aren't facts; neither the ones that tell us how deficient we are—NUTs (Negative Unconscious Thoughts)—nor the ones that tell us how great we are. To start reversing behavioral bad habits, we need to identify the cues in our internal or external environments, investigate the body's emotional response, and replace it with a healthier activity. One of the most powerful forces of change is people, and so it's helpful to join forces with others to undo bad habits. As we approach these habits with an eye of curiosity and learning, the brain becomes primed to notice them as they're occurring. The moment we notice it, we've stepped into a space of awareness in which we can choose that healthier response.

Part 2: The Five Natural Antidepressants

CHAPTER 3:
CHANGE THE BRAIN THROUGH MINDFULNESS

The foundation of your natural antidepressants starts with mindfulness, also known as awareness. It's the act of intentionally paying attention to the here and now while putting aside our programmed biases. We know that negative self-judgments are major cues for the depressive loop. The brain's strategy to see the depressive loop as a problem and attempt to fix it by rehashing past events or rehearsing future ones only digs us deeper into the loop. Neuroscientists are finding that rumination and mindfulness are inversely correlated. Try worrying about yourself while being fully present to the flavor of your tea. It doesn't work. Scientists have also found that mindfulness training can make us less reactive to things that are startling. This has important implications for training our brains to be less reactive to depressive cues and planting the seeds of contentment, calm, and joy.

CHAPTER 4:
NURTURE SELF-COMPASSION AND ITS WONDERFUL SIDE EFFECTS

Neuroscience has shown us that when we're feeling good, the left side of the prefrontal cortex, right behind our foreheads, lights up; and when we're feeling depressed, the right side lights up. We now know that the skill of compassion allows us to intentionally activate the states of the brain that provide an experience of resiliency. Studies also point to the notion that we can train our brains to react to suffering with compassion as opposed to aversion or disgust. When we naturally react to our suffering with self-compassion instead of self-loathing, we flip the depressive loop on its head. Self-compassion is a skill, and we can learn how to apply self-compassion breaks to uncover this natural antidepressant. We can also learn to experience self-compassion's wonderfully resilient side effects and uncover happiness with hope, gratitude, joy, patience, forgiveness, connection, and wisdom.

CHAPTER 5:
LIVE WITH PURPOSE—KNOW WHY YOU MATTER
AND WHAT YOU CAN DO ABOUT IT

Multiple research studies have confirmed that money can't buy happiness, except if you're giving it away. Depression is a self-absorbed experience of disconnection where we can't get away from ourselves. Purpose is a 180-degree shift. It's about getting outside of yourself and discovering what you have to contribute to the world. You begin to understand that you're not an island and that your actions have ripple effects. Purpose is akin to the act of compassion—knowing others are less fortunate or suffering, and choosing to help. Science shows that compassion and altruism support health and well-being. Discovering how you'd like to be remembered can help get you in touch with your values and what matters most to you. It can kick this natural antidepressant into gear. You can start with Twenty-One Days of Purpose.

CHAPTER 6:
GO OUT AND PLAY—REDISCOVERING THE JOY OF LIFE

One of the great play researchers of all time, Brian Sutton-Smith, argues that the opposite of play is not work, it's depression. Play includes having novel things to engage with in our environments (toys) and people to enjoy them with (playmates). Research shows that when toys and playmates are taken away from people, they experience symptoms of depression. The depression loop is fueled by negative emotions, self-judgments, disengagement, helplessness, and isolation. Play inspires the exact opposite qualities and siphons off this fuel. The act of play is filled with positive emotions, and is engaging, satisfying, connecting, and social. Play opens up a more flexible mind, beckoning us to seek out novel thoughts and actions in response to the task at hand. As we continue to play, we become more flexible and creative in the way that we approach things, including the depression loop—fostering a happier and more resilient brain.

CHAPTER 7:
LEARN TO GET BETTER AND BETTER

The common definition of mastery is a feeling of personal control, and who wouldn't want more of that? However, what most people don't think about is the most effective approach to mastery. Research shows that cultivating mastery over something is most successful when we approach it with the mindset of learning versus performance. A learning mindset not only helps you to be more creative when overcoming obstacles but also allows you to achieve more—and it's a lot more fun, too. This is the golden thread that weaves together all the previous steps and sets you up for success. You begin to engage a form of activity scheduling where you take a look at what you're *doing* in the day and begin to replace neutral or depleting activities with what you've learned through the previous steps in this book. This takes some effort, but with a learning mindset, you will be less affected by obstacles and more forgiving and resilient about the inevitable bumps in the road.

Uncovering Happiness: The Discussion Guide

Change is best experienced when we get to bounce ideas around with other people. You might have thoughts and questions, and you might want to share your own stories that have come up while reading this book. There may have been things you connected with while reading, and others you didn't. Maybe ideas and experiences that have helped you weren't mentioned here. Interacting with other people around *Uncovering Happiness* makes the wisdom within you come alive, which will benefit you and others. Here are twenty questions to start the conversation.

1. Has Elisha Goldstein convinced you that you actually have natural antidepressants that can be cultivated like a skill? If so, which ones have you experienced at this point? If not, why?

2. In what way have your natural antidepressants affected you personally, in your relationships, as a parent, with colleagues, or even in your spiritual life? What are some real-life examples?

3. Which of the steps did you find easy? Which ones were more difficult? Do you find yourself going after the "easy successes,"

engaging mostly with the simple steps? What are some possible things you can learn from engaging in the more difficult steps?

4. In terms of mental bad habits, what have you found are your top five NUTs? Do you notice that other people have these same voices in their minds? What happens to you when you recognize you're not alone?

5. What behavioral bad habits have you identified that cue the depressive loop? Have you been able to identify what you really need in moments of depression? What are some ideas and ways you can learn to swap out unhealthy habits for healthier ones?

6. Have you been able to engage in any mindfulness in your daily life? How is this different from how you normally pay attention throughout the day? How can you see this as being a helpful moment when the brain gets cued into a depressive loop? Do you have any real-life stories of incorporating mindfulness?

7. What is your current "go-to" practice to widen that space between stimulus and response? If you don't have one, what are some ideas that you can begin to integrate into your life?

8. This book holds self-compassion as a primary healing element for uncovering happiness and cultivating an antidepressant brain. Have there been any moments where you have had the opportunity to practice self-compassion? If so, what did it look like, and what did you notice? If not, why? What were the obstacles?

9. How might you structure your environment to encourage self-compassion? Are there any signs you can put up to remind you? Are there people you can have more contact with that support this way of relating to yourself? Who are those people? How can you contact them more?

10. When thinking about what you have to contribute to this world, what comes up for you? Is there a space for purpose in the work that you do? Where does it come in with family and friends? Can you relate to this as an act of compassion?

11. *Uncovering Happiness* devotes an entire section to purposeful living. At work, at home, with your friends, are you living a purposeful life? Given all you have to do in a day, where can you fit in purposeful acts?

12. The Tool Kit includes an invitation to experiment with Twenty-One Days of Purpose. Can you start it now or get a few people together and try this out? What is more important than engaging what matters most in life, and if you are waiting, why?

13. Has there ever been anything that falls under the category of play that you've avoided for reasons such as "It's a waste of my time" or "It seems too indulgent"? See if you can become aware of the obstacles. How can you move past them?

14. Are you in a position to delegate any tasks that may free up some time to pursue the things you really want to pursue?

15. Is there anything you've ever wanted to learn or master that you have set aside because of self-defeating thoughts such as "There

isn't enough time" or "I'll never be good at that" or "I'd rather watch television"? If thoughts aren't facts, what's really getting in your way? What would be there if these thoughts weren't there?

16. Elisha talks about the difference between a fixed mindset and a growth mindset. What things does your mind say you "can't" do? What is the evidence for that, and what is the evidence against that? Is there a possibility that the thought is not a fact? Can you learn to get better?

17. Elisha laid out the importance of noticing your personal depression loop, reversing bad habits, and cultivating the natural antidepressants of mindfulness, self-compassion, purpose, play, and mastery. Is there anything else you find to be a natural antidepressant that already resides in you?

18. Our ability goes up dramatically when we believe we can change. Belief goes up dramatically when we're part of a community that believes in us. Would finding others to take this journey with you support you in doing the work to nourish an antidepressant brain and uncover happiness?

19. Is Elisha underplaying the difficulty of depression? Does his view of natural antidepressants seem too Pollyannaish?

20. What are the things that make you truly happy? Now reflect on the past week and consider how many moments were dedicated to doing those things? Can you learn to bring more of them into your life?

What are some questions that you've come up with? Write them down here and bring them into the group discussion.*

_____

_____

_____

_____

---

* You may or may not know that I blog frequently to bring together the community. If you have any additional questions, send them to me at elisha@elishagoldstein.com.

Find Out More

The essence of uncovering happiness is staying connected. I know that approaches to depression are evolving constantly. I'm a big believer in the wisdom of community and am also interested in what you have to say about what works for you and how you can integrate it in ways that will be supportive to many people. Please feel free to contact me personally at elisha@elishagoldstein .com and let me know your thoughts. Your interactions here can have ripple effects that support thousands of others.

You can also get up-to-date information, writings, audio, video, info on where I'll be in person, and access to my news-letter with 365 Daily Now Moments to keep you honest at www.elishagoldstein.com.

Acknowledgments

This is not *my* book, it is the book of countless people before me who have talked about, written about, researched, and lived the elements of uncovering happiness. This book wouldn't exist if it weren't for my teachers, friends and colleagues, who, through their direct guidance, have helped me uncover what it means to live mindfully and compassionately in daily life: Viktor Frankl, Thich Nhat Hanh, Jack Kornfield, Jon Kabat-Zinn, Bob Stahl, Dan Siegel, Rick Hanson, Susan Kaiser Greenland, Pema Chodron, Tara Brach, Tim Ryan, Jim Gimian, Barry Boyce, Trudy Goodman, Christiane Wolf, Roger Nolan, Ron Alexander, Richard Davidson, Zindel Segal, Mark Williams, John Teasdale, Kristin Neff, Christopher Germer, Brene Brown, Sharon Salzberg, Stephen Porges, Pat Ogden, James Baraz, Mark Feenstra, and Dacher Keltner. I am also indebted to Babette Rothschild, a renowned trauma therapist, who originally came to me with the idea of writing a book on depression. I feel deep gratitude to Julia Cameron for helping me uncover my creative soul, and to Jaak Panksepp, Mihalyi Csikzentmihalyi, and Stuart Brown for their incredible work in bringing the importance of play back into adult life. I also want to acknowledge some great journalists: Charles Duhigg for providing all his research into the power of

259

habits and Daniel Pink for reminding us that our greatest motivators are on the inside. Carol Dweck's work confirmed for me the important thread that is woven throughout the book: seeing life through the lens of learning is the most powerful way to gain mastery and confidence with uncovering happiness.

I hold deep gratitude for my patients and students, who have trusted me enough to let me into their hearts and have given me permission to use some of their stories in this book (with pseudonyms), and have also been some of my greatest teachers.

I am so grateful to have found Leah Pearlman of Dharmacomics .com, who is not only incredibly gifted in creating the comics in this book, but has an enormous heart of generosity. Stefanie Goldstein gave up many of her evenings and afternoons to create the wonderful drawings in this book; I can't thank her enough. I also want to acknowledge Beatrice Dumin and Ashley Graber for extending themselves to bring my work out into the world. To my friends Ari and Olisa Klaristenfeld at We Are A-OK for listening to my ideas and creating an amazing presence for them on the web.

Thank you to John Grohol, CEO of PsychCentral.com, all the editors at *The Huffington Post*, and Barry Boyce at Mindful.org for allowing me to write for them all these years on the intersection of mindfulness and psychotherapy. Thank you to all who are part of The Now Effect community and the regular readers of my blogs; I've enjoyed interacting with you along the way. Your comments, questions, and stories have created wisdom that I've benefited from.

A long list of friends, family, colleagues, and students read early drafts of *Uncovering Happiness* or added input at various stages: Beatrice Dumin, Therese Borchard, Lisa Ray, Jan Goldstein, Stefanie Goldstein, Bonnie Goldstein, Jane Wick, Steve Nelson, Donna Gregory, Stephanie Tade, Daniel Siegel, and Tony

Yollin gave me helpful suggestions. Special thanks to Alice Lesch Kelly, who did a wonderful job with her incredible editing, guidance, and creative idea for the acronym NUTs.

I am blessed to have a brilliant and loving literary agent in Stephanie Tade, who has been a great gift, being there for me to talk out ideas, bat around titles, and carefully guide me with great love. We're fortunate to have a wonderful editor at Atria Books, Johanna Castillo, along with her assistant Kaitlyn Zafonte, both of whom have great eyes for how to make good things great.

I couldn't have written this without the support of my parents, Jan, Jane, Steve, and Bonnie, for their consistent love, support, and belief in me. My sisters Yaffa, Batsheva, and Shira, and my brother, Ari, have also opened up doors of inspiration, creativity, and hope. All of my nieces and nephews, including Asher, Isabella, Chaz, Shai, Tali, Max, Gabrielle, Jonas, Hillel, and Destiny, are great guides in the art of play. Marion and Matt Solomon have gone above and beyond for me personally and professionally, and for that I feel deep gratitude. Thank you to my in-laws, Judy and George Nassif, who have also encouraged and loved me along the way. I also want to thank my in-laws Audrey and Karl Jacobs and Randy Kessel.

I chose to dedicate this book to my two favorite boys on this planet, Lev and Bodhi, who are in every way my teachers for uncovering happiness. They give me so many opportunities to practice mindfulness, self-compassion, purpose, play, and mastery. May you continue a lifetime of uncovering happiness. The threads of your lives are woven in my heart forever.

Finally, to my greatest supporter, advocate, friend, and partner in this life, Stefanie Goldstein. She is my guide in living with a wise and open heart. I have also found so much joy and meaning in sharing our work of service together that has so far led to our eight-week program CALM—Connecting Adolescents to Learning Mindfulness and eventually will expand to helping others with *Raising a Mindful Family*. I am so blessed and happy to share this life with you.

To you, the reader, for intentionally making the active choice to take time out of all your daily busyness to pay attention to your life and uncover your happiness. This is a radical act of self-love. Thank you, thank you, thank you.

Notes

Introduction

xi *once described depression as a dryness of the heart*: Mahatma Gandhi in a letter dated April 22, 1914, hinting at domestic discord, though the addressee is not known, *The Collected Works of Mahatma Gandhi*, Supplementary Volume (Government of India, 1994).

xi *Dalai Lama referred to it as*: Dalai Lama, "Countering Stress and Depression," *Hindustan Times* (India), January 3, 2011.

xi *Writer John Keats*: Robert Gittings, ed., *John Keats: Selected Letters,* rev. ed. (New York: Oxford University Press, 2009).

xi *twenty-five million Americans have an episode of major depression*: *Major Depression Fact Sheet* (Arlington, VA, National Association of Mental Illness, April 2013), www.nami.org/factsheets/depression_factsheet.pdf.

xv *decades-old assumption*: Alix Spiegel interviews a number of experts, "When It Comes to Depression, Serotonin Isn't the Whole Story," *Morning Edition*, National Public Radio NPR, January 23, 2012, www.npr.org/blogs /health/2012/01/23/145525853/when-it-comes-to-depression-serotonin-isnt-the-whole-story. While we know it's not as simple as balancing brain chemicals, some science suggests that SSRIs can facilitate supportive neuroplastic change. See also Katsunori Kobayashi, Yumiko Ikeda, and Hidenori Suzuki, "Behavioral Destabilization Induced by the Selective Serotonin Reuptake Inhibitor Fluoxetine," *Molecular Brain* 4, no. 12 (March 16, 2011), 4–12.

xvi *helpful in reducing the risk of relapse*: J. Piet and E. Hougaard, "The Effect of Mindfulness-Based Cognitive Therapy for Prevention of Relapse in Recurrent Major Depressive Disorder: A Systematic Review and Meta-analysis," *Clinical Psychology Review* 31, no 6 (August 2011): 1032–40.

xvi *alternative to or support for medication*: Zindel Segal et al., "Antidepressant Monotherapy vs. Sequential Pharmacotherapy and Mindfulness-Based Cognitive Therapy, or Placebo, for Relapse Prophylaxis in Recurrent Depression, *Archives of General Psychiatry* 67, no. 12 (December 2010): 1256–64. Also, the following study found that people who engaged with mindfulness had a 47 percent relapse rate, while people who just used medication had a 60 percent relapse rate: Willem

263

Kuyken et al., "Mindfulness-Based Cognitive Therapy to Prevent Relapse in Recurrent Depression," *Journal of Consulting and Clinical Psychology* 76, no. 6 (December 2008): 966–78.

xvii *wired with an automatic negativity bias*: Roy F. Baumeister et al., "Bad Is Stronger Than Good," *Review of General Psychology* 5, no. 4 (December 2001): 323–70. Also, Paul Rozin and Edward B. Royzman, "Negativity Bias, Negativity Dominance, and Contagion," *Personality and Social Psychology Review* 5, no. 4 (November 2001): 296–320. Another study shows how the brain recognizes negative stimuli quicker: J. S. Morris et al., "A Differential Neural Response in the Human Amygdala to Fearful and Happy Facial Expressions," *Nature* 383, no. 6603 (October 31, 1996): 812–15. Tiffany Ito, Jeff Larsen, Kyle Smith, and John Cacioppo conducted the study "Negative Information Weighs More Heavily on the Brain: The Negativity Bias in Evaluative Categorizations," *Journal of Personality and Social Psychology* 75, no. 4 (October 1998): 887–900.

xix *Learned helplessness is a mental state*: The term *learned helplessness* was originally coined by psychologist Martin Seligman in his work with dogs. You will discover more of this in the text. The original study was Martin E. P. Seligman and Steven F. Maier, "Failure to Escape Traumatic Shock," *Journal of Experimental Psychology* 74, no. 1 (May 1967): 1–9. Since this time, he has been a founder of the positive psychology movement, publishing texts such as *Learned Optimism: How to Change Your Mind and Your Life* (New York: Vintage Books, 2006) and *Flourish: A Visionary New Understanding of Happiness and Well-Being* (New York: Free Press, 2011).

xx *we can actually grow new neural connections*: One of the most memorable earlier human studies of neuroplasticity, using London taxi drivers as subjects, showed growth in the hippocampus—the part of the brain responsible for learning and memory. As you'll discover, the hippocampus is also associated with stress and depression. Eleanor A. Maguire et al., "Navigation-Related Structural Change in the Hippocampi of Taxi Drivers," *Proceedings of the National Academy of Sciences of the United States of America* 97, no. 8 (April 11, 2000): 4398–403. Most parts of the brain are split up into a right side and a left side. There is debate in the field of neuroscience as to the roles of either side, so for simplicity's sake, throughout the book, I refer to the brain structures in the singular. Also see Sharon Begley, *Train Your Mind, Change Your Brain: How a New Science Reveals Our Extraordinary Potential to Transform Ourselves* (New York: Ballantine Books, 2007); Norman Doidge, *The Brain That Changes Itself: Stories of Personal Triumph from the Frontiers of Brain Science* (New York: Penguin Books, 2007).

xxiii *I began running mindfulness-based stress reduction (MBSR)*: Mindfulness-based stress reduction is an eight-week program designed by Jon Kabat-Zinn and is the most researched program available today when it comes to mindfulness. Much of the neuroscience is based on MBSR. Many other programs have come after this, including mindfulness-based cognitive therapy (MBCT) and mindfulness-based relapse prevention (MBRP), among others. See the website of the University of Massachusetts Medical School Center for Mindfulness in Medicine, Health Care, and Society, www.umassmed.edu/cfm/index.aspx; or see Bob Stahl, PhD, and Elisha Goldstein, PhD, *A Mindfulness-Based Stress Reduction Workbook* (Oakland: New Harbinger, 2010).

xxiii *and mindfulness-based cognitive therapy (MBCT) programs*: Mindfulness-based

NOTES

cognitive therapy is an eight-week program designed by Zindel Segal, PhD, Mark Williams, PhD, and John Teasdale, PhD. MBCT is structured after MBSR but integrates more cognitive therapy to help prevent the relapse of depression. This is an excellent program. See the MBCT website, www.MBCT.com; also, for an interesting read on what mediates the effects of MBCT, see Willem Kuyken et al., "How Does Mindfulness-Based Cognitive Therapy Work?," *Behaviour Research and Therapy* 48, no. 11 (November 2010): 1105–112.

Step 1: Understand the Depression Loop

6 *It is so prevalent that nearly 7 percent of adults*: Ronald C. Kessler et al., "Prevalence, Severity, and Comorbidity of Twelve-Month DSM-IV Disorders in the National Comorbidity Survey Replication (NCS-R)," *Archives of General Psychiatry* 62, no. 6 (June 2005): 617–27. Also, *U.S. Census Bureau Population Estimates by Demographic Characteristics* (Washington, DC: U.S. Census Bureau), table 2, "Annual Estimates of the Population by Selected Age Groups and Sex for the United States: April 1, 2000 to July 1, 2004" (NC-EST 2004-02).

8 *Although women are 70 percent more likely than men to become depressed*: Ronald C. Kessler et al., "The Epidemiology of Major Depressive Disorder: Results from the National Comorbidity Survey Replication (NCS-R)," *Journal of the American Medical Association* 289, no. 23 (June 18, 2003): 3095–105.

10 *Depression can sometimes be caused by medical conditions*: Many medical conditions incline us toward depression; here are a few studies containing scientific examples: Mirella P. Hage and Sami T. Azar, "The Link Between Thyroid Function and Depression," *Journal of Thyroid Research* 2012, article ID 590648 (2012), doi:10.1155/2012/590648; Wei Jiang and Jonathan R. T. Davidson, "Antidepressant Therapy in Patients with Ischemic Heart Disease," *American Heart Journal* 150, no. 5 (November 2005): 871–81; Sherita Hill Golden et al., "Examining a Bidirectional Association Between Depressive Symptoms and Diabetes," *JAMA* 299, no. 23 (June 18, 2008): 2751–59. There are also a number of studies showing the side effects of drugs leading to depression, including: Kevin P. Conway et al., "Lifetime Comorbidity of DSM-IV Mood and Anxiety Disorders and Specific Drug Use Disorders: Results from the National Epidemiologic Survey on Alcohol and Related Conditions," *Journal of Clinical Psychiatry* 67, no. 2 (February 2006): 247–57; David R. Rubinow, Peter J. Schmidt, and Catherine A. Roca, "Estrogen-Serotonin Interactions: Implications for Affective Regulation," *Biological Psychiatry* 44, no. 9 (November 1, 1998): 839–50.

13 *it's called* experience-dependent neuroplasticity: Eric R. Kandel, *In Search of Memory: The Emergence of a New Science of Mind* (New York: W. W. Norton, 2007); Joseph LeDoux, *Synaptic Self: How Our Brains Become Who We Are* (New York: Penguin Books, 2003); Maguire et al., "Navigation-Related Structural Change in the Hippocampi," 4398–403.

13 neurons, *are interacting with what some have said are a trillion connections*: David J. Linden, *The Accidental Mind: How Brain Evolution Has Given Us Love, Memory, Dreams, and God* (Cambridge, MA: Belknap Press of Harvard University Press, 2007).

14 *This is called top-down processing*: Daniel J. Siegel, *Developing Mind: How Relationships and the Brain Interact to Shape Who We Are*, 2nd ed. (New York: Guilford Press, 2012).

16 self-directed *neuroplasticity*: Jeffrey M. Schwartz and Sharon Begley, *The Mind and the Brain: Neuroplasticity and the Power of Mental Force* (New York: HarperCollins, 2003).

16 *something called learned helplessness*: The first study was one that I mentioned previously in the notes, Seligman and Maier, "Failure to Escape Traumatic Shock." The second study was Martin Seligman, "Learned Helplessness," *Annual Review of Medicine* 23, no. 1 (February 1972): 407–12.

17 *Years later, researchers conducted similar studies with people*: As female subjects in an experiment were faced with repeated impossible tasks, they showed a reduction in activity in an area that many scientists group with the prefrontal cortex (anterior cingulate), responsible for goal-directed activity. Herbert Bauer et al., "Functional Neuroanatomy of Learned Helplessness," *NeuroImage* 20, no. 2 (October 2003): 927–39.

19 *They split rats into three groups*: Juan A. Varela et al., "Control over Stress Induces Plasticity of Individual Prefrontal Cortical Neurons: A Conductance-Based Neural Simulation," *Nature Precedings* (2011), doi:10.1038/npre.2011.6267.1.

19 *The amygdala is an almond-shaped structure*: Daniel J. Siegel, *The Mindful Brain: Reflection and Attunement in the Cultivation of Well-Being* (New York, W. W. Norton, 2007).

19 *tells the body how to react*: While the amygdala gathers both positive and negative stimuli, it reacts more to negative stimuli. This obviously has implications on relapsing into depression. See William A. Cunningham and Tobias Brosch, "Motivational Salience: Amygdala Tuning from Traits, Needs, Values, and Goals," *Current Directions in Psychological Science* 21, no. 1 (February 2012): 54–59; Israel Liberzon et al., "Extended Amygdala and Emotional Salience: A PET Activation Study of Positive and Negative Affect," *Neuropsychopharmacology* 28, no. 4 (April 2003): 726–33; Stephan B. Hamann et al., "Ecstasy and Agony: Activation of the Human Amygdala in Positive and Negative Emotion," *Psychological Science* 13, no. 2 (March 2002): 135–41.

19 *often enlarged in a depressed brain*: Richard Davidson, Diego Pizzagalli, and Jack Nitschke, "The Representation and Regulation of Emotion in Depression: Perspectives from Affective Neuroscience," in *Handbook of Depression*, 2nd ed., eds. Ian Gotlib and Constance Hammen (New York: Guilford Press, 2009), 218–48.

20 *The prefrontal cortex (PFC) is located in the front of the brain*: The structures of the brain that make up the prefrontal cortex are up for debate. For example, a number of scientists consider the anterior cingulate cortex (ACC) a substructure of the prefrontal cortex. The ACC is involved in assessing and responding to the emotional and cognitive input and decides which matters to address. In major depression, science has found decreased activation in the ACC. Helen Mayberg et al., "Paralimbic Hypoperfusion in Unipolar Depression," *Journal of Nuclear Medicine* 35, no. 6 (June 1994): 929–34. Other studies have shown increased activation of the ACC during recovery: Helen Mayberg et al., "Cingulate Function in Depression: A Potential Predictor of Treatment Response," *NeuroReport* 8, no. 4 (March 3, 1997): 1057–61. Why is this important for depression? An impaired ACC means that our brain is not monitoring our internal and external environments very well. When the ACC is functioning normally, it may notice some disparity between our behav-

ior and a situation (such as an outburst of crying at work) and then call for further processing within the PFC for impulse control. This suggests that our ability to cope with overwhelming emotions is blunted, and we're more likely to make poor choices that keep us stuck in a depression loop. The good news is that science also shows that regular meditation can increase ACC activity. Fadel Zeidan et al., "Neural Correlates of Mindfulness Meditation–Related Anxiety Relief," *Social Cognitive and Affective Neuroscience* 9, no. 6 (June 2014): 751–59.

Another part of the PFC, the insula: Another area of the brain that many believe to be part of the PFC is the insula. Sara Lazar, PhD, an instructor at Harvard Medical School, has called this part of the brain "the seat of awareness" and states that it can be strengthened through meditation. Sara Lazar et al., "Meditation Experience Is Associated with Increased Cortical Thickness," *NeuroReport* 16, no. 17 (November 28, 2005): 1893–97. Others say it is critical for emotional self-awareness and decision making, which seem vital to working with depression. Helen Mayberg, MD, from Emory University, and colleagues have conducted some fascinating experiments showing how we may be able to predict which treatments are best for different people, depending on changes in insula activity when undergoing different interventions. Callie L. McGrath et al., "Toward a Neuroimaging Treatment Selection Biomarker for Major Depressive Disorder," *JAMA Psychiatry* 70, no. 8 (August 2013): 821–29. The insula has been found to activate with awareness of the physical body (interoception), which is inversely correlated with the ruminative mind. When we're mindful of bodily sensations, rumination, which is often the fuel for the depressive loop, goes down. Norman A. S. Farb et al., "Minding One's Emotions: Mindfulness Training Alters the Neural Expression of Sadness," *Emotion* 10, no. 1 (February 2010): 25–33; Norman Farb, Zindel Segal, and Adam Anderson. "Mindfulness Meditation Training Alters Cortical Representations of Interoceptive Attention," *Social Cognitive and Affective Neuroscience* 8, no. 1 (January 2013): 15–26.

20 *show a general reduction in PFC activity*: Davidson, Pizzagalli, and Nitschke, "Representation and Regulation of Emotion in Depression," 218–48.

20 *less activity in the left prefrontal cortex*: Richard J. Davidson et al., "Regional Brain Function, Emotion and Disorders of Emotion," *Current Opinion in Neurobiology* 9, no. 2 (April 1999): 228–34; Richard Davidson, Daren C. Jackson, and Ned H. Kalin, "Emotion, Plasticity, Context, and Regulation: Perspectives from Affective Neuroscience," *Psychological Bulletin* 126, no. 6 (November 2000): 890–909.

21 *This may be why in a depressed brain*: Stephanie L. Willard et al., "Cell Number and Neuropil Alterations in Subregions of the Anterior Hippocampus in a Female Monkey Model of Depression," *Biological Psychiatry* 74, no. 12 (December 15, 2013): 890–907; Sanjaya Saxena et al., "Cerebral Metabolism in Major Depression and Obsessive-Compulsive Disorder Occurring Separately and Concurrently," *Biological Psychiatry* 50, no. 3 (August 1, 2001): 159–70.

29 *simple process of putting feelings into words*: Matthew D. Lieberman et al., "Putting Feelings into Words: Affect Labeling Disrupts Amygdala Activity to Affective Stimuli," *Psychological Science* 18, no. 5 (May 2007): 421–28.

31 *if you can name them, you can tame them*: Daniel Siegel originally said, "Name it to tame it." See *The Mindful Brain*.

Step 2: Reverse Bad Habits

35 *these five seem to earn the highest marks*: The mind traps of doubt, emptiness, irritation, sluggishness, and restlessness come from the five hindrances in Buddhism. Traditionally, these are five mental factors that hinder our ability to progress with meditation. However, in daily life, these factors seem to block us from advancing in just about anything and seem to be universal. To learn more, you can look to Gil Fronsdal, *Unhindered: A Mindful Path Through the Five Hindrances* (Redwood City, CA: Tranquil Books, 2013).

40 *In 1996 Jill Bolte Taylor*: Jill Bolte Taylor, *My Stroke of Insight: A Brain Scientist's Personal Journey* (New York: Plume, 2009).

43 *I feel as though I'm up against the world*: Steven D. Hollon and Philip C. Kendall. "Cognitive Self-Statements in Depression: Development of an Automatic Thoughts Questionnaire," *Cognitive Therapy and Research* 4, no. 4 (December 1980): 383–95.

45 *a series of questions adapted from American speaker and author Byron Katie*: Byron Katie with Stephen Mitchell, *Love What Is: Four Questions That Can Change Your Life* (New York: Three Rivers Press, 2003).

47 *habits are formed in a lump of neurological tissue*: While the basal ganglia is an oval of cells made up of multiple parts, I describe it as a single structure for ease of language. Gregory Ashby and John Ennis, "The Role of the Basal Ganglia in Category Learning," *Psychology of Learning and Motivation* 46 (2006): 1–36; F. Gregory Ashby, Benjamin O. Turner, and Jon C. Horvitz, "Cortical and Basal Ganglia Contributions to Habit Learning and Automaticity," *Trends in Cognitive Sciences* 14, no. 5 (May 2010): 208–15; Claudio Da Cunha and Mark G. Packard, "Preface: Special Issue on the Role of the Basal Ganglia in Learning and Memory," *Behavioural Brain Research* 199, no. 1 (April 12, 2009): 1–2; Ann M. Graybiel, "The Basal Ganglia: Learning New Tricks and Loving It," *Current Opinion in Neurobiology* 15, no. 6 (December 2005): 638–44; Mark G. Packard, "Role of Basal Ganglia in Habit Learning and Memory: Rats, Monkeys, and Humans," in *Handbook of Basal Ganglia Structure and Function: A Decade of Progress*, eds. Heinz Steiner and Kuei Y. Tseng (London: Academic Press, 2010), 561–69.

48 *inherent negativity bias*: Tiffany A. Ito et al., "Negative Information Weighs More Heavily on the Brain: The Negativity Bias in Evaluative Categorizations," *Journal of Personality and Social Psychology* 75, no. 4 (October 1998): 887–900.

48 *science also shows that it opens our mind up to greater possibilities*: Steven M. Southwick and Dennis S. Charney, "The Science of Resilience: Implications for the Prevention and Treatment of Depression," *Science* 338, no. 6103 (October 5, 2012): 79–82; Michael A. Cohn et al., "Happiness Unpacked: Positive Emotions Increase Life Satisfaction by Building Resiliency," *Emotion* 9, no. 1 (June 2009): 361–68; Michele M. Tugade and Barbara L. Fredrickson, "Regulation of Positive Emotions: Emotion Regulation Strategies That Promote Resilience," *Journal of Happiness Studies* 8, no. 3 (September 2007): 311–33. For more on encouraging the good in us, see Rick Hanson *Hardwiring Happiness: The New Brain Science of Contentment, Calm, and Confidence* (New York: Harmony Books, 2014).

50 *Dopamine, also a key contributor to our habits*: Nora D. Volkow et al., "Overlapping Neuronal Circuits in Addiction and Obesity: Evidence of Systems Pathology," *Philosophical Transactions of the Royal Society* 363, no. 1507 (October 2008): 3191–210; Nora D. Volkow et al., "Prediction of Reinforcing Responses to Psychostimulants

in Humans by Brain Dopamine D2 Receptor Levels," *American Journal of Psychiatry* 156, no. 9 (September 1999): 1440–43; Nora D. Volkow et al., "Brain DA D2 Receptors Predict Reinforcing Effects of Stimulants in Humans: Replication Study," *Synapse* 46, no. 2 (November 2002): 79–82.

52 *Acceptance comes when there is a sense of feeling*: I am indebted to the work of Tara Brach, an inspiring human being and teacher. This notion of acceptance comes from her book *Radical Acceptance: Embracing Your Life with the Heart of a Buddha* (New York: Bantam Books, 2004).

54 *abnormally low activity in the prefrontal cortex*: Davidson, Pizzagalli, and Nitschke, "Representation and Regulation of Emotion in Depression," 218–48.

54 *In one study, he and his colleagues*: Antoine Bechara et al., "Deciding Advantageously Before Knowing the Advantageous Strategy," *Science* 275, no. 5304 (February 28, 1997): 1293–95.

56 *the story of Charles Duhigg*: Charles Duhigg, *The Power of Habit: Why We Do What We Do in Life and Business* (New York: Random House, 2012).

57 *practice visualizing the process*: Alvara Pascual-Leone, "Reorganization of Cortical Motor Outputs in the Acquisition of New Motor Skills," in *Recent Advances in Clinical Neurophysiology*, eds. Jun Kinura and Hiroshi Shibasaki (Amsterdam: Elsevier Science, 1996), 304–8; Alvara Pascual-Leone et al., "Modulation of Muscle Responses Evoked by Transcranial Magnetic Stimulation During the Acquisition of New Fine Motor Skills," *Journal of Neurophysiology* 74, no. 3 (September 1995): 1037–45.

59 *one of my therapy strategies: Forgive and Invite*: Mark Williams et al., *The Mindful Way Through Depression: Freeing Yourself from Chronic Unhappiness* (New York: Guilford Press, 2007).

60 *placebo rates in randomized controlled trials*: Timothy Walsh et al., "Placebo Response in Studies of Major Depression: Variable, Substantial, and Growing," *Journal of the American Medical Association* 287, no. 14 (April 10, 2002): 1840–47.

Step 3: Change the Brain Through Mindfulness

66 *The social psychologist Ellen Langer*: *The Power of Mindful Learning* (New York: Da Capo Press, 1998). Also see Ellen Langer's *Mindfulness: 25th Anniversary Edition* (New York: Da Capo Lifelong Books, 2014).

67 *research has shown that when people cultivate mindfulness*: The science that suggests the benefits of mindfulness is far too vast and growing exponentially at this point to cover adequately. However, here are a few studies that report the benefits listed. For research on mindfulness with cognitive flexibility, see Andrew C. Hafenbrack, Zoe Kinias, and Sigal G. Barsade, "Debiasing the Mind Through Meditation: Mindfulness and the Sunk-Cost Bias," *Psychological Science* 25, no. 2 (February 2014): 369–76. For research on mindfulness and focus, see Adam Moore and Peter Malinowski, "Meditation, Mindfulness and Cognitive Flexibility," *Consciousness and Cognition* 18, no. 1 (March 2009): 176–86. For research on mindfulness and stress reduction, see Richard J. Davidson et al., "Alterations in Brain and Immune Function Produced by Mindfulness Meditation," *Psychosomatic Medicine* 65, no. 4 (July–August 2003): 564–70. For research on reducing rumination, see Norman A. S. Farb et al., "Attending to the Present: Mindfulness Meditation Reveals Distinct Neural Modes of Self-Reference," *Social Cognitive and Affective Neuroscience* 2, no. 4 (December 2007): 313–22; Farb et al., "Minding One's Emotions,"

25–33. For research on mindfulness and empathy, see Shauna L. Shapiro, Gary E. Schwartz, and Ginny Bonner, "Effects of Mindfulness-Based Stress Reduction on Medical and Premedical Students," *Journal of Behavioral Medicine* 21, no. 6 (December 1998): 581–99. For research on mindfulness and compassion, see Shauna L. Shapiro et al., "Mindfulness-Based Stress Reduction for Health Care Professionals: Results from a Randomized Trial," *International Journal of Stress Management* 12, no. 2 (May 2005): 164–76. For research on mindfulness and communication, see Mathias Dekeyser et al., "Mindfulness Skills and Interpersonal Behaviour," *Personality and Individual Differences* 44, no. 5 (April 2008): 1235–45. For research on mindfulness and higher quality of life, see Jeanette Sawyer Cohen and Lisa Miller, "Interpersonal Mindfulness Training for Well-Being: A Pilot Study with Psychology Graduate Students," *Teachers College Record* 111, no. 12 (2009): 2760–74.

74 *"Breathing in, I have arrived; breathing out, I am home"*: Thich Nhat Hanh has made informal mindfulness practices such as this famous. You can find more like this at the website for Deer Park Monastery in Escondido, California, http://deerparkmonastery.org/mindfulness-practice/practicing-mindfulness-at-deer-park.

75 *induces real changes in the brain*: Eileen Luders et al., "The Underlying Anatomical Correlates of Long-Term Meditation; Larger Hippocampal and Frontal Volumes of Gray Matter," *NeuroImage* 45, no. 3 (April 15, 2009): 672–78; Britta Hölzel et al., "Investigation of Mindfulness Meditation Practitioners with Voxel-Based Morphometry," *Social Cognitive and Affective Neuroscience* 3, no. 1 (March 2008): 55–61; Sara W. Lazar et al., "Meditation Experience Is Associated with Increased Cortical Thickness," *NeuroReport* 16, no. 17 (November 28, 2005): 1893–97.

75 *For example, in one study*: Farb et al., "Minding One's Emotions," 25–33.

76 *In a 2003 study, Richie Davidson*: Richard Davidson et al., "Alteration in Brain and Immune Function Produced by Mindfulness Meditation," *Psychosomatic Medicine* 65, no. 4 (July 2003): 564–70.

77 *right prefrontal cortex of negative emotions*: The right side of the PFC has been associated with avoidance, withdrawal, and inhibition. Hugh Garavan, Thomas Ross, and Elliot Stein, "Right Hemispheric Dominance of Inhibitory Control: An Event-Related Functional MRI Study," *Proceedings of the National Academy of Sciences of the United States of America* 96, no. 14 (July 6, 1999): 8301–6. In another study demonstrating how the neurobiology of depression is interpersonal, depressed mothers who were seen as withdrawn rarely shared positive emotions with their baby. During this study, the child also exhibited a decrease in left prefrontal activation and an increase in right prefrontal activation. If this activity persists, this could affect the child in the years to come. Miguel A. Diego et al., "Withdrawn and Intrusive Maternal Interaction Style and Infant Frontal EEG Asymmetry Shifts in Infants of Depressed and Non-depressed Mothers," *Infant Behavior and Development* 29, no. 2 (April 2006): 220–29.

77 *In 2012, Dr. Fadel Zeiden*: Fadel Zeidan et al., "Neural Correlates of Mindfulness Meditation–Related Anxiety Relief," *Social Cognitive and Affective Neuroscience* 9, no. 6 (June 2014): 751–59. Other studies have also shown mindfulness as a path to pain control, including Tim Gard et al., "Pain Attenuation Through Mindfulness Is Associated with Decreased Cognitive Control and Increased Sensory Processing in the Brain," *Cerebral Cortex* 22, no. 11 (November 1, 2012): 2692–702.

78 *A study out of Richie Davidson's lab*: Perla Kaliman et al., "Rapid Changes in

Histone Deacetylases and Inflammatory Gene Expression in Expert Meditators,"
Psychoneuroendocrinology 40 (February 2014): 96–107.

84 *more detail in my previous book,* The Now Effect: Elisha Goldstein, *The Now Effect: How a Mindful Moment Can Change the Rest of Your Life* (New York: Atria Books, 2012).

84 *In his book* The Miracle of Being Awake: Thich Nhat Hanh, *The Miracle of Being Awake* (Sri Lanka: Buddhist Publication Society, 1976).

Step 4: Nurture Self-Compassion and Its Wonderful Side Effects

89 *change the activity in our brains*: While there is no current science pointing to self-compassion inducing shifts in our brain activity, my theory is that it has similar neurobiological effects as seen in compassion research. Olga M. Klimecki et al., "Differential Pattern of Functional Brain Plasticity After Compassion and Empathy Training," *Social Cognitive and Affective Neuroscience* 9, no. 6 (June 2014): 873–79.

89 *interrupting the depression loop*: Tobias Krieger et al., "Self-Compassion in De-pression: Associations with Depressive Symptoms, Rumination, and Avoidance in Depressed Outpatients," *Behavior Therapy* 44, no. 3 (September 2013): 501–13.

89 *cling like Velcro to our negative voices*: Rick Hanson does a beautiful job exploring this in his book *Buddha's Brain: The Practical Neuroscience of Happiness, Love, and Wisdom* (Oakland, New Harbinger, 2009).

89 *John Cacioppo, PhD, put this question*: Ito et al., "Negative Information Weighs More Heavily on the Brain."

90 *Barbara Fredrickson, PhD, of the University of North Carolina*: Barbara Fredrickson, *Positivity: Top-Notch Research Reveals the 3-to-1 Ratio That Will Change Your Life* (New York: Three Rivers Press, 2009).

90 *John Gottman, PhD, one of the leading researchers*: John M. Gottman and Robert W. Levenson, "Marital Processes Predictive of Later Dissolution: Behavior, Physiology, and Health," *Journal of Personality and Social Psychology* 63, no. 2 (August 1992): 221–33; John Mordechai Gottman and Robert Wayne Levenson, "A Two-Factor Model for Predicting When a Couple Will Divorce: Exploratory Analyses Using 14-Year Longitudinal Data," *Family Process* 41, no. 1 (Spring 2002): 83–96.

92 *Albert Einstein wrote: A human being*: Albert Einstein, letter excerpted in the *New York Post*, November 28, 1972. p. 12.

92 *Kristin Neff, PhD, a researcher*: Kristin Neff, *Self-Compassion: The Proven Power of Being Kind to Yourself* (New York: William Morrow, 2011).

94 *Self-Compassion Inventory*: You can further test how self-compassionate you are at Kristin Neff's website: www.self-compassion.org/test-your-self-compassion-level .html.

95 *Oxytocin is released into the bloodstream*: A general source for reviewing oxytocin literature is www.oxytocin.org/refs/index.html.

95 *research studies suggest that the act of self-compassion*: Many studies focus on the reception of kindness or warm touch associated with oxytocin levels, such as Ju-lianne Holt-Lunstad, Wendy A. Birmingham, and Kathleen C. Light, "Influence of a 'Warm Touch' Support Enhancement Intervention Among Married Couples on Ambulatory Blood Pressure, Oxytocin, Alpha Amylase, and Cortisol," *Psycho-somatic Medicine* 70, no. 9 (November–December 2008): 976–85. It is my theory that treating ourselves with kindness and compassion also cues a similar biological

reaction. This has been suggested before in Dacher Keltner, *Born to Be Good: The Science of a Meaningful Life* (New York: W. W. Norton, 2009), and Linda Graham, *Bouncing Back: Rewiring Your Brain for Maximum Resilience and Well-Being* (Novato, CA: New World Library, 2013). These books also contain wonderful exercises, which the authors suggest raise oxytocin levels.

95 *Let It Linger*: It's been found that encouraging the good in our lives can make us more resilient. Barbara L. Fredrickson et al., "What Good Are Positive Emotions in Crisis? A Prospective Study of Resilience and Emotions Following the Terrorist Attacks on the United States on September 11th, 2001," *Journal of Personality and Social Psychology* 84, no. 2 (February 2003): 365–76; Barbara L. Fredrickson and Robert W. Levenson, "Positive Emotions Speed Recovery from the Cardiovascular Sequelae of Negative Emotions," *Cognition and Emotion* 12, no. 2 (March 1, 1998): 191–220. You can find more on "taking in the good" of life in Rick Hanson's book *Hardwiring Happiness*.
Note of caution: If someone struggles with bipolar disorder, it's important to be aware of the intensity and duration of the positive mood, as it may be leading to a manic episode. June Gruber, "Can Feeling Too Good Be Bad? Positive Emotion Persistence (PEP) in Bipolar Disorder," *Current Directions in Psychological Science* 20, no. 4 (August 2011): 217–21.

96 *Stan Tatkin, author of*: Stan Tatkin, *Wired for Love: How Understanding Your Partner's Brain and Attachment Style Can Help You Defuse Conflict and Build a Secure Relationship* (Oakland, New Harbinger, 2012).

96 *We can nurture self-compassion*: You can find the metaphors of the stick and the carrot and the scenario of talking to children about their grades in Kristin Neff's book *Self-Compassion*. I adapted this by adding the metaphor of the cake to highlight the difference between self-compassion (carrot) and self-indulgence (cake).

98 *Paul Gilbert, a professor of psychology*: Paul Gilbert and Choden, *Mindful Compassion: How the Science of Compassion Can Help You Understand Your Emotions, Live in the Present, and Connect Deeply with Others* (Oakland: New Harbinger, 2014); Paul Gilbert, "Introducing Compassion-Focused Therapy," *Advances in Psychiatric Treatment* 15, no. 3 (May 2009): 199–208.

99 *In 2006 Dr. Gilbert published a study*: Paul Gilbert and Sue Procter, "Compassionate Mind Training for People with High Shame and Self-Criticism: A Pilot Study of a Group Therapy Approach," *Clinical Psychology and Psychotherapy* 13, no. 6 (November–December 2006): 353–79.

102 *we are more effective in the face of support*: Ed Diener and Micaela Y. Chan, "Happy People Live Longer: Subjective Well-Being Contributes to Health and Longevity," *Applied Psychophysiology* 3, no. 1 (March 2011): 1–43; Barbara L. Fredrickson et al., "Open Hearts Build Lives: Positive Emotions, Induced Through Meditation, Build Consequential Personal Resources," *Journal of Personality and Social Psychology* 95, no. 5 (November 2008): 1045–62; Theodore A. Powers, Richard Koestner, and David C. Zuroff, "Self-Criticism, Goal Motivation, and Goal Progress," *Journal of Social and Clinical Psychology* 26, no. 7 (2007): 826–40; Barbara L. Fredrickson, "The Role of Positive Emotions in Positive Psychology: The Broaden-and-Build Theory of Positive Emotions," *American Psychologist* 56, no. 3 (March 2001): 218–26.

103 *Understanding your needs*: To learn more about uncovering your needs, you can

go to the website of the Center for Nonviolent Communication, at www.cnvc.org /Training/needs-inventory.

105 *a critical bundle of fibers*: Stephen W. Porges, *The Polyvagal Theory: Neurophysiological Foundations of Emotions, Attachment, Communication, and Self-Regulation* (New York: W. W. Norton, 2011).

105 *The vagus nerve is also entwined with our oxytocin network*: Keltner, *Born to Be Good*.

105 *stimulate the vagus nerve and help relieve depressive*: Charles R. Conway et al., "Association of Cerebral Metabolic Activity Changes with Vagus Nerve Stimulation Antidepressant Response in Treatment-Resistant Depression," *Brain Stimulation* 6, no. 5 (September 2013): 788–97.

105 *The vagus nerve is also active when we feel compassion*: Keltner, *Born to Be Good*.

106 *Take Self-Compassion Breaks*: In this book, I use the term "self-compassion break" to refer to an opportunity to recognize a difficult moment and be kind to yourself in a variety of ways. The term "self-compassion break" is also a specific meditation in Mindful Self-Compassion, an 8-week program created by Kristin Neff, PhD, and Christopher Germer, PhD. In their program, the term refers to a specific meditation where you say the following: (1) "This is a moment of suffering," (2) "Suffering is a part of living," and (3) "May I be kind to myself." You can find a very clear description on the Mindful Self-Compassion website at www.mindfulselfcompassion .org/handouts/SelfCompassionBreak.pdf.

108 *multiple opportunities to befriend yourself*: These phrases come from a classic lovingkindness practice. This practice has been shown to relieve depressive symptoms. Fredrickson et al., "Open Hearts Build Lives."

109 Benefits of Laughter Yoga: While I'm not aware of any specific study showing that laughter activates a left prefrontal shift, we can infer from Richie Davidson's research that this positive experience would be associated with that shift. In Daniel Goleman's book *Destructive Emotions: How Can We Overcome Them? A Scientific Dialogue with the Dalai Lama* (New York: Bantam Books, 2003), his work showed how enthusiasm creates a left prefrontal shift. You can find more about the benefits of laughter yoga on the Laughter Yoga International website, www.laughteryoga .org/english.

110 *science shows that it also serves as a natural antidepressant*: Social engagement has been found to change our neurobiology to alleviate depression. Porges, *Polyvagal Theory*.

117 *an "upward spiral"*: Fredrickson, "Role of Positive Emotions in Positive Psychology," 218–26.

118 *a skill that we can encourage and cultivate*: C. R. Snyder, "Hypothesis: There Is Hope," in *Handbook of Hope: Theory, Measures, and Applications*, ed. C. R. Snyder (San Diego: Academic Press, 2000, 3–21.

118 *you are likely to become grateful for the relief*: Robert A. Emmons and Michael E. McCullough, "Counting Blessings Versus Burdens: An Experimental Investigation of Gratitude and Subjective Well-Being in Daily Life," *Journal of Personality and Social Psychology* 84, no. 2 (February 2003): 377–89.

121 *he administered mild electrical shocks*: James A. Coan, Hillary S. Schaefer, and Richard J. Davidson, "Lending a Hand: Social Regulation of the Neural Response to Threat," *Psychological Science* 17, no. 12 (December 2006): 1032–39.

Step 5: Live with Purpose—Know Why You
Matter and What You Can Do About It

124 *In his acclaimed book*: Viktor E. Frankl, *Man's Search for Meaning* (Boston: Beacon Press, 2006).

125 *In the United States alone, seventy-eight million*: U.S. Census Bureau Facts for Features, "Oldest Baby Boomers Turn 60!" news release no. CB06-FFSE.01-2, January 3, 2006, www.census.gov/newsroom/releases/pdf/cb06-ffse01-2.pdf.

126 *Sometimes you hear a voice*: Jalāl al Dīn Rūmī, *The Essential Rumi*, rev. ed., trans. Coleman Barks (New York: HarperOne, 2004).

127 *That's what happened in a 2009 study*: Tait D. Shanafelt et al., "Career Fit and Burnout Among Academic Faculty," *Archives of Internal Medicine* 169, no. 10 (May 25, 2009): 990–95.

128 *sense of purpose have stronger immune systems and experience less cellular inflammation*: Barbara Fredrickson et al. "A Functional Genomic Perspective on Human Well-Being," *Proceedings of the National Academy of Sciences of the United States of America* 110, no. 33 (August 13, 2013): 13684–89.

128 *Makes us happier*: Michele M. Tugade and Barbara L. Fredrickson, "Regulation of Positive Emotions: Emotion Regulation Strategies That Promote Resilience," *Journal of Happiness Studies* 8, no. 3 (September 2007): 311–33.

128 *Speeds up recovery from disease*: Steve W. Cole et al., "Social Regulation of Gene Expression in Human Leukocytes," *Genome Biology* 8, no. 9 (September 2007): R189; Fredrickson et al., "Functional Genomic Perspective on Human Well-Being."

128 *Activates the pleasure centers of the brain*: Jorge Moll et al., "Human Fronto-Mesolimbic Networks Guide Decisions About Charitable Donation," *Proceedings of the National Academy of Sciences of the United States of America* 103, no. 42 (October 17, 2006): 15623–28.

128 *Serves as a buffer against stress*: Michael J. Poulin et al., "Giving to Others and the Association Between Stress and Mortality," *American Journal of Public Health* 103, no. 9 (September 2013): 1649–55.

128 *Reduces cellular inflammation*: Fredrickson, "Functional Genomic Perspective on Human Well-Being."

128 *Increases our sense of connection with others*: Cendri A. Hutcherson, Emma M. Seppala, and James J. Gross, "Lovingkindness Meditation Increases Social Connectedness," *Emotion* 8, no. 5 (October 2008): 720–24.

128 *May lengthen our life spans*: Sara Konrath et al., "Motives for Volunteering Are Associated with Mortality Risk in Older Adults," *Health Psychology* 31, no. 1 (January 2012): 87–96; Julianne Holt-Lunstad, Timothy B. Smith, and J. Bradley Layton, "Social Relationships and Mortality Risk: A Meta-analytic Review," *PLOS Medicine* 7, no. 7 (July 27, 2010): e1000316.

129 *at your own retirement party*: The exercise of imagining yourself at your own retirement party or funeral and turning values into verbs is adapted from acceptance and commitment therapy (ACT). ACT is an evidence-based psychological approach that integrates mindfulness and acceptance strategies to work with a host of psychological disorders. Steve Hayes and Spencer Smith, *Get out of Your Mind and into Your Life: The New Acceptance and Commitment Therapy* (Oakland: New Harbinger, 2005).

133 *perceived the hill as being less steep*: Simone Schnall et al., "Social Support and the

Perception of Geographical Slant," *Journal of Experimental Social Psychology* 44, no. 5 (September 2008): 1246–55; Mukul Bhalla and Dennis R. Proffitt, "Visual-Motor Recalibration in Geographical Slant Perception," *Journal of Experimental Psychology: Human Perception and Performance* 25, no. 4 (August 1999): 1076–96.

135 *Philip Burguieres, who became one of the youngest Fortune 500 CEOs*: PBS conducted a wonderful interview with Philip and others in its award-winning documentary film *Depression: Out of the Shadows*, which is worth looking at: www.pbs.org/wgbh/takeonestep/depression.

138 *intrinsic goals were happier than those chasing extrinsic goals*: Christopher P. Niemiec, Richard M. Ryan, and Edward L. Deci, "The Path Taken: Consequences of Attaining Intrinsic and Extrinsic Aspirations in Post-College Life," *Journal of Research and Personality* 73, no. 3 (June 2009): 291–306.

139 *respond to stress better with eudaimonic well-being*: Fredrickson, "Functional Genomic Perspective on Human Well-Being."

140 *decided to offer it as a book*: Elisha Goldstein, ed., *A Mindful Dialogue: A Path Toward Working with Stress, Pain and Difficult Emotions* (Newburyport, MA, Psychcentral, 2011).

140 *he first asked them how happy they were*: Elizabeth W. Dunn, Lara B. Aknin, and Michael I. Norton, "Spending Money on Others Promotes Happiness," *Science* 319, no. 5870 (March 21, 2008): 1687–88.

142 *in the form of "compassion fatigue"*: Babette Rothschild with Marjorie Rand, *Help for the Helper: The Psychophysiology of Compassion Fatigue and Vicarious Trauma* (New York: W. W. Norton, 2006); Charles R. Figley, ed., *Compassion Fatigue: Coping with Secondary Traumatic Stress Disorder in Those Who Treat the Traumatized* (New York: Routledge, 1995).

142 *First, we did a mountain meditation*: This is a practice that comes out of Mindfulness-Based Stress Reduction. The short version described here is adapted from Thich Nhat Hanh's mountain meditation. You can learn more about this wonderful man at the website of Plum Village Mindfulness Practice Centre, http://plumvillage.org.

Step 6: Go Out and Play—Rediscovering the Joy of Life

147 *the absence of play in adults contributes to depression*: Jaak Panksepp and Lucy Biven, *The Archaeology of Mind: Neuroevolutionary Origins of Human Emotions* (New York: W. W. Norton, 2012); Jaak Panksepp, "Affective Neuroscience of the Emotional BrainMind: Evolutionary Perspectives and Implications for Understanding Depression," *Dialogues in Clinical Neuroscience* 12, no. 4 (December 2010): 533–45; Stuart Brown and Christopher Vaughan, *Play: How It Shapes the Brain, Opens the Imagination, and Invigorates the Soul* (New York: Avery, 2009).

148 *Play is happening when you are so engrossed*: "Discovering the Importance of Play Through Personal Histories and Brain Images: An Interview with Stuart L. Brown," *American Journal of Play* 1, no. 4 (Spring 2009): 399–412.

148 *Mihaly Csikszentmihalyi*: Mihaly Csikszentmihalyi, *Flow: The Psychology of Optimal Experience* (New York: Harper & Row, 1990).

151 *an essential truth in our human experience*: You can read this study in detail in chapters 10 and 11 of Mihaly Csikszentmihalyi, *Beyond Boredom and Anxiety: Experiencing Flow in Work and Play*, 25th anniversary ed. (San Francisco: Jossey-Bass, 2000).

151 *collecting more than six thousand "play histories"*: "Discovering the Importance of Play," 405.

154 *Diamond and her colleagues took thirty-six rats*: Marian C. Diamond, David Krech, and Mark R. Rosenzweig, "The Effects of an Enriched Environment on the Histology of the Rat Cerebral Cortex," *Journal of Comparative Neurology* 123, no. 1 (August 1964): 111–19.

156 *studies suggest is low when feeling depressed*: Kay M. Tye et al., "Dopamine Neurons Modulate Neural Encoding and Expression of Depression-Related Behaviour," *Nature* 483, no. 7433 (January 24, 2013): 537–41; Francis Lavergne and Thérèse M. Jay, "A New Strategy for Antidepressant Prescription," *Frontiers in Neuroscience* 4 (November 19, 2010): doi:10.3389/fnins.2010.00192.

156 *ran mazes faster and more efficiently*: Lena C. Hoffmann et al., "Effect of 'Enriched Environment' During Development on Adult Rat Behavior and Response to the Dopamine Receptor Agonist Apomorphine," *Neuroscience* 158, no. 4 (February 2009): 1589–98.

156 *needed less glucose to function*: Marian Diamond, *Enriching Heredity: The Impact of the Environment on the Anatomy of the Brain* (New York: Free Press, 1988).

156 *increased survival of nerve cells in the hippocampus*: Nerve cells, like all other things, can survive and die. As nerve cells survive in the brain it maintains the functionality of that area of the brain. In this case increased survival of nerve cells in the hippocampus, means a better functioning hippocampus. Rachel B. Speisman et al., "Environmental Enrichment Restores Neurogenesis and Rapid Acquisition in Aged Rats," *Neurobiology of Aging* 34, no. 1 (January 2013): 263–74.

157 *Julia Cameron's book* The Artist's Way: Julia Cameron, *The Artist's Way: A Spiritual Path to Higher Creativity*, 10th anniversary ed. (New York: Jeremy P. Tarcher/ Putnam, 2002). Another good book on creativity is Ellen Langer's *On Becoming Yourself Through Mindful Creativity* (New York: Ballantine Books, 2006).

157 *brought along a poetry book by e. e. cummings*: e. e. cummings, *Selected Poems*, ed. Richard S. Kennedy (New York: Liveright, 1994).

163 *Three Steps to Savoring*: Other wonderful books that speak to the art of savoring are Hanson, *Hardwiring Happiness;* Thich Nhat Hanh and Lilian Cheung, *Savor: Mindful Eating, Mindful Life* (New York: HarperOne, 2011).

164 coined the term "foreboding joy": Brené Brown, *Daring Greatly: How the Courage to Be Vulnerable Transforms the Way We Live, Love, Parent, and Lead* (New York: Gotham Books, 2012).

Step 7: Learn to Get Better and Better

167 *the most dramatic changes in the brain*: Bogdan Draganski et al., "Temporal and Spatial Dynamics of Brain Structure Changes During Extensive Learning," *Journal of Neuroscience* 26, no. 23 (June 7, 2006): 6314–17.

169 *two different types of mindset*: Carol S. Dweck, *Mindset: The New Psychology of Success* (New York: Ballantine Books, 2006); Carol S. Dweck, *Self-Theories: Their Role in Motivation, Personality, and Development* (Philadelphia: Psychology Press: 2000).

170 *In her book* Self-Theories: Dweck, *Self-Theories*.

170 *Dweck enlisted college students*: This study is explained in detail in chapter 2 of Dweck's *Mindset*, which is the source of all the quotations here.

172 *She even started a course*: Betty Edwards, *Drawing on the Right Side of the Brain,* 4th ed. (New York: Tarcher, 2012). Find out more about this course at www.drawright .com.

175 *It's time to figure out your mindset*: This series of statements is adapted from Carol Dweck's mindset assessment. Dweck, *Mindset.*

178 *your brain is literally depleted of neurochemicals*: Lavergne and Jay, "New Strategy."

179 *being strategic about increasing activity*: A large number of studies point to the efficacy of being more strategic with activity to prevent relapse. See Andrew C. Butler and Aaron T. Beck, "Cognitive Therapy for Depression," *Clinical Psychologist* 48, no. 3 (Summer 1995): 3–5.

179 *The strategy is called activity scheduling*: You will also find a version of activity scheduling in mindfulness-based cognitive therapy (MBCT) and mindful compassion cognitive therapy (MCCT).

187 *reliable predictor of reduction in depression relapse*: Patrick J. Smith et al., "Effects of Exercise and Weight Loss on Depressive Symptoms Among Men and Women with Hypertension," *Journal of Psychosomatic Medicine* 63, no. 5 (November 2007): 463–69.

188 *the benefits of prolonged endurance training*: Brett Klika and Chris Jordan, "High-Intensity Circuit Training Using Body Weight: Maximum Results with Minimal Investment," *ACSM's Health & Fitness Journal* 17, no. 3 (May–June 2013): 8–13.

189 *packed with vitamins and* antioxidants: Mariangela Rondanelli et al., "Effect of Omega-3 Fatty Acids Supplementation on Depressive Symptoms and on Health-Related Quality of Life in the Treatment of Elderly Women with Depression: A Double-Blind, Placebo-Controlled, Randomized Clinical Trial," *Journal of the American College of Nutrition* 29, no. 1 (February 2010): 55–64.

189 *vitamins B_{12} and B_6, and another B vitamin, folate*: Kimberly A. Skarupski et al., "Longitudinal Association of Vitamin B-6, Folate, and Vitamin B-12 with Depressive Symptoms Among Older Adults Over Time" *American Journal of Clinical Nutrition* 92, no. 2 (August 2010): 330–35.

189 *they recalled 81 percent of the words with negative connotations*: Matthew P. Walker and Els van der Helm, "Overnight Therapy? The Role of Sleep in Emotional Brain Processing," *Psychological Bulletin* 135, no. 5 (September 2009): 731–48.

190 *associated with weaker immune systems*: Hataikarn Nimitphong and Michael F. Holick, "Vitamin D, Neurocognitive Functioning and Immunocompetence," *Current Opinion in Clinical Nutrition and Metabolic Care* 14, no. 1 (January 2011): 7–14.

190 *twenty minutes a day outdoors in good weather*: Matthew C. Keller et al., "A Warm Heart and a Clear Head: The Contingent Effects of Weather on Mood and Cognition," *Psychological Science,* 16, no. 9 (September 2005): 724–31; George MacKerron and Susana Mourato, "Happiness Is Greater in Natural Environments," *Global Environmental Change* 23, no. 5 (October 2013): 992–1000.

190 *twenty-minute exposure to the sun's ultraviolet (UV) rays reduced blood pressure*: Donald Liu et al., "UVA Irradiation of Human Skin Vasodilates Arterial Vasculature and Lowers Blood Pressure Independently of Nitric Oxide Synthase," *Journal of Investigative Dermatology* 134, no. 7 (July 2014): 1839–46.

190 *a strong connection with family and friends can dramatically reduce depressive re-*

lapse: Tegan Cruwys et al., "Feeling Connected Again: Interventions That Increase Social Identification Reduce Depression Symptoms in Community and Clinical Settings," *Journal of Affective Disorders* 159 (April 20, 2014): 139–46.

204 *loneliness also spreads three degrees*: John T. Cacioppo, James H. Fowler, and Nicholas A. Christakis, "Alone in the Crowd: The Structure and Spread of Loneliness in a Large Social Network," *Journal of Personality and Social Psychology* 97, no. 6 (December 2009): 977–91.

207 *the average American slept ten hours*: *Sleep Facts and Stats* (Arlington, VA: National Sleep Foundation, 2007).

207 *people sleep an average of just six hours and forty minutes*: The 2011 Sleep in America poll took a sample of 1,508 adults between ages thirteen and sixty-four. The poll used the validated Epworth Sleepiness Scale for all participants. National Sleep Foundation, "Annual Sleep in America Poll Exploring Connections with Communications Technology Use and Sleep," news release, March 7, 2011, http://sleepfoundation.org/media-center/press-release/annual-sleep-america-poll-exploring-connections-communications-technology-use-.

212 *the Twitter version of your purpose*: This exercise is adapted from the funeral practice in acceptance and commitment therapy (ACT). Hayes, *Get Out of Your Mind*.

214 *hope is built from having a goal in mind*: Snyder, "Hypothesis: There Is Hope."

215 *Make It Pocketsize*: The idea behind creating something pocketsize to carry around with you as a reminder comes out of my work in mindfulness-based relapse prevention (MBRP). To look into this program more and the science behind it, go to the MBRP website, www.mindfulrp.com.

217 *Science journalist Daniel Pink*: For a wonderfully in-depth and interesting read on motivation, see Daniel Pink, *Drive: The Surprising Truth About What Motivates Us* (New York: Riverhead Books, 2009).

220 *Three Yoga Poses for Depression*: I am indebted to Amy Weintraub, who has done extensive work on yoga for depression. Please discover more about this with her book *Yoga for Depression: A Compassionate Guide to Relieve Suffering Through Yoga* (New York: Broadway Books, 2004). I am also indebted to Denise Kaufman, who has trailblazed the "Squat Revolution." Find out more about this incredible woman and the benefits of squatting at www.denisekaufman.com.

230 *Studies find that the more intentional attention we give to these practices, the more we see brain change*: Joshua A. Grant et al., "Cortical Thickness and Pain Sensitivity in Zen Meditators," *Emotion* 10, no. 1 (February 2010): 43–53; Hölzel et al., "Investigation of Mindfulness Meditation Practitioners."

232 *The Compassionate Body Scan*: You can also find a different version of the Compassionate Body Scan in Kristin Neff and Christopher Germer's program mindful self-compassion.

242 *Sky of Awareness Meditation*: Although *Uncovering Happiness* is a secular book, it draws from many of the world's wisdom traditions. A reference to making your mind as vast as the sky can be found in the Buddhist scripture *Majjhima Nikaya*, in which the Buddha reportedly said, "Develop a mind that is vast like space, where experiences both pleasant and unpleasant can appear and disappear without conflict, struggle, or harm. Rest in a mind like a vast sky."

Index

INDEX

Get email updates on

ELISHA GOLDSTEIN,

exclusive offers,

and other great book recommendations

from Simon & Schuster.

Visit **newsletters.simonandschuster.com**

or

scan below to sign up: